A BEGINNER'S GUIDE TO

TALMAGE

JAMES EDWARD TALMAGE
1862–1933

A BEGINNER'S GUIDE TO
TALMAGE

EXCERPTS FROM THE WRITINGS *of* JAMES E. TALMAGE

Compiled by Calvin R. Stephens

DESERET
BOOK

© 2013 Deseret Book Company

Visit us at DeseretBook.com

Library of Congress Cataloging-in-Publication Data

Talmage, James E. (James Edward), 1862–1933, author.
  [Works. Selections (Beginner's guide to Talmage)]
  A beginner's guide to Talmage : excerpts from the writings of James E. Talmage / Calvin R. Stephens, compiler.
       pages cm
  Includes bibliographical references and index.
  ISBN 978-1-60907-397-8 (paperbound : alk. paper)
  1. The Church of Jesus Christ of Latter-day Saints—Doctrines. 2. Mormon Church—Doctrines.
  I. Stephens, Calvin R., 1946– editor. II. Title.
  BX8635.3.T35 2013
  230'.93—dc23   2013009075

Printed in the United States of America
Publisher's Printing, Salt Lake City, UT

10   9   8   7   6   5   4   3   2   1

CONTENTS

CONTENTS

CONTENTS

CONTENTS

CONTENTS

CONTENTS

INTRODUCTION

In paying tribute to Elder James E. Talmage, Elder Melvin J. Ballard, who served with him for fourteen years in the Quorum of the Twelve Apostles of The Church of Jesus Christ of Latter-day Saints, said:

"He produced many volumes that shall be read until the end of time, because that which he has written is so clear and so impressive that it shall be among the cherished treasures of those who love the works of God. Yet those contributions he gave freely to the Church, without any earthly reward" (*Deseret News,* Aug. 5, 1933).

Elder James E. Talmage was a gifted scholar, scientist, teacher, author, orator, and apostle, whose writings made a significant contribution to the published doctrines of the Church. Schooled in the laws, principles, and doctrines of the Church, he was a faithful Latter-day Saint and great defender of the faith. "Seen only through the medium of his writings on theology, Dr. Talmage may appear as a somewhat stern and always serious-minded man, but in life he was not only warm and understanding but also possessed of a rich sense of humor" (Talmage, *Talmage Story,* 229). Although some may think of his writing as difficult to understand, his experiences, attitudes, and teachings provide great lessons for Latter-day Saints today.

Whether then or now, the adversary has always fought ferociously to prevent the growth of the Lord's Church. Even at a young age, James courageously stood firm in his convictions against these opposing forces. Foreordained to become a vital leader in the earthly kingdom of God, he must have posed a serious threat to Satan. On June 15, 1873, when James was ten years old, his father planned to baptize him after dark not far from their home to avoid persecution from those who opposed the Church. James recalled, "As father stood in the water and took my hand, . . . we were veritably horror-stricken by a combined shriek, yell, scream, howl—I know not how to describe the awful noise such as none of us had ever heard. It seemed to be a combination of every fiendish [noise] we could conceive of. I remember how I trembled at the awful manifestation, which had about it the sharpness and volume of a thunderclap followed by an angry roar, which died away as a hopeless groan. . . . Father . . . asked me if I was too frightened to be baptized; . . . I answered by stepping into the water" ("An Unusual Accompaniment to a Baptism," *Improvement Era,* June 1922, 675–76).

James's unquenchable thirst for knowledge and his passion for learning began in his youth. Although a third-generation member of the Church, like all Saints, he had to gain his own testimony. He said, "I seem to have been born with a testimony yet in my early adolescence I was led to question whether that testimony was really my own or derived from my parents. I set about investigating the claims of the

Church and pursued the investigation by prayer, fasting, and research with all the ardor of an investigator on the outside. While such a one investigates with a view of coming into the Church if its claims be verified, I was seeking a way out of the Church if its claims should prove to me to be unsound. After months of such inquiry, I found myself in possession of an assurance beyond all question that I was in solemn fact a member of The Church of Jesus Christ. I was convinced once and for all, and this knowledge is so fully an integral part of my being that without it I would not be myself" (Bryant S. Hinckley, "Greatness in Men—James E. Talmage," *Improvement Era*, July 1932, 524).

As he grew to adulthood, it became clear that James was brilliant, capable of great accomplishments and worthy of recognition; however, whether in his pursuit of education or in the performance of his Church duties or callings, he was both selfless and humble. Having been advised by President John Taylor to seek his education in the East and return home promptly, James did not focus on attaining degrees and academic honors for himself. Instead, he was like a bee, going forth to gather honey that he could then bring back to the hive. He sought knowledge primarily to bless the lives of others (Talmage, *Talmage Story*, 230).

Humility and integrity also characterized his feelings about each of his callings in the Church, including his call to serve in the Quorum of the Twelve Apostles:

"Every call I have received to an office in the priesthood has come to me because someone was needed to fill a particular place, and was in no sense a matter of advancement or honor to myself as an individual. . . . Early in life I realized that I would have to live with myself more than with anybody else, and I have tried to so live that I would be in good company when alone" (Hinckley, "Greatness in Men—James E. Talmage," 524).

James E. Talmage was a prolific author and a powerful orator. He wrote several volumes related to geology and minerals, but his most influential works relate to Church doctrine and principles. His best-known books were written at the request of the First Presidency, and others were drawn from lectures delivered to the University Sunday School or other audiences. Concerned about his writing being part of the permanent record and doctrine of the Church, he specifically requested that a "committee on criticism" be appointed to review and approve all material before it was published.

The excerpts in *A Beginner's Guide to Talmage* are from the following writings and speeches:

Articles of Faith was published in 1899. Church President Lorenzo Snow announced: "During the early part of April there will be issued by the Deseret News a Church work, entitled 'The Articles of Faith,' the same being a series of lectures on the principal doctrines of the Church of Jesus Christ of Latter-day Saints, by Dr. James E. Talmage. The lectures were prepared by appointment of the First Presidency, and the book will be published by the Church. It is intended for use as a text book in Church schools, Sunday schools, [Mutual] Improvement associations, quorums of the Priesthood, and other Church organizations in which the study of Theology is pursued, and also for individual use among the members of the Church. The work has been approved by the First Presidency, and I heartily commend it to the members of the Church" ("Official Announcement," *Deseret Evening News,* Mar. 10, 1899, 4).

The Story and the Philosophy of Mormonism combines two separate works. Originally a series of lectures given at the University of Michigan and then at Cornell and other universities, "The Story of 'Mormonism'" was printed in installments in the *Improvement Era* in 1901. The *Improvement Era* also published "The Philosophical Basis of 'Mormonism,'" a 1915 address to the Philosophical Society of Denver. These two works were later published together in one volume.

The Great Apostasy was published in 1909 to provide evidence of the decline and extinction of the primitive Church of Jesus Christ. Its preface declares: "If the alleged apostasy of the primitive Church was not reality, The Church of Jesus Christ of Latter-day Saints is not the divine institution its name proclaims" (iii).

The House of the Lord was written in response to a 1911 blackmail attempt by unscrupulous individuals who had managed to take pictures of the interior of the Salt Lake Temple. Dr. Talmage wrote to the First Presidency to suggest that the Church respond to this attempted blackmail by publishing a book explaining the purposes of ancient and modern temples and the ordinances performed in them, together with high-quality photographs of the interior and the exterior of several temples. This book was approved and written, and it was published in September 1912.

Jesus the Christ, perhaps Dr. Talmage's most frequently studied work, was based on a series of lectures he had given from 1904 to 1906 about Jesus Christ. The First Presidency requested that he compile the lectures into a book for general Church use, but the writing was postponed nearly a decade because of special assignments given to Dr. Talmage during that time, including his call to the Council of the Twelve Apostles in December 1911. He was unable to commence writing until September 14, 1914, when in an effort to minimize interruptions, the First Presidency provided him a room in the Salt Lake Temple to use for writing. His manuscript was completed just over seven months later on April 19, 1915.

The review committee for *Jesus the Christ* included the full body of the General Authorities of the Church. President Joseph F. Smith and his counselors wrote on its publication: "This important work has been prepared by appointment, and is to be published by the Church. The field of treatment is indicated on the title-page as 'A study of the Messiah and his mission, according to Holy Scriptures both ancient and modern.' The book is more than a 'Life of Christ' in the ordinary acceptation of that title. . . . The sacred subject of our Savior's life and mission is presented as it is accepted and proclaimed by the Church that bears his Holy Name. We desire that the work, 'Jesus the Christ' be read and studied by the Latter-day Saints, in their families, and in the organizations that are devoted wholly or in part to theological study. We commend it especially for use in our Church schools, as also for the advanced theological classes in Sunday schools and priesthood quorums, for the instruction of our missionaries, and for general reading" ("Official Announcement," *Deseret Evening News,* Aug. 14, 1915, 4).

The Vitality of Mormonism originated as short essays that were printed weekly during a two-year period. The essays were collected and published in 1919.

The Parables of James E. Talmage contains parables told by Elder Talmage that appeared in the *Improvement Era* beginning in January 1914. Albert L. Zobell Jr. compiled them into a small book published in 1973.

In addition to writing these books, Elder Talmage spoke in general conferences of the Church from April 1912 through October 1924. He did not speak in general conference during the years 1925–27 while he was serving as president of the European Mission, but he again spoke in conference sessions from April 1928 until April 1933.

"The power of Dr. Talmage's pen lives on in his published works and is felt by succeeding generations" (Talmage, *Talmage Story*, 230). Whether a century ago or today, members of the Church come to know Jesus Christ through the testimony and teachings of the apostles (see John 17:20), who are responsible to teach the doctrine of Christ and maintain its purity. Elder James E. Talmage possessed a powerful knowledge and testimony of Jesus Christ, and he generously imparted it to generations of Church members through his lectures and writing.

Eight months before he passed away, Elder Talmage again proclaimed his powerful testimony of the Savior and the plan of salvation. His testimony, published in an article entitled "Our Lord—the Christ," included this passage:

"We acclaim Jesus Christ as the veritable Son of the Eternal Father in both spirit and body. He lived as a Man among men yet was wholly unique in that He combined within Himself the attributes of mortality as the heritage from a mortal mother and the powers of Godhood received as a birthright from His immortal Father. Thus He became capable of death and died, yet had power over death, and so held death in abeyance until He willed to die. . . . Through Him Redemption is assured and Salvation made possible to every soul. . . . A Redeemer and Savior is essential to the accomplishment of the Father's work and glory—'to bring to pass the immortality and eternal life of man.' Sometime, somewhere, the knowledge of the Lord shall come to every soul with saving or convicting effect; then every knee shall bow, and every tongue confess that He is the Christ, the Son of the Living God" (*Improvement Era,* Dec. 1932, 69).

Elder Talmage would certainly hope for every member of the Church to have an abiding testimony of our Redeemer and Savior. His invitation to learn more of the Savior was originally extended in 1915 in *Jesus the Christ,* but it applies equally well to us today: A careful study of the text will help the reader to grow in faith, understand the plan of salvation more fully, have an increased desire to obey God, and gain greater knowledge of the life and mission of Jesus Christ. "To comprehend the works of Christ, one must know Him as the Son of God: to the man who has not yet learned to know, to the honest soul who would inquire after the Lord the invitation is ready; let him 'Come and See'" (*Jesus the Christ,* 143). As we study the teachings of Elder James E. Talmage along with the scriptures, our own understanding and testimony of the Savior will be profoundly expanded and deepened.

LIFE SKETCH

James Edward Talmage was born on Sunday, September 21, 1862, at Hungerford, Berkshire, England, a third-generation member of The Church of Jesus Christ of Latter-day Saints. He and his family left England May 24, 1876, arriving in the Salt Lake Valley on June 19. The Talmages soon afterward moved to Provo. There, at the age of thirteen, James enrolled in Brigham Young Academy, where he received instruction from Karl G. Maeser and others.

An avid student, James had obtained his early schooling in his home district in England, where he became an Oxford diocesan prize scholar in 1874. After arriving in Utah, James continued his education at Brigham Young Academy from 1876 to 1879, although it was interrupted at times for various reasons.

On June 15, 1879, his name was enrolled as one of twelve candidates for a normal (teaching) diploma. He had had to take theoretical examinations that lasted five days. "At the end of those five days, James emerged with an official grade of 99 per cent in efficiency and 100 per cent in standing" and received a certificate for 100 percent efficiency for composition (*Talmage Story*, 12).

Two months later, at the age of sixteen, James was hired to teach at Brigham Young Academy. The first year he taught grammar, penmanship, drawing, physiology, Latin reading, and phonography (shorthand). A year later geology, philosophy, and chemistry were added to his teaching responsibilities.

Desiring further education, James approached President John Taylor for counsel. President Taylor encouraged him to enter a university in the East and laid his hands on the young man's head to give him a blessing, which was fully realized.

In 1882–83, James took courses in chemistry and geology at Lehigh University, Bethlehem, Pennsylvania. "Though a special student and not a candidate for a degree, he passed during his single year of residence nearly all the examinations in the four-year course and was later graduated; and in 1883–84 he was engaged in advanced work at John Hopkins University, Baltimore, Maryland" (Jenson, *Biographical Encyclopedia*, 3:788).

In the fall of 1884, James returned to Provo and Brigham Young Academy, where he became professor of geology and chemistry. At the same time he served in Provo City as councilman, alderman, and justice of the peace. In 1888 he moved to Salt Lake City to become the principal of the Salt Lake Stake Academy, later called the Latter-day Saints College. He held that position until 1893.

In 1894, the University of Deseret was renamed the University of Utah, and James became both professor of geology and president of the university. In 1896 he received the degree of doctor of philosophy from

Illinois Wesleyan University. His thesis for the doctorate was entitled "The Past and Present of the Great Salt Lake." In 1897 he resigned as president of the University of Utah but continued there as a professor of geology for ten more years. In 1907 he resigned to pursue a private practice as a consulting mining geologist.

Meanwhile, in 1888, while serving as principal of the Salt Lake Stake Academy, James courted Merry May Booth, at one time his student and by then a teacher in Kaysville, Utah. The courtship lasted five months, and the young couple was married June 14, 1888, by President Daniel H. Wells in the Manti Temple. James and May, as she was called, became the parents of eight children—four boys and four girls. May was a devoted companion to her husband and served faithfully in various callings in the Church, including forty years as a member of the general board of the Young Women's Mutual Improvement Association.

Dr. Talmage was an active member of The Church of Jesus Christ of Latter-day Saints from his youth. He was called as a member of the Quorum of the Twelve Apostles on December 7, 1911, to fill the vacancy caused by Elder Charles W. Penrose who was called as a counselor in the First Presidency. The next day, James E. Talmage was ordained an apostle under the hands of President Joseph F. Smith, assisted by his counselors Anthon H. Lund and Charles W. Penrose. Francis M. Lyman, Hyrum M. Smith, George F. Richards and Joseph Fielding Smith, all members of the Quorum of Twelve, participated in the ordination.

As a special witness of the Savior, Elder Talmage was a dedicated disciple of Jesus Christ and loyal to His appointed prophet, who presided over the Church. President Alvin R. Dyer recalled:

"I remember, as a boy, attending a priesthood meeting with my father. I sat close by with my hand in his most of the meeting, especially since the speaker, Apostle James E. Talmage, spoke of the perils and deceptions of the last days which would try the faith of members. One of the men in the meeting stood and asked Brother Talmage the question: 'What will be the best thing for us to do in that day?' I shall never forget his answer.

"'My brother, see that you follow the counsel and direction of the prophet, for he is God's representative upon the earth, and he will know'" (Conference Report, Oct. 1965, 19).

Elder Talmage was a gifted speaker as well as a gifted writer. Elder Orson F. Whitney, a contemporary in the Quorum of the Twelve, stated: "Dr. Talmage is also a writer and speaker of great ability and skill. He is an absolute master of English both by pen and tongue, and possess a musical eloquence of marvelous fluency and precision. His style of oratory, though not stentorian, is wonderfully impressive, and his well stored mind, capacious memory, quick recollection and remarkable readiness of speech, render him a beau-ideal instructor, in public or in private" (*History of Utah*, 4:360).

Articles of Faith and *Jesus the Christ*, two of Elder Talmage's most important works, have been used throughout the Church for more than one hundred years. Even today they are a standard for missionaries to use in preparing to teach the gospel of Jesus Christ among the nations of the earth.

Church President Heber J. Grant observed that Elder Talmage's "book 'Jesus the Christ' will live forever. His 'Articles of Faith' has probably been more widely circulated than any other book that has ever been written by one of the apostles of the church" (*Deseret News,* Aug. 5, 1933).

President J. Reuben Clark Jr. summarized the ministry of Elder Talmage: "He was a diligent searcher after all truth. As a scientist he was not content with one field alone. He distinguished himself in chemistry, geology, mineralogy, entomology, biology, and microscopy. He conducted fruitful original experimentation in radio activity. He had the true scientific spirit—a love for truth, a near hatred for error.

"But in some respects his surpassing quality was this: He brought to bear all his surpassing powers of investigation, of analysis, and of discovery to blend all truth into one harmonious whole. To him God's Gospel Plan was truth and all truth. Whatever fell outside that Plan was error" (*Deseret News,* Aug. 5, 1933; paragraphing altered).

Elder James E. Talmage died at the age of seventy on July 27, 1933, at his home in Salt Lake City. His funeral was held August 5 in the Salt Lake Tabernacle. Eight thousand people attended. The concluding speaker was President Grant, who said he delighted in what Elder Talmage had written because he made things so plain and had a perfect knowledge of the work that he had been so valiant in. President Grant gave this benediction on the earthly ministry of Elder Talmage: "I commend to brother Talmage's family that they read all of section 76 of the Doctrine and Covenants, and I assure them that every promise of glory and exaltation that is there made to the faithful he will receive; he will attain to all the blessings promised in that wonderful vision given to Joseph Smith and Sidney Rigdon" (*Deseret News,* Aug. 5, 1933).

Key to Abbreviations

AF = *Articles of Faith*

CR = Conference Reports of The Church of Jesus Christ of
Latter-day Saints

GA = *The Great Apostasy*

HL = *The House of the Lord*

JTC = *Jesus the Christ*

PJT = *The Parables of James E. Talmage*

SPM = *The Story and the Philosophy of Mormonism*

VM = *The Vitality of Mormonism*

1

PLAN OF SALVATION

PRE-EARTH LIFE

Mankind Is the Spirit Offspring of God. The spirits of mankind are
the offspring of God. The Church of Jesus Christ of Latter-day Saints
so affirms on the basis of scriptural certainty, and as wholly reasonable
and consistent.

The preexistent or antemortal state of man has been heretofore
demonstrated. God the Eternal Father is the actual and literal Parent
of spirits. That many of these spirits in their embodied state manifest
more of human weakness than of Divine heritage, that they grasp the
earthly present with little regard for the heavenly past and with less for
the yet greater possibilities of the heavenly future, is no proof to the
contrary of the revealed truth that man belongs to the lineage of God
(*VM*, 233–34).

Mankind Lived First as Spirit Children with God. We hold it to be reasonable, scriptural and true, that man's period of earth-life is but one stage in the general plan of the soul's progression; and that birth is no more the beginning than is death the close of individual existence. God created all things spiritually before they were created temporally upon the earth; and the spirits of all men lived as intelligent beings, endowed with the capacity of choice and the rights of free agency, before they were born in flesh. They were the spirit-children of God (*SPM,* 115).

Scriptures Teach of Pre-Earth Life. It is a grievous error to assume that mortal birth marks the beginning of one's individual existence. Quite as reasonable is it to hold that death means annihilation of the soul. The preexistent or antemortal state of man is as plainly affirmed by Scripture as is the fact of life beyond the grave.

We are too prone to regard the body as the man, and this mistake breeds the thought that life in the flesh is all there is to existence. There is in man an immortal spirit that existed as an intelligent being before the body was begotten, and that shall continue to exist as the same immortal individual after the body has gone to decay. Divine revelation attests the solemn truth that man is eternal (*VM,* 228).

The Logic of a Pre-Earth Life. We hear much nowadays as to the speculative ideas of men concerning the condition beyond the grave; but the admission that there is an individual existence beyond the grave, is a declaration that there must have been an individual, intelligent creation before we came here in the flesh. Life beyond the grave postulates a pre-existent state . . . While the world admits the pre-existence of Christ and points to Him as one who before mortal birth shared with His Father in the honors of the godhead and in the powers of the Creator, they deny to the souls that are now upon the earth, and those that had lived as mortals, a pre-existent condition. I want to read to you one scripture bearing upon that subject and I read to you from the Book of Abraham, a scripture with which some of our people are better acquainted today than they were a year ago, because of the futile attempts that have been made to discredit it. By the failures that have resulted in these attempts, the strength of the faith of our people has been increased. The great patriarch says: "Now, the Lord had shown unto me, Abraham, the intelligences that were organized before the world was, and among all these there were many of the noble and great ones; and God saw these souls that they, were good, and He stood in the midst of them and He said, 'These I will make my rulers,' for He stood among those that were spirits, and He saw that they were good, and He said unto me, Abraham, 'Thou are one of them; thou wast chosen before thou wast born'" (CR, Oct. 1913, 120).

Many Foreordained for Service on the Earth. Everyone of us was known by name and character to the Father, who is "the God of the spirits of all flesh" (Numbers 16:22, 27:16), in our antemortal or primeval childhood; and from among the hosts of His unembodied children God chose for special service on earth such as were best suited to the accomplishment of His purposes. In illustration consider the Lord's definite revelation to Jeremiah the prophet: "Before I formed thee in the belly I knew thee; and before thou camest forth out of the womb I

17

sanctified thee, and I ordained thee a prophet unto the nations." (Jer. 1:5.) (*VM,* 229).

War in Heaven. The cause of the great antemortal "war in Heaven" was the rebellion of Lucifer following the rejection of his plan whereby it was proposed that mankind be saved from the dangers and sins of their mortality, not through the merit of struggle and endeavor against evil, but by compulsion. Satan sought to destroy the free agency of man; and in the primeval council of the angels and the Gods he was discredited; while the offer of the Well Beloved Son, Jehovah, afterwards Jesus the Christ, to insure the free agency of man in the mortal state, and to give Himself a sacrifice and propitiation for the sins of the race, was accepted, and was made the basis of the plan of Salvation *(SPM,* 118).

CREATION

All Things Were First Created Spiritually. The Scriptures aver that all things existing upon earth, including man, were created spiritually prior to their embodiment in earthly tabernacles; and furthermore, that mortal man is fashioned after the image of God. In short, all earthly existences are material expressions of preexistent entities. The human body, so far as it is normal, undeformed and unimpaired, is a presentment of the spirit itself.

One of the essential and distinguishing characteristics of life is the power to select and utilize in its own tabernacle, whether plant, animal, or human, the material elements within its reach, so far as such are necessary to its growth and development. This is true alike of the unborn embryo and of the mature being.

Man's spirit, therefore, is in the likeness of its Divine and Eternal Father, and in the operations of the functions of life it shapes the body to conform with itself. How could the spirit be otherwise than in the image of God if it be divinely begotten and born?

The conformation of the body to the likeness of the preexistent spirit is attested in a revelation to an ancient prophet and seer, wherein the Lord Jesus Christ, then in the unembodied state, showed Himself to His mortal servant, saying: "Seest thou that ye are created after mine own image? Yea, even all men were created in the beginning, after mine own image. Behold, this body, which ye now behold, is the body of my spirit; and man have I created after the body of my spirit; and even as I appear unto thee to be in the spirit, will I appear unto my people in the flesh." (Book of Mormon, Ether, 3:15, 16.)

The Church of Jesus Christ of Latter-day Saints teaches that the spirit of man being the offspring of Deity, and the human body though of earthly composition yet being, in its perfect condition, the very image of God, man, even in his present and so-called fallen condition, possesses inherited traits, tendencies, and powers that tell of his Divine descent; and that these attributes may be developed as to make him, even while mortal, in a measure Godlike. If this be not true we have to explain a vital exception to what we regard as an inviolable law of organic nature—that like begets like, and that perpetuation of species is in compliance with the condition "each after his kind" (*VM*, 234–35).

Earth Created for Man. The earth was created primarily for the carrying out of the divine purposes respecting man. The astronomer regards it as one of the stellar units; the geologist looks upon it as the field for his investigation; but beyond such conceptions we regard it as one of the many spheres created with definite purpose, in which the destiny of the human race is the chief element and was the principal concern of the Creator, in bringing it into existence. We read, as the Lord revealed unto his friend and servant, Abraham, that before the earth was framed the Creator and those immediately associated with him looked out into space and said: We will take of these materials, and we will make an earth whereon these unembodied spirits may dwell; and we will prove them herewith, to see if they will do whatsoever the Lord their God shall command them.

Now, that being the purpose for which this world was created, we can readily understand that there is a very close relationship between earth and man (CR, Oct. 1923, 48–49).

THE FALL

Adam Had His Agency in the Garden of Eden. In the day of Eden, the first man had placed before him commandment and law, with an explanation of the penalty which would follow a violation of that law. No law could have been given him in righteousness, had he not been free to act for himself. 'Nevertheless thou mayest choose for thyself, for it is given unto thee, but remember that I forbid it,' said the Lord God to Adam. Concerning His dealings with the first patriarch of the race,

God has declared in this day, 'Behold I gave unto him that he should be an agent unto himself' (*GA, 35*).

Fall of Adam and Eve. "And I, the Lord God, commanded the man, saying: Of every tree of the garden thou mayest freely eat, But of the tree of the knowledge of good and evil, thou shalt not eat of it; nevertheless, thou mayest choose for thyself, for it is given unto thee; but remember that I forbid it, for in the day thou eatest thereof thou shalt surely die."

The Temptation to disobey this injunction soon came. Satan presented himself before Eve in the garden, and, speaking by the mouth of the serpent, questioned her about the commandments that God had given respecting the tree of knowledge of good and evil. Eve answered that they were forbidden even to touch the fruit of that tree, under penalty of death. Satan then sought to beguile the woman, contradicting the Lord's statement and declaring that death would not follow a violation of the divine injunction; but that, on the other hand, by doing that which the Lord had forbidden she and her husband would become like unto the gods, knowing good and evil for themselves. The woman was captivated by these representations; and, being eager to possess the advantages pictured by Satan, she disobeyed the command of the Lord, and partook of the fruit forbidden. She feared no evil, for she knew it not. Then, telling Adam what she had done, she urged him to eat of the fruit also.

Adam found himself in a position that made it impossible for him to obey both of the specific commandments given by the Lord. He and his wife had been commanded to multiply and replenish the earth. Adam had not yet fallen to the state of mortality, but Eve already had; and in such dissimilar conditions the two could not remain together, and therefore could not fulfil the divine requirement as to procreation. On the other hand, Adam would be disobeying another commandment by yielding to Eve's request. He deliberately and wisely decided to stand by the first and greater commandment; and, therefore, with understanding of the nature of his act, he also partook of the fruit that grew on the tree of knowledge. The fact that Adam acted understandingly in this matter is affirmed by scripture. Paul, in writing to Timothy, explained that "Adam was not deceived, but the woman being deceived was in the transgression." The prophet Lehi, in expounding the scriptures to his sons, declared: "Adam fell that men might be; and men are that they might have joy" (*AF*, 64–65).

The Fall of Adam and Eve Brought Mortality. It would be unreasonable to suppose that the transgression of Eve and Adam came as a surprise to the Creator. By His infinite foreknowledge, God knew what would be the result of Satan's temptation to Eve, and what Adam would do under the resulting conditions. Further, it is evident that the fall was foreseen to be a means whereby man could be brought into direct experience with both good and evil, so that of his own agency he might elect the one or the other, and thus be prepared by the experiences of a mortal probation for the exaltation provided in the beneficent plan of his creation: *"For behold, this is my work and my glory—to bring to pass the immortality and eternal life of man"* spake the Lord unto Moses. It was the purpose of God to place within the reach of the spirits begotten by Him in the heavens the means of individual effort, and the opportunity of winning not merely redemption from death but also salvation and even exaltation, with the powers of eternal progression and increase. Hence it was necessary that the spiritual offspring of God should leave the scenes of their primeval childhood and enter the school of mortal experience, meeting, contending with, and overcoming evil, according to their several degrees of faith and strength. Adam and Eve could never have been the parents of a mortal posterity had they not themselves become mortal; mortality was an essential element in the divine plan respecting the earth and its appointed inhabitants; and, as a means of introducing mortality, the Lord placed before the progenitors of the race a law, knowing what would follow (*AF,* 68–69).

The Fall a Natural Process. Here, let me say, that therein consisted the fall—the eating of things unfit, the taking into the body of the things that made of that body a thing of earth: and I take this occasion to raise my voice against the false interpretation of scripture, which in some instances has been adopted by certain people, and is current in their minds, and is referred to in a hushed and half-secret way, that the fall of man consisted in some offense against the laws of chastity and of virtue. Such a doctrine is an abomination. What right have we to turn the scriptures from their proper sense and meaning? What right have we to declare that God meant not what He said? The fall was a natural process, resulting through the incorporation into the bodies of our first parents of the things that came from food unfit, through the violation of the command of God regarding what they should eat. Don't go around whispering that the fall consisted in the mother of the race losing her chastity and her virtue. It is not true; the human race is not

23

born of fornication. These bodies that are given unto us are given in the way that God has provided. Let it not be said that the patriarch of the race, who stood with the gods before he came here upon the earth, and his equally royal consort, were guilty of any such foul offense. The adoption of that belief has led many to excuse departures from the path of chastity and the path of virtue, by saying that it is the sin of the race, it is as old as Adam. It was not introduced by Adam. It was not committed by Eve. It was the introduction of the devil and came in order that he might sow the seeds of early death in the bodies of men and women, that the race should degenerate as it has degenerated whenever the laws of virtue and of chastity have been transgressed.

Our first parents were pure and noble, and when we pass behind the veil we shall perhaps learn something of their high estate, more than we know now. . . . The fall consisted in disobedience of the commands as to what things were fit for the body (CR, Oct. 1913, 118–19).

Original Sin. If the expression "original sin" has any definite signification it must be taken to mean the transgression of our parents in Eden. We were not participators in that offense. We are not inheritors of original sin, though we be subjects of the consequences (*VM,* 46).

Gospel Plan Eternal. The gospel of Jesus Christ is given of God: it is eternal. Have you ever formed a single passage in Holy Writ that indicates in the least degree any revision or alteration of the fundamental laws and principles of the gospel? Have you ever found it necessary for God to amend Himself and His words? Men make constitutions and enact laws, and then have to repeal and alter them, but the fundamental laws of truth are eternal: they will never be amended, they will never be changed. As declared to Adam, so is it declared unto the world today: Except ye have faith in God and in His Son Jesus Christ, as the one and only Savior and Redeemer of mankind: except we repent of our sins with a real and genuine repentance: except ye be baptized by immersion in water, at the hands of one having authority, and receive the gift of the Holy Ghost by the authorized laying on of hands, there is no possibility of your finding place in the kingdom of God. We look in vain for modification or qualification. The gospel is as simple today as it ever has been, and it will never be less simple (CR, Oct. 1918, 60–61).

Gospel Taught in All Dispensations. Be it known that the gospel, so far as this earth and its inhabitants are concerned, dates from Adam. Unto him was taught the necessity of faith in the Lord Jesus Christ, not merely mental belief, but abiding, impelling, living faith, the necessity of repentance, the indispensability of baptism in water by immersion for the remission of sins, the indispensability of the bestowal of the Holy Ghost. These principles and ordinances were taught unto Adam, administered unto him, and by him were taught and administered to others. So was it also with Enoch, with Noah, with Abraham, with Moses, and with the hosts of God's righteous servants in the early dispensations, who in many instances laid down their lives in defense of the principles which they promulgated (CR, Apr. 1918, 159–60).

Simplicity of the Gospel. We rejoice in simplicity. The Gospel of Jesus Christ is won-fully [wonderfully] simple. We as a people value, I believe, scholastic attainments at their full worth. While we foster and encourage the training and development of the mind, I was about to say to the full limit, certainly almost to the limit, of our material ability, as witness the unceasing effort and continuous expenditure of vast sums in the maintenance of church schools, and the willingness with which the Latter-day Saints as members of the community impose upon themselves, in common with their fellow citizens, taxes for the support of schools under state control and direction, we nevertheless hold that scholastic attainments are not essential to a full understanding of the Gospel of Jesus Christ. We do not believe that a diploma from a theological seminary is an essential part of the credentials of a teacher or preacher of the word of God. Nevertheless we endeavor to encourage and aid in a material way the training of the mind and the development of all the faculties that shall be conducive to educational advancement in the truest sense of the term, but we hold the Gospel is simple that all may understand it who will (CR, Apr. 1916, 129–30).

MARRIAGE

Marriage a Part of God's Eternal Plan. But the bringing of children into the world is but part of God's beneficent plan of uplift and development through honorable marriage. Companionship of husband and wife is a divinely appointed means of mutual betterment; and according to the measure of holy love, mutual respect and honor with which that companionship is graced and sanctified, do man and woman develop toward the spiritual stature of God. It is plainly the Divine intent that husband and wife should be each the other's great incentive to effort and achievement in good works.

Blessed indeed are the wedded pair who severally find in each a help meet for the other (*VM,* 215).

Marriage an Eternal Law. Grand as may seem the achievements of a man who is truly great, the culmination of his glorious career lies in his leaving posterity to continue, and enhance the triumphs of their sire. And if such be true of mortals with respect to the things of earth, transcendently greater is the power of eternal increase, as viewed in the light of revealed truth concerning the unending progression of the future state. Truly the apostle was wise when he said: "Neither is the man without the woman, neither the woman without the man, in the Lord."

The Latter-day Saints accept the doctrine that marriage is honorable, and apply it as a requirement to all who are not prevented by physical or other disability from assuming the sacred responsibilities of the wedded state. They consider, as part of the birthright of every worthy man, the privilege and duty to stand as the head of a household, the father of a posterity, which by the blessing of God may never become extinct; and equally strong is the right of every worthy woman to be wife and mother in the family of mankind (*AF,* 443–44).

ATONEMENT

The Atonement, a Necessary Part of the Plan of Salvation, Was Based on God's Foreknowledge. The Eternal Father well understood the diverse natures and varied capacities of His spirit-offspring; and His infinite foreknowledge made plain to Him, even in the beginning, that in the school of life some of His children would succeed and others would fail; some would be faithful, others false; some would choose the good, others the evil; some would seek the way of life while others would elect to follow the road to destruction. He further foresaw that death would enter the world, and that the possession of bodies by His children would be of but brief individual duration. He saw that His commandments would be disobeyed and His law violated; and that men, shut out from His presence and left to themselves, would sink rather than rise, would retrograde rather than advance, and would be lost to the heavens. It was necessary that a means of redemption be provided, whereby erring man might make amends, and by compliance with established law achieve salvation and eventual exaltation in the eternal worlds. The power of death was to be overcome, so that, though men would of necessity die, they would live anew, their spirits clothed with immortalized bodies over which death could not again prevail (*JTC*, 17–18).

PERFECTION

Perfection Is a Commandment and Can Be Obtained. We believe in the more than imperial status of the human race. We believe that our spirits are the offspring of Deity, and we hold that when Christ said to His apostles, "Be ye therefore perfect, even as your Father which is in heaven is perfect," He was not talking of a merely idealistic yet impossible achievement; but that on the contrary He meant that it was possible for men to advance until they shall become like unto the Gods in their powers and in their attainments, through righteousness (CR, Apr. 1915, 123).

Faithful Members Can Become like Their Heavenly Parents. The doctrine of the relationship between God and men, as made plain through the word of revelation, is today as it was of old, though in the light of later scripture we are enabled to read the meaning more clearly. It is provided that we, the sons and daughters of God, may advance until we become like unto our Eternal Father and our Eternal Mother, in that we may become perfect in our spheres as they are in theirs (CR, Apr. 1915, 123).

Perfection Is Comparative. Many have stumbled over that admonition of Christ, "Be ye perfect even as your Father which is in heaven is perfect." Men have asked: How can that be? We are not like Him; we are still mortal, with all our frailties. Even those who believe in the eternal progression of man so reason, so argue, and they would make out that Christ uttered fable and fiction; for to so admonish in the face of impossibility would be nothing less. But Christ told the people in that day, and He has repeated the admonition and injunction unto us: Be perfect in the sense in which your Father in heaven is perfect. What man calls "perfection" is after all comparative. Plainly a man in mortality cannot be perfect in power nor in influence nor in righteousness, in all details in the sense in which God the Father and His Son Jesus Christ are perfect. Both of Them are resurrected men, both of Them have passed through conditions strictly analogous to those of mortality through which we are passing, both of whom have died, both of whom have been resurrected, both of whom are glorified, supremely so. In the sense in which They are perfect you and I cannot aspire to be so here in the flesh. But we can be perfect if we will in our sphere, as They are perfect in Their sphere; and perfection in the lesser is the greatest possible preparation for perfection in the greater (CR, Apr. 1918, 160–61).

Perfection Is Possible. Our Lord's admonition to men to become perfect, even as the Father is perfect (Matt. 5:48) cannot rationally be construed otherwise than as implying the possibility of such achievement. Plainly, however, man cannot become perfect in mortality in the sense in which God is perfect as a supremely glorified Being. It is possible, though, for man to be perfect in his sphere in a sense analogous to that in which superior intelligences are perfect in their several spheres; yet the relative perfection of the lower is infinitely inferior to that of the higher. A college student in his freshman or sophomore year may be perfect as freshman or sophomore; his record may possibly be a hundred per cent on the scale of efficiency and achievement; yet the honors of the upper classman are beyond him, and the attainment of graduation is to him remote, but of assured possibility, if he do but continue faithful and devoted to the end (*JTC,* 248).

As an impressive and profound climax to one division of the sublime discourse, The Sermon on the Mount, the Master said: "Be ye therefore perfect, even as your Father which is in heaven is perfect." (Matt. 5:48.) . . . The law of the Gospel is a perfect law; and the sure effect of full obedience thereto is perfection. Of those who attain exaltation in the celestial kingdom Christ has declared: "These are they who are just men made perfect through Jesus the Mediator of the new covenant, who wrought out this perfect Atonement through the shedding of his own blood." ([D&C] 76:69) (*VM,* 264–65).

Destiny of Man. As a necessary consequence, man may advance by effort and by obedience to higher and yet higher laws as he may learn them in the eternities to come, until he attains the rank and status of Godship. "Mormonism" is so bold as to declare that such is the possible destiny of the human soul. And why not? Is this possibility unreasonable? Would not the contrary be opposed to what we recognize as natural law? Man is of the lineage of the Gods. He is the spirit-offspring of the Eternal One, and by the inviolable law that living beings perpetuate after their kind, the children of God may become like unto their Parents in kind if not in degree. The human soul is a God *in embryo* (*SPM,* 141–42).

SALVATION OFFERED TO THE DEAD

At Death All Go to the Spirit World. To the penitent transgressor crucified by His side, who reverently craved remembrance when the Lord should come into His kingdom, Christ had given the comforting assurance: "Verily I say unto thee, Today shalt thou be with me in paradise." The spirit of Jesus and the spirit of the repentant thief left their crucified bodies and went to the same place in the realm of the departed. On the third day following, Jesus, then a resurrected Being, positively stated to the weeping Magdalene: "I am not yet ascended to my Father." He had gone to paradise but not to the place where God dwells. Paradise, therefore, is not Heaven, if by the latter term we understand the abode of the Eternal Father and His celestialized children. Paradise is a place where dwell righteous and repentant spirits between bodily death and resurrection. Another division of the spirit world is reserved for those disembodied beings who have lived lives of wickedness and who remain impenitent even after death. Alma, a Nephite prophet, thus spake of the conditions prevailing among the departed (*JTC,* 671).

Plan of Salvation Includes Those in the Spirit World. We learn that the ministry of Christ was not confined to the few who lived in mortality during the short period of His earthly life, nor to them and the generations then future; but to all, dead, living, and yet unborn. It cannot be denied that myriads had lived and died before the meridian of time, and of these multitudes, as of the many since born, unnumbered hosts have died without a knowledge of the Gospel and its prescribed plan of salvation. What is their condition, as indeed what shall be the state of the present inhabitants of earth, and of the multitudes yet future, who shall die in ignorance and without the faith that saves? Let us ask again, how can those who know not Christ have faith in Him, and how, while lacking both knowledge and faith can they avail themselves of the provision made for their salvation?

The Church of Jesus Christ of Latter-day Saints affirms that the plan of salvation is not bounded by the grave; but that the Gospel is deathless and everlasting, reaching back into the ages that have gone, and forward into the eternities of the future. The ministry of the Savior among the dead doubtless included the revelation of His own atoning death, the inculcation of faith in Himself and in the divinely-appointed plan He represented, and the necessity of a repentance acceptable unto God. It is reasonable to believe that the other essential requirements comprised within the *laws and ordinances of the Gospel* were made known (*HL*, 70).

Salvation for the Dead Commenced by Jesus Christ. The inauguration of this work among the dead was wrought by Christ in the interval between His death and resurrection (*HL*, 91).

Prophecy Concerning the Dead. Christ's realm was not bounded by the grave; even the dead were wholly dependent upon Him for their salvation; and to the terrified ears of His dumbfounded accusers He proclaimed the solemn truth, that even then the hour was near in which the dead should hear the voice of the Son of God. Ponder His profound affirmation: "Verily, verily, I say unto you, The hour is coming, and now is, when the dead shall hear the voice of the Son of God: and they that hear shall live" (*JTC*, 209–10).

Salvation Offered to the Living and the Dead. The victory of Christ over death and sin would be incomplete were its effects confined to the small minority who have heard, accepted, and lived the gospel of salvation in the flesh. Compliance with the laws and ordinances of the gospel is essential to salvation. Nowhere in scripture is a distinction made in this regard between the living and the dead. The dead are those who have lived in mortality upon earth; the living are mortals who yet shall pass through the ordained change which we call death. All are children of the same Father, all to be judged and rewarded or punished by the same unerring justice, with the same interposition of benign mercy. Christ's atoning sacrifice was offered, not alone for the few who lived upon the earth while He was in the flesh, nor for those who were born in mortality after His death, but for all inhabitants of earth then past, present, and future. He was ordained of the Father to be a judge of both quick and dead; He is Lord alike of living and dead, as men speak of dead and living, though all are to be placed in the same position before Him; there will be but a single class, for all live unto Him. While His body reposed in the tomb, Christ was actively engaged in the further accomplishment of the Father's purposes, by offering the boon of salvation to the dead, both in paradise and in hell (*JTC*, 676).

Temples a Necessary Part of the Plan of Salvation. The Gospel of Jesus Christ is given for the salvation of human-kind; its requirements apply alike to the living whose blessed privilege it is to hear its glad tidings while in the flesh, and to the dead who may accept the truth in the spirit world. The genius of the Gospel is that of altruism unbounded; its power to save extends beyond the portals of death. As the vicarious work for the dead can be done only in sanctuaries specially devoted thereto, there will be an ever-present need for Temples so long as there are souls awaiting this ministry (*HL*, 233).

Purpose for Building Temples. To me there is special significance in our assembling upon this block, by the great temple that is consecrated mostly to the work for the dead. For be it known that this great labor of temple-building, for which the Latter-day Saints are so well known and so widely famed, is very largely, though not entirely, a work in behalf of the dead. They are not giving of their substance to erect these great buildings for themselves, for aggrandizement, nor for the beautification of earth. The temple-building spirit manifested among the Latter-day Saints is the spirit of absolute unselfishness; it is the spirit of Elijah, the spirit by which the feelings of the children are turned toward the fathers, and the feelings of the fathers are directed toward the children; for no man stands upon this earth alone. We talk of independence. No man is independent. We are all interdependent; and we shall only rise as we carry others with us, and as we are assisted by others. My own mind is led to that great subject, and I have thought of it much as I have sat through the exercises of the morning, because of the fact that it was at the glorious Easter time the work for the dead was inaugurated; it was at this season the great missionary labor in the spirit world was begun, and the doors were there opened and a means of deliverance preached unto those who had been sitting in darkness, some of them even from the days of Noah (CR, Apr. 1912, 126–27).

Ordinance Work for the Dead Done in the Temples. Largely for the administration of ordinances in behalf of the dead the Latter-day Saints build and maintain Temples, wherein the living posterity enter the waters of baptism and receive the laying on of hands for the gift of the Holy Ghost, as representatives of their departed progenitors. This labor was foretold through Malachi as a necessary and characteristic feature of the last dispensation, preceding the advent of Christ in glory and judgment. Thus, the dead fathers and living children are turned toward one another in the affection of a kinship that is to endure throughout eternity. (See Malachi 4:5–6.) (*VM,* 247).

RESURRECTION

A Literal Resurrection. Easter stands today for Christian belief, profession, and hope. It is the gladsome day of the year; and we believe that in this present year the anniversary comes at very nearly the actual and correct date. It is the anniversary of the greatest event in all history, the most effective miracle known to man—a miracle surpassing all that the mind of man could of itself conceive. It was upon the day we now commemorate that victory over the tomb was proclaimed and the glad tidings of eternal life were made known.

The Latter-day Saints believe in a literal resurrection of the body. They accept the biblical doctrine in all its beauty and simplicity. They do not invest it with foreign mysteries, nor do they read into the sacred record interpretation and meaning not inherent therein. The Latter-day Saints believe that this life is a necessary part of the education of the soul, that it is a stage marking advancement and progression; that only those of the sons and daughters of God who were worthy were permitted to take upon themselves mortal tabernacles upon the earth. They believe that death is just as much a part of the divine plan as is birth; and that death is but a passing from one necessary stage to another yet more advanced. They believe, without question or doubt, that the body and the spirit shall again be united in a literal resurrection; and be it remembered, the resurrection of the body is the controlling thought and the central idea of Easter service. The man who believes in the resurrection of the body must base his belief upon revelation; and the man who so believes is inconsistent if he questions the truth declared in absolute and literal revelation from God (CR, Apr. 1912, 124–25).

Nature of a Resurrected Being. Behold my hands and my feet, that it is I myself; handle me and see; for a spirit hath not flesh and bones, as ye see me have." And yet they could scarcely believe for the joy of it! The demonstrated fact seemed to them too good to be true. To make plain that he was a corporeal being in the sense of having a tangible body, no mere outward shape or semblance only, he asked if they had anything to eat, and they brought honey and other food to him and he did eat before them, demonstrating that his body was complete, with internal organs as well as external parts.

Can a resurrected being eat food of earth? A resurrected being can function upon any lower plane. A resurrected personage can do anything that a mortal personage can do, and much besides (CR, Apr. 1928, 93).

Resurrection Is Universal. As the scriptures conclusively prove, the resurrection is to be universal. While it is true that the dead shall be brought forth in order, each as he is prepared for the first or a later stage, yet everyone who has tabernacled in the flesh shall again assume his body; and, with spirit and body reunited, he shall be judged. The Book of Mormon is definite in the description of the literal and universal resurrection (*AF,* 391).

Resurrection of the Just and the Unjust. Two General Resurrections are mentioned in the scriptures, and these may be specified as first and final, or as the resurrection of the just and the resurrection of the unjust. The first was inaugurated by the resurrection of Jesus Christ; immediately following which many of the saints came forth from their graves. A continuation of this, the resurrection of the just, has been in operation since, and will be greatly extended, or brought to pass in a general way, in connection with the coming of Christ in His glory. The final resurrection will be deferred until the end of the thousand years of peace, and will be in connection with the last judgment (*AF*, 385).

Earth Will Die and Be Resurrected. According to the scriptures the earth has to undergo a change analogous to death, and is to be regenerated in a way comparable to a resurrection. References to the elements melting with heat, and to the earth being consumed and passing away, such as occur in many scriptures already cited, are suggestive of death; and the new earth, really the renewed or regenerated planet, may be likened to a resurrected organism (*AF*, 378).

JUDGMENT

Factors Involved with the Judgment. "The Father of souls has endowed His children with the divine birthright of free agency; He does not and will not control them by arbitrary force; He impels no man toward sin; He compels none to righteousness. Unto man has been given freedom to act for himself; and, associated with this independence, is the fact of strict responsibility and the assurance of individual accountability. In the judgment with which we shall be judged, all the conditions and circumstances of our lives shall be considered. The inborn tendencies due to heredity, the effect of environment whether conducive to good or evil, the wholesome teachings of youth, or the absence of good instruction—these and all other contributory elements must be taken into account in the rendering of a just verdict as to the soul's guilt or innocence. Nevertheless, the divine wisdom makes plain what will be the result with given conditions operating on known natures and dispositions of men, while every individual is free to choose good or evil within the limits of the many conditions existing and operative" (*JTC*, 29).

Time of Final Judgment. The final judgment, at which all men shall appear before the bar of God, is to follow their resurrection from the dead. We shall stand in our resurrected bodies of flesh and bones to receive from Jesus Christ, who shall judge the world, the sentence we individually merit, whether it be "Come ye blessed of my Father" or "Depart from me ye cursed." (See Matt. 25:31–46.) (*VM*, 64).

KINGDOMS OF GLORY

Kingdoms of Glory. The three kingdoms of widely differing glories are severally organized on a plan of gradation. The Telestial kingdom comprises subdivisions; this also is the case, we are told, with the Celestial; and, by analogy, we conclude that a similar condition prevails in the Terrestrial. Thus the innumerable degrees of merit amongst mankind are provided for in an infinity of graded glories. The Celestial kingdom is supremely honored by the personal ministrations of the Father and the Son. The Terrestrial kingdom will be administered through the higher, without a fulness of glory. The Telestial is governed through the ministrations of the Terrestrial, by "angels who are appointed to minister for them" (*AF*, 409).

Varying Degrees of Salvation. Some degree of salvation will come to all who have not forfeited their right to it; exaltation is given to those only who by righteous effort have won a claim to God's merciful liberality by which it is bestowed. Of the saved, not all will be exalted to the higher glories; rewards will not be bestowed in violation of justice; punishments will not be meted out to the ignoring of mercy. No one can be admitted to any order of glory, in short, no soul can be saved until justice has been satisfied for violated law. Our belief in the universal application of the atonement implies no supposition that all mankind will be saved with like endowments of glory and power. In the kingdom of God there are numerous degrees or gradations provided for those who are worthy of them; in the house of our Father there are many mansions, into which only those who are prepared are admitted (*AF,* 91).

Earth Will Be a Celestial Planet. Yet we learn that Eden was in reality a feature of our planet, and that the earth is destined to become a celestialized body fit for the abode of the most exalted intelligences. The Millennium, with all its splendor, is but a more advanced stage of preparation, by which the earth and its inhabitants will approach foreordained perfection (*AF,* 375).

KINGDOM PRESENTED TO THE FATHER

Celestial Consummation. The vanquishment of Satan and his hosts shall be complete. The dead, small and great, all who have breathed the breath of life on earth, shall be resurrected—every soul that has tabernacled in flesh, whether good or evil—and shall stand before God, to be judged according to the record as written in the books. So shall be brought to glorious consummation the mission of the Christ. "Then cometh the end, when he shall have delivered up the kingdom to God, even the Father; when he shall have put down all rule and all authority and power. For he must reign, till he hath put all enemies under his feet. The last enemy that shall be destroyed is death. For he hath put all things under his feet." Then shall the Lord Jesus "deliver up the kingdom, and present it unto the Father spotless, saying—I have overcome and have trodden the wine-press alone, even the wine-press of the fierceness of the wrath of Almighty God. Then shall he be crowned with the crown of his glory, to sit on the throne of his power to reign for ever and ever." The earth shall pass to its glorified and celestialized condition, an eternal abode for the exalted sons and daughters of God. Forever shall they reign, kings and priests to the Most High, redeemed, sanctified, and exalted through their Lord and God JESUS THE CHRIST (*JTC*, 792).

Jesus Christ Subject to the Father. But when he saith all things are put under him, it is manifest that he is excepted, which did put all things under him. And when all things shall be subdued unto him, then shall the Son also himself be subject unto him that put all things under him, that God may be all in all" (*AF*, 379).

2

THE GODHEAD

EVIDENCE OF GOD

History and Tradition. History as written by man, and authentic tradition as transmitted from generation to generation prior to the date of any written record now extant, give evidence of the actuality of Deity and of close and personal dealings between God and man in the early epochs of human existence. One of the most ancient records known, the Holy Bible, names God as the Creator of all things, and moreover, declares that He revealed Himself to our first earthly parents and to many other holy personages in the early days of the world (*AF,* 30).

Nature Testifies of God. Human Reason, operating upon observations of nature, strongly declares the existence of God. The mind, already imbued with the historical truths of the divine existence and its close relationship with man, will find confirmatory evidence in nature on every side; and even to him who rejects the testimony of the past, and assumes to set up his own judgment as superior to the common belief of ages, the multifarious evidences of design in nature appeal. The observer is impressed by the manifest order and system in creation; he notes the regular succession of day and night providing alternate periods of work and rest for man, animals, and plants; the sequence of the seasons, each with its longer periods of activity and recuperation; the mutual dependence of animals and plants; the circulation of water from sea to cloud, from cloud to earth again, with beneficent effect. As man proceeds to the closer examination of things he finds that by study and scientific investigation these proofs are multiplied many fold. He may learn of the laws by which the earth and its associated worlds are governed in their orbits; by which satellites are held subordinate to planets, and planets to suns; he may behold the marvels of vegetable and animal anatomy, and the surpassing mechanism of his own body; and with such appeals to his reason increasing at every step, his wonder as to who ordained all this gives place to adoration for the Creator whose presence and power are thus so forcefully proclaimed; and the observer becomes a worshiper.

Everywhere in nature is the evidence of cause and effect; on every side is the demonstration of means adapted to end. But such adaptations, says a thoughtful writer, "indicate contrivance for a given purpose, and contrivance is the evidence of intelligence, and intelligence is the attribute of mind, and the intelligent mind that built the stupendous universe is God." To admit the existence of a designer in the evidence of design, to say there must be a contriver in a world of intelligent contrivance, to believe in an adapter when man's life is directly dependent upon the most perfect adaptations conceivable, is but to accept self-evident truths. The burden of proof as to the non-existence of God rests upon him who questions the solemn truth that God lives. "Every house is builded by some man; but he that built all things is God." Plain as is the truth so expressed, there are among men a few who profess to doubt the evidence of reason and to deny the author of their own being. Strange, is it not, that here and there one, who finds in the contrivance exhibited by the ant in building her house, in the architecture of the honey-comb, and in the myriad instances of orderly instinct among the least of living things, a proof of intelligence from which man may learn and be wise, will yet question the operation of intelligence in the creation of worlds and in the constitution of the universe?

Man's consciousness tells him of his own existence; his observation proves the existence of others of his kind and of uncounted orders of organized beings. From this we conclude that something must have existed always, for had there been a time of no existence, a period of nothingness, existence could never have begun, for from nothing, nothing can be derived. The eternal existence of something, then, is a fact beyond dispute; and the question requiring answer is, what is that eternal something—that existence which is without beginning and without end? Matter and energy are eternal realities; but matter of itself is neither vital nor active, nor is force of itself intelligent; yet vitality and activity are characteristic of living things, and the effects of intelligence are universally present. Nature is not God; and to mistake the one for the other is to call the edifice the architect, the fabric the designer, the marble the sculptor, and the thing the power that made it. The system of nature is the manifestation of an order that argues a directing intelligence; and that intelligence is of an eternal character, coeval with existence itself. Nature herself is a declaration of a superior Being, whose will and purpose she exhibits in her varied aspects. Beyond and above nature stands nature's God (*AF*, 32–34).

A Fool Denies There Is a God. Human reason, so liable to err in dealing with subjects of lesser import, may not of itself lead its possessor to a convincing knowledge of God; yet its exercise will aid him in his search, strengthening and confirming his inherited instinct toward his Maker. "The fool hath said in his heart, There is no God." In this passage as in scriptural usage elsewhere, the fool is a wicked man, one who has forfeited his wisdom by wrongdoing, bringing darkness over his mind in place of light, and ignorance instead of knowledge. By such a course, the mind becomes depraved and incapable of appreciating the finer arguments in nature. A wilful sinner grows deaf to the voice of both intuition and reason in holy things, and loses the privilege of communing with his Creator, thus forfeiting the strongest means of attaining a personal knowledge of God (*AF*, 35–36).

GODHEAD—THREE DISTINCT INDIVIDUALS

Godhead Composed of Three Personages. Three personages composing the great presiding council of the universe have revealed themselves to man: (1) God the Eternal Father; (2) His Son, Jesus Christ; and (3) the Holy Ghost. That these three are separate individuals, physically distinct from each other, is demonstrated by the accepted records of divine dealings with man. On the occasion of the Savior's baptism,

John recognized the sign of the Holy Ghost; he saw before him in a tabernacle of flesh the Christ, unto whom he had administered the holy ordinance; and he heard the voice of the Father. The three personages of the Godhead were present, manifesting themselves each in a different way, and each distinct from the others. Later the Savior promised His disciples that the Comforter, who is the Holy Ghost, should be sent unto them by His Father; here again are the three members of the Godhead separately defined. Stephen, at the time of his martyrdom, was blessed with the power of heavenly vision, and he saw Jesus standing on the right hand of God. Joseph Smith, while calling upon the Lord in fervent prayer, saw the Father and the Son, standing in the midst of light that shamed the brightness of the sun; and one of these declared of the other, "This is My Beloved Son. Hear Him!" Each of the members of the Trinity is called God, together they constitute the Godhead (*AF*, 39–40).

Unity of the Godhead. The Godhead is a type of unity in the attributes, powers, and purposes of its members. Jesus, while on earth and in manifesting Himself to His Nephite servants, repeatedly testified of the unity existing between Himself and the Father, and between them both and the Holy Ghost. This cannot rationally be construed to mean that the Father, the Son, and the Holy Ghost are one in substance and in person, nor that the names represent the same individual under different aspects. A single reference to prove the error of any such view may suffice: Immediately before His betrayal, Christ prayed for His disciples, the Twelve, and other converts, that they should be preserved in unity, "that they all may be one" as the Father and the Son are one.

We cannot assume that Christ prayed that His followers lose their individuality and become one person, even if a change so directly opposed to nature were possible. Christ desired that all should be united in heart, spirit, and purpose; for such is the unity between His Father and Himself, and between them and the Holy Ghost.

This unity is a type of completeness; the mind of any one member of the Trinity is the mind of the others; seeing as each of them does with the eye of perfection, they see and understand alike. Under any given conditions each would act in the same way, guided by the same principles of unerring justice and equity. The one-ness of the Godhead, to which the scriptures so abundantly testify, implies no mystical union of substance, nor any unnatural and therefore impossible blending of personality. Father, Son, and Holy Ghost are as distinct in their persons and individualities as are any three personages in mortality. Yet their unity of purpose and operation is such as to make their edicts one, and their will the will of God (*AF*, 40–41).

GOD THE FATHER

Elohim. The name *Elohim* is of frequent occurrence in the Hebrew texts of the Old Testament, though it is not found in our English versions. In form the word is a Hebrew plural noun; but it connotes the plurality of excellence or intensity, rather than distinctively of number. It is expressive of supreme or absolute exaltation and power. *Elohim,* as understood and used in the restored Church of Jesus Christ, is the name-title of God the Eternal Father, whose firstborn Son in the spirit is *Jehovah*—the Only Begotten in the flesh, Jesus Christ (*JTC*, 38).

God the Father Once Mortal. It would appear unnecessary to cite at greater length in substantiating our affirmation that Jesus Christ was God even before He assumed a body of flesh. During that antemortal period there was essential difference between the Father and the Son, in that the former had already passed through the experiences of mortal life, including death and resurrection, and was therefore a Being possessed of a perfect, immortalized body of flesh and bones, while the Son was yet unembodied. Through His death and subsequent resurrection Jesus the Christ is today a Being like unto the Father in all essential characteristics (*JTC,* 38–39).

God the Father Has a Physical Body. We affirm that to deny the materiality of God's person is to deny God; for a thing without parts has no whole, and an immaterial body cannot exist. The Church of Jesus Christ of Latter-day Saints proclaims against the incomprehensible God, devoid of "body, parts, or passions," as a thing impossible of existence, and asserts its belief in and allegiance to the true and living God of scripture and revelation (*AF,* 48).

God's Knowledge of His Children. Our Heavenly Father has a full knowledge of the nature and dispositions of each of His children, a knowledge gained by long observation and experience in the past eternity of our primeval childhood; a knowledge compared with which that gained by earthly parents through mortal experience with their children is infinitesimally small. By reason of that surpassing knowledge, God reads the future of child and children, of men individually and of men collectively as communities and nations; He knows what each will do under given conditions, and sees the end from the beginning. His fore-knowledge is based on intelligence and reason. He foresees the future as a state which naturally and surely will be; not as one which must be because He has arbitrarily willed that it shall be (*GA*, 20).

Appearance of God the Father. A general consideration of scriptural evidence leads to the conclusion that God the Eternal Father has manifested Himself to earthly prophets or revelators on very few occasions, and then principally to attest the divine authority of His Son, Jesus Christ. As before shown, the Son was the active executive in the work of creation; throughout the creative scenes the Father appears mostly in a directing or consulting capacity. Unto Adam, Enoch, Noah, Abraham and Moses the Father revealed Himself, attesting the Godship of the Christ, and the fact that the Son was the chosen Savior of mankind. On the occasion of the baptism of Jesus, the Father's voice was heard, saying, "This is my beloved Son, in whom I am well pleased"; and at the transfiguration a similar testimony was given by the Father. On an occasion yet later, while Jesus prayed in anguish of soul, submitting Himself that the Father's purposes be fulfilled and the Father's name glorified, "Then came there a voice from heaven, saying, I have both glorified it, and will glorify it again." The resurrected and glorified Christ was announced by the Father to the Nephites on the western hemisphere, in these words: "Behold my beloved Son, in whom I am well pleased, in whom I have glorified my name: hear ye him." From the time of the occurrence last noted, the voice of the Father was not heard again among men, so far as the scriptures aver, until the spring of 1820, when both the Father and the Son ministered unto the prophet Joseph Smith, the Father saying, "This is my beloved Son, hear him!" These are the instances of record in which the Eternal Father has been manifest in personal utterance or other revelation to man apart from the Son. God the Creator, the Jehovah of Israel, the Savior and Redeemer of all nations, kindreds and tongues, are the same, and He is Jesus the Christ (*JTC*, 39–40).

JESUS CHRIST

Jesus Christ Is the Executive of the Father. The Father operated in the work of creation through the Son, who thus became the executive through whom the will, commandment, or word of the Father was put into effect. It is with incisive appropriateness therefore, that the Son, Jesus Christ, is designated by the apostle John as the Word; or as declared by the Father "the word of my power." The part taken by Jesus Christ in the creation, a part so prominent as to justify our calling Him the Creator, is set forth in many scriptures. The author of the Epistle to the Hebrews refers in this wise distinctively to the Father and the Son as separate though associated Beings: "God, who at sundry times and in divers manners spake in time past unto the fathers by the prophets, hath in these last days spoken unto us by his Son, whom he hath appointed heir of all things, by whom also he made the worlds." Paul is even more explicit in his letter to the Colossians, wherein, speaking of Jesus the Son, he says: "For by him were all things created, that are in heaven, and that are in earth, visible and invisible, whether they be thrones, or dominions, or principalities, or powers: all things were created by him, and for him: and he is before all things, and by him all things consist." And here let be repeated the testimony of John, that by the Word, who was with God, and who was God even in the beginning, all things were made; "and without him was not anything made that was made."

That the Christ who was to come was in reality God the Creator was revealed in plainness to the prophets on the western hemisphere. Samuel, the converted Lamanite, in preaching to the unbelieving Nephites justified his testimony as follows: "And also that ye might know of the coming of Jesus Christ, the Son of God, the Father of heaven and of earth, the Creator of all things, from the beginning; and that ye might know of the signs of his coming, to the intent that ye might believe on his name."

To these citations of ancient scripture may most properly be added the personal testimony of the Lord Jesus after He had become a resurrected Being. In His visitation to the Nephites He thus proclaimed Himself: "Behold, I am Jesus Christ the Son of God. I created the heavens and the earth, and all things that in them are. I was with the Father from the beginning. I am in the Father, and the Father in me; and in me hath the Father glorified his name" (*JTC*, 33–34).

Divine Investiture. At this point Philip interposed with the request, "Lord, shew us the Father, and it sufficeth us." Jesus answered with pathetic and mild reproof: "Have I been so long time with you, and yet hast thou not known me, Philip? he that hath seen me hath seen the Father; and how sayest thou then, Shew us the Father?" He was grieved by the thought that His nearest and dearest friends on earth, those upon whom He had conferred the authority of the Holy Priesthood, should be yet ignorant of His absolute oneness with the Father in purpose and action. Had the Eternal Father stood amongst them, in Person, under the conditions there existing, He would have done as did the Well Beloved and Only Begotten Son, whom they knew as Jesus, their Lord and Master. So absolutely were the Father and the Son of one heart and mind, that to know either was to know both; nevertheless the Father could be reached only through the Son (*JTC*, 602).

All Power Given to Jesus Christ. To those assembled on the mount Jesus declared: "All power is given unto me in heaven and in earth." This could be understood as nothing less than an affirmation of His absolute Godship. His authority was supreme, and those who were commissioned of Him were to minister in His name, and by a power such as no man could give or take away (*JTC*, 694–95).

Millions Proclaim Jesus the Christ. The solemn testimonies of millions dead and of millions living unite in proclaiming Him as divine, the Son of the Living God, the Redeemer and Savior of the human race, the Eternal Judge of the souls of men, the Chosen and Anointed of the Father—in short, the Christ (*JTC*, 1–2).

HOLY GHOST

Holy Ghost a Spirit Man. The Holy Ghost, called also Spirit, and Spirit of the Lord, Spirit of God, Comforter, and Spirit of Truth, is not tabernacled in a body of flesh and bones, but is a personage of spirit; yet we know that the Spirit has manifested Himself in the form of a man. Through the ministrations of the Spirit the Father and the Son may operate in their dealings with mankind; through Him knowledge is communicated, and by Him the purposes of the Godhead are achieved. The Holy Ghost is the witness of the Father and the Son, declaring to man their attributes, bearing record of the other personages of the Godhead (*AF*, 42).

Holy Ghost Is the Minister of the Godhead. The Holy Ghost may be regarded as the minister of the Godhead, carrying into effect the decisions of the Supreme Council.

In the execution of these great purposes, the Holy Ghost directs and controls the varied forces of nature, of which indeed a few, and these perhaps of minor order wonderful as even the least of them appears to man, have thus far been investigated by mortals. Gravitation, sound, heat, light, and the still more mysterious and seemingly supernatural power of electricity, are but the common servants of the Holy Ghost in His operations (*AF*, 160).

The Holy Ghost Has Appeared to Man. The Holy Ghost undoubtedly possesses personal powers and affections; these attributes exist in Him in perfection. Thus, He teaches and guides, testifies of the Father and the Son, reproves for sin, speaks, commands, and commissions, makes intercession for sinners, is grieved, searches and investigates, entices, and knows all things. These are not figurative expressions, but plain statements of the attributes and characteristics of the Holy Ghost. That the Spirit of the Lord is capable of manifesting Himself in the form and figure of man, is indicated by the wonderful interview between the Spirit and Nephi, in which He revealed Himself to the prophet, questioned him concerning his desires and belief, instructed him in the things of God, speaking face to face with the man. "I spake unto him," says Nephi, "as a man speaketh; for I beheld that he was in the form of a man; yet nevertheless, I knew that it was the Spirit of the Lord; and he spake unto me as a man speaketh with another." However, the Holy Ghost does not possess a body of flesh and bones, as do both the Father and the Son, but is a personage of spirit (*AF,* 159–60).

Power and Office of the Holy Ghost. He is a teacher sent from the Father; and unto those who are entitled to His tuition He will reveal all things necessary for the soul's advancement. Through the influences of the Holy Spirit the powers of the human mind may be quickened and increased, so that things past may be brought to remembrance. He will serve as a guide in things divine unto all who will obey Him, enlightening every man, in the measure of his humility and obedience; unfolding the mysteries of God, as the knowledge thus revealed may effect greater spiritual growth; conveying knowledge from God to man; sanctifying those who have been cleansed through obedience to the requirements of the Gospel; manifesting all things; and bearing witness unto men concerning the existence and infallibility of the Father and the Son.

Not alone does the Holy Ghost bring to mind the past and explain the things of the present, but His power is manifested in prophecy concerning the future. "He will shew you things to come," declared the Savior to the apostles in promising the advent of the Comforter. Adam, the first prophet of earth, under the influence of the Holy Ghost "predicted whatsoever should befall his posterity unto the latest

generation." The power of the Holy Ghost then, is the spirit of prophecy and revelation; His office is that of enlightenment of the mind,
quickening of the intellect, and sanctification of the soul (*AF*, 162–63).

ATTRIBUTES OF DEITY

Have All Attributes in Their Perfection. The individual members of
the Holy Trinity are united in purpose, plan, and method. To conceive
of disagreement, differences, or dissension among them would be to
regard them as lacking in the attributes of perfection that characterize
Godhood. But that this unity involves any merging of personality is
nowhere attested in Scripture, and the mind is incapable of apprehend-
ing such a union (*VM*, 43).

Father and Son Resurrected. The Father is a personal being, possessing a definite form, with bodily parts and spiritual passions. Jesus
Christ, who was with the Father in spirit before coming to dwell in
the flesh, and through whom the worlds were made, lived among men
as a man, with all the physical characteristics of a human being; after
His resurrection He appeared in the same form; in that form He ascended into heaven; and in that form He has manifested Himself to
the Nephites, and to modern prophets. We are assured that Christ was
in the express image of His Father, after which image man also has
been created. Therefore we know that both the Father and the Son
are in form and stature perfect men; each of them possesses a tangible
body, infinitely pure and perfect and attended by transcendent glory,
nevertheless a body of flesh and bones (*AF*, 41–42).

Foreknowledge of God. As it became apparent that Israel had chosen the evil alternative, the Lord brought before them again and again the picture of impending distress. He pleaded with them as a father with a wayward son; He commanded and threatened, but they would not heed. In time came the Assyrian captivity, later the Babylonian, and then subjugation by Rome. In accord with the fateful prophecy voiced by Amos, Israel has been scattered amongst the nations "like as corn is sifted in a sieve."

All this was foreknown to Israel's God—yes, and more, for beyond the dispersion He saw the gathering of His people, now in progress. Did Jehovah, whose prescience embraced the events of centuries and millenniums, bring the curse upon Israel, or did Israel bring it upon themselves?

God reads the future of child and children, of men individually and of men collectively as communities and nations; He knows what each will do under given conditions and sees the end from the beginning. His foreknowledge springs from intelligence and supreme wisdom. He sees the future as a state which in the sequence of events will be, not as one which must be because He has willed that it shall be.

The predicted judgments of the last days, now manifest, are just and, withal, beneficent. They were divinely foretold, and the way of escape or protection was prepared aforetime *(PJT,* 52–53).

Foreknowledge Not a Determining Cause. It is not fair to blame the Lord, even in thought, because he gives us warning of what is to come. It is most irrational and illogical so to do. He, with his omniscience, knows what is to come to individuals and nations, and he gives warnings. Many of us take that warning to be an expression of divine determination to punish and to afflict. Well, others besides the Lord are subjects of ill-directed blame sometimes. I have suffered from it. On one occasion I undertook to warn a merry party of intending picnickers not to set out on their jaunt, because a storm was coming, a violent storm. I had consulted the instruments that told of its coming. But they knew better and they went, and they came back in some fashion. I wish you could have seen them. But the tragical part of it was they blamed it all on me (CR, Apr. 1933, 109).

God Is Omnipresent. There is no part of creation, however remote, into which God cannot penetrate; through the medium of the Spirit the Godhead is in direct communication with all things at all times. It has been said, therefore, that God is everywhere present; but this does not mean that the actual person of any one member of the Godhead can be physically present in more than one place at one time. The senses of each of the Trinity are of infinite power; His mind is of unlimited capacity; His powers of transferring Himself from place to place are infinite; plainly, however, His person cannot be in more than one place at any one time. Admitting the personality of God, we are compelled to accept the fact of His materiality; indeed, an "immaterial being," under which meaningless name some have sought to designate the condition of God, cannot exist, for the very expression is a contradiction in terms. If God possesses a form, that form is of necessity of definite proportions and therefore of limited extension in space. It is impossible for Him to occupy at one time more than one space of such limits; and it is not surprising, therefore, to learn from the scriptures that He moves from place to place (*AF*, 42–43).

God Is Omniscient. By Him matter has been organized and energy directed. He is therefore the Creator of all things that are created; and "Known unto God are all his works from the beginning of the world." His power and His wisdom are alike incomprehensible to man, for they are infinite. Being Himself eternal and perfect, His knowledge cannot be otherwise than infinite. To comprehend Himself, an infinite Being, He must possess an infinite mind. Through the agency of angels and ministering servants He is in continuous communication with all parts of creation, and may personally visit as He may determine (*AF*, 43–44).

God Is Omnipotent. He is properly called the Almighty. Man can discern proofs of the divine omnipotence on every side, in the forces that control the elements of earth and guide the orbs of heaven in their prescribed courses. Whatever His wisdom indicates as necessary to be done God can and will do. The means through which He operates may not be of infinite capacity in themselves, but they are directed by an infinite power. A rational conception of His omnipotence is power to do all that He may will to do (*AF*, 44).

Some of God's Personal Attributes. God is kind, benevolent, and loving—tender, considerate, and long-suffering, bearing patiently with the frailties of His children. He is just and merciful in judgment, yet combining with these gentler qualities firmness in avenging wrongs.

He is jealous of His own power and the reverence paid to Him; that is to say, He is zealous for the principles of truth and purity, which are nowhere exemplified in a higher degree than in His personal attributes. This Being is the author of our existence, Him we are permitted to approach as Father. Our faith will increase in Him as we learn of Him (*AF,* 44).

Knowledge Is Power. In such wise did God make known anciently the power by virtue of which He is supreme over all the intelligences that exist—the fact that He is more intelligent than any and all others. In the heavens as upon the earth the aphorism holds good that Knowledge is Power, providing that by "knowledge" we mean application, and not merely mental possession, of truth. In a revelation through Joseph Smith the prophet given in 1833, the character of Divine authority and power is thus sublimely summarized: "The Glory of God is Intelligence." (Doctrine and Covenants 93:36.)

The context of the passage shows that the intelligence therein referred to as an attribute of Deity is spiritual light and truth; and that man may attain to a measure of this exalting light and truth is thus made certain: "He that keepeth His commandments receiveth truth and light, until he is glorified in truth and knoweth all things. . . . Intelligence, or the light of truth, was not created or made, neither indeed can be. All truth is independent in that sphere in which God has placed it, to act for itself, as all intelligence also" (*VM,* 267).

Righteous Anger an Attribute of Deity. The incident of Christ's forcible clearing of the temple is a contradiction of the traditional conception of Him as of One so gentle and unassertive in demeanor as to appear unmanly. Gentle He was, and patient under affliction, merciful and long-suffering in dealing with contrite sinners, yet stern and inflexible in the presence of hypocrisy, and unsparing in His denunciation of persistent evil-doers. His mood was adapted to the conditions to which He addressed Himself; tender words of encouragement or burning expletives of righteous indignation issued with equal fluency from His lips. His nature was no poetic conception of cherubic sweetness ever present, but that of a Man, with the emotions and passions essential to manhood and manliness. He, who often wept with compassion, at other times evinced in word and action the righteous anger of a God. But of all His passions, however gently they rippled or strongly surged, He was ever master. Contrast the gentle Jesus moved to hospitable service by the needs of a festal party in Cana, with the indignant Christ plying His whip, and amidst commotion and turmoil of His own making, driving cattle and men before Him as an unclean herd (*JTC*, 158).

3

JESUS THE CHRIST

PROPHETS TESTIFY OF CHRIST

Advent of Jesus Christ Foretold. The occasion of the Savior's advent was preappointed; and the time thereof was specifically revealed through authorized prophets on each of the hemispheres (*JTC*, 58).

Prophets Knew of the Coming of Christ. The Lord's revelation to Adam making known the ordained plan whereby the Son of God was to take upon Himself flesh in the meridian of time, and become the Redeemer of the world, was attested by Enoch, son of Jared and father of Methuselah. From the words of Enoch we learn that to him as to his great progenitor, Adam, the very name by which the Savior would be known among men was revealed—"which is Jesus Christ, the only name which shall be given under heaven, whereby salvation shall come unto the children of men." The recorded covenant of God with Abraham, and the reiteration and confirmation thereof with Isaac and in turn with Jacob—that through their posterity should all nations of the earth be blessed—presaged the birth of the Redeemer through that chosen lineage. Its fulfillment is the blessed heritage of the ages.

In pronouncing his patriarchal blessing upon the head of Judah, Jacob prophesied: "The sceptre shall not depart from Judah, nor a lawgiver from between his feet, until Shiloh come; and unto him shall the gathering of the people be." That by Shiloh is meant the Christ is evidenced by the fulfillment of the conditions set forth in the prediction, in the state of the Jewish nation at the time of our Lord's birth.

Moses proclaimed the coming of a great Prophet in Israel, whose ministry was to be of such importance that all men who would not accept Him would be under condemnation; and that this prediction had sole reference to Jesus Christ is conclusively shown by later scriptures (*JTC*, 44–45).

GENEALOGY

Genealogy of Mary and Joseph. Two genealogical records purporting to give the lineage of Jesus are found in the New Testament, one in the first chapter of Matthew, the other in the third chapter of Luke. These records present several apparent discrepancies, but such have been satisfactorily reconciled by the research of specialists in Jewish genealogy. No detailed analysis of the matter will be attempted here; but it should be borne in mind that the consensus of judgment on the part of investigators is that Matthew's account is that of the royal lineage, establishing the order of sequence among the legal successors to the throne of David, while the account given by Luke is a personal pedigree, demonstrating descent from David without adherence to the line of legal succession to the throne through primogeniture or nearness of kin. Luke's record is regarded by many, however, as the pedigree of Mary, while Matthew's is accepted as that of Joseph. The all important fact to be remembered is that the Child promised by Gabriel to Mary, the virginal bride of Joseph, would be born in the royal line. A personal genealogy of Joseph was essentially that of Mary also, for they were cousins. Joseph is named as son of Jacob by Matthew, and as son of Heli by Luke; but Jacob and Heli were brothers, and it appears that one of the two was the father of Joseph and the other the father of Mary and therefore father-in-law to Joseph. That Mary was of Davidic descent is plainly set forth in many scriptures; for since Jesus was to be born of Mary, yet was not begotten by Joseph, who was the reputed, and, according to the law of the Jews, the legal, father, the blood of David's posterity was given to the body of Jesus through Mary alone. Our Lord, though repeatedly addressed as Son of David, never repudiated the title but accepted it as rightly applied to Himself. Apostolic testimony stands in positive assertion of the royal heirship of Christ through earthly lineage, as witness the affirmation of Paul, the scholarly Pharisee: "Concerning his Son Jesus Christ our Lord, which was made of the seed of David according to the flesh"; and again: "Remember that Jesus Christ of the seed of David was raised from the dead" (*JTC*, 85–86).

Mary the Mother of Jesus Christ. What marvelous and sacred secrets were treasured in that mother's heart; and what new surprises and grave problems were added day after day in the manifestations of unfolding wisdom displayed by her more than mortal Son! Though she could never have wholly forgotten, at times she seemingly lost sight of, her Son's exalted personality. That such conditions should exist was perhaps divinely appointed. There could scarcely have been a full measure of truly human experience in the relationship between Jesus and His mother, or between Him and Joseph, had the fact of His divinity been always dominant or even prominently apparent. Mary appears never to have fully understood her Son; at every new evidence of His uniqueness she marveled and pondered anew. He was hers, and yet in a very real sense not wholly hers. There was about their relation to each other a mystery, awful yet sublime, a holy secret which that chosen and blessed mother hesitated even to tell over to herself. Fear must have contended with joy within her soul because of Him (*JTC*, 115–16).

Character of Joseph, Guardian of the Son of God. When Joseph greeted his promised bride after her three months' absence, he was greatly distressed over the indications of her prospective maternity. Now, the Jewish law provided for the annulment of a betrothal in either of two ways—by public trial and judgment, or by private agreement attested by a written document signed in the presence of witnesses. Joseph was a just man, a strict observer of the law, yet no harsh extremist; moreover he loved Mary and would save her all unnecessary humiliation, whatever might be his own sorrow and suffering. For Mary's sake he dreaded the thought of publicity; and therefore determined to have the espousal annulled with such privacy as the law allowed. He was troubled and thought much of his duty in the matter, when, "behold, the angel of the Lord appeared unto him in a dream, saying, Joseph, thou son of David, fear not to take unto thee Mary thy wife: for that which is conceived in her is of the Holy Ghost. And she shall bring forth a son, and thou shalt call his name Jesus: for he shall save his people from their sins."

Great was Joseph's relief of mind; and great his joy in the realization that the long predicted coming of the Messiah was at hand; the words of the prophets would be fulfilled; a virgin, and she the one in the world most dear to him, had conceived, and in due time would bring forth that blessed Son, Emmanuel, which name by interpretation means "God with us." The angel's salutation was significant; "Joseph, thou son of David," was the form of address; and the use of that royal title must have meant to Joseph that, though he was of kingly lineage, marriage with Mary would cast no shadow upon his family status (*JTC*, 84–85).

BIRTH

Only Begotten Son. Mary's promised Son was to be "The Only Begotten" of the Father in the flesh; so it had been both positively and abundantly predicted. True, the event was unprecedented; true also it has never been paralleled; but that the virgin birth would be unique was as truly essential to the fulfillment of prophecy as that it should occur at all. That Child to be born of Mary was begotten of Elohim, the Eternal Father, not in violation of natural law but in accordance with a higher manifestation thereof; and, the offspring from that association of supreme sanctity, celestial Sireship, and pure though mortal maternity, was of right to be called the "Son of the Highest." In His nature would be combined the powers of Godhood with the capacity and possibilities of mortality; and this through the ordinary operation of the fundamental law of heredity, declared of God, demonstrated by science, and admitted by philosophy, that living beings shall propagate—after their kind. The Child Jesus was to inherit the physical, mental, and spiritual traits, tendencies, and powers that characterized His parents—one immortal and glorified—God, the other human—woman (*JTC*, 81).

Heaven Announced the Birth of the Son of God. From the period of its beginning, Bethlehem had been the home of people engaged mostly in pastoral and agricultural pursuits. It is quite in line with what is known of the town and its environs to find at the season of Messiah's birth, which was in the springtime of the year, that flocks were in the field both night and day under the watchful care of their keepers. Unto certain of these humble shepherds came the first proclamation that the Savior had been born. Thus runs the simple record: "And there were in the same country shepherds abiding in the field, keeping watch over their flock by night. And, lo, the angel of the Lord came upon them, and the glory of the Lord shone round about them: and they were sore afraid. And the angel said unto them, Fear not: for, behold, I bring you good tidings of great joy, which shall be to all people. For unto you is born this day in the city of David a Saviour, which is Christ the Lord. And this shall be a sign unto you: Ye shall find the babe wrapped in swaddling clothes, lying in a manger. And suddenly there was with the angel a multitude of the heavenly host praising God, and saying, Glory to God in the highest, and on earth peace, good will toward men."

Tidings of such import had never before been delivered by angel or received by man—good tidings of great joy, given to but few and those among the humblest of earth, but destined to spread to all people. There is sublime grandeur in the scene, as there is divine authorship in the message, and the climax is such as the mind of man could never have conceived—the sudden appearance of a multitude of the heavenly host, singing audibly to human ears the briefest, most consistent and most truly complete of all the songs of peace ever attuned by mortal or spirit choir. What a consummation to be wished—Peace on earth! But how can such come except through the maintenance of good will toward men? And through what means could glory to God in the highest be more effectively rendered?

The trustful and unsophisticated keepers of sheep had not asked for sign or confirmation; their faith was in unison with the heavenly communication; nevertheless the angel had given them what he called a sign, to guide them in their search. They waited not, but went in haste, for in their hearts they believed, yea, more than believed, they knew, and this was the tenor of their resolve: "Let us now go even unto Bethlehem, and see this thing which is come to pass, which the Lord hath made known unto us." They found the Babe in the manger, with the mother and Joseph nearby; and, having seen, they went out and testified to the truth concerning the Child. They returned to their flocks, glorifying and praising God for all they had heard and seen.

There is meaning as deep as the pathos that all must feel in the seemingly parenthetical remark by Luke. "But Mary kept all these things, and pondered them in her heart." It is apparent that the great truth as to the personality and mission of her divine Son had not yet unfolded itself in its fulness to her mind. The whole course of events, from the salutation of Gabriel to the reverent testimony of the shepherds concerning the announcing angel and the heavenly hosts, was largely a mystery to that stainless mother and wife (*JTC,* 94–95).

Date of the Birth of Jesus Christ. As to the season of the year in which Christ was born, there is among the learned as great a diversity of opinion as that relating to the year itself. It is claimed by many Biblical scholars that December 25th, the day celebrated in Christendom as Christmas, cannot be the correct date. We believe April 6th to be the birthday of Jesus Christ as indicated in a revelation of the present dispensation already cited, in which that day is made without qualification the completion of the one thousand eight hundred and thirtieth year since the coming of the Lord in the flesh. This acceptance is admittedly based on faith in modern revelation, and in no wise is set forth as the result of chronological research or analysis. We believe that Jesus Christ was born in Bethlehem of Judea, April 6, 1 B.C. (*JTC,* 104).

BOYHOOD

Jesus Christ's Boyhood. Concerning the home life of Joseph and his family in Nazareth, the scriptural record makes but brief mention. The silence with which the early period of the life of Jesus is treated by the inspired historians is impressive; while the fanciful accounts written in later years by unauthorized hands are full of fictitious detail, much of which is positively revolting in its puerile inconsistency. None but Joseph, Mary, and the other members of the immediate family or close associates of the household could have furnished the facts of daily life in the humble home at Nazareth; and from these qualified informants Matthew and Luke probably derived the knowledge of which they wrote. The record made by those who knew is marked by impressive brevity. In this absence of detail we may see evidence of the genuineness of the scriptural account. Inventive writers would have supplied, as, later, such did supply, what we seek in vain within the chapters of the Gospels. With hallowed silence do the inspired scribes honor the boyhood of their Lord; he who seeks to invent circumstances and to invest the life of Christ with fictitious additions, dishonors Him. Read thoughtfully the attested truth concerning the childhood of the Christ: "And the child grew, and waxed strong in spirit, filled with wisdom: and the grace of God was upon him."

In such simplicity is the normal, natural development of the Boy Jesus made clear. He came among men to experience all the natural conditions of mortality; He was born as truly a dependent, helpless babe as is any other child; His infancy was in all common features as the infancy of others; His boyhood was actual boyhood, His development was as necessary and as real as that of all children. Over His mind had fallen the veil of forgetfulness common to all who are born to earth, by which the remembrance of primeval existence is shut off. The Child grew, and with growth there came to Him expansion of mind, development of faculties, and progression in power and understanding. His advancement was from one grace to another, not from gracelessness to grace; from good to greater good, not from evil to good; from favor with God to greater favor, not from estrangement because of sin to reconciliation through repentance and propitiation (*JTC,* 111–12).

Development and Growth. Our knowledge of Jewish life in that age justifies the inference that the Boy was well taught in the law and the scriptures, for such was the rule. He garnered knowledge by study, and gained wisdom by prayer, thought, and effort. Beyond question He was trained to labor, for idleness was abhorred then as it is now; and every Jewish boy, whether carpenter's son, peasant's child, or rabbi's heir, was required to learn and follow a practical and productive vocation. Jesus was all that a boy should be, for His development was unretarded by the dragging weight of sin; He loved and obeyed the truth and therefore was free (*JTC,* 112).

Jesus Christ at the Age of Twelve. The amazement of Mary and her husband on finding the Boy in such distinguished company, and so plainly the object of deference and respect, and the joy of seeing again the beloved One who to them had been lost, did not entirely banish the memory of the anguish His absence had caused them. In words of gentle yet unmistakable reproof the mother said: "Son, why hast thou thus dealt with us? behold, thy father and I have sought thee sorrowing." The Boy's reply astonished them, in that it revealed, to an extent they had not before realized, His rapidly maturing powers of judgment and understanding. Said He: "How is it that ye sought me? wist ye not that I must be about my Father's business?"

Let us not say that there was unkind rebuke or unfilial reproof in the answer of this most dutiful of sons to His mother. His reply was to Mary a reminder of what she seems to have forgotten for the moment—the facts in the matter of her Son's paternity. She had used the words "thy father and I"; and her Son's response had brought anew to her mind the truth that Joseph was not the Boy's father. She appears to have been astonished that One so young should so thoroughly understand His position with respect to herself. He had made plain to her the inadvertent inaccuracy of her words; His Father had not been seeking Him; for was He not even at that moment in His Father's house, and particularly engaged in His Father's business, the very work to which His Father had appointed Him?

He had in no wise intimated a doubt as to Mary's maternal relationship to Himself; though He had indisputably shown that He recognized as His Father, not Joseph of Nazareth, but the God of Heaven. Both Mary and Joseph failed to comprehend the full import of His words. Though He understood the superior claim of duty based on His divine Sonship, and had shown to Mary that her authority as earthly mother was subordinate to that of His immortal and divine Father, nevertheless He obeyed her (*JTC*, 114–15).

Veil Removed Gradually. Christ's realization that He was the chosen and foreordained Messiah came to Him gradually (*JTC*, 128).

INCARNATE GOD

Jesus Christ Had a Physical Body. Jesus found a resting place near the stern of the ship and soon fell asleep. A great storm arose; and still He slept. The circumstance is instructive as it evidences at once the reality of the physical attributes of Christ, and the healthy, normal condition of His body. He was subject to fatigue and bodily exhaustion from other causes, as are all men; without food He grew hungry; without drink He thirsted; by labor He became weary. The fact that after a day of strenuous effort He could calmly sleep, even amidst the turmoil of a tempest, indicates an unimpaired nervous system and a good state of health. Nowhere do we find record of Jesus having been ill. He lived according to the laws of health, yet never allowed the body to rule the spirit; and His daily activities, which were of a kind to make heavy demands on both physical and mental energy, were met with no symptoms of nervous collapse nor of functional disturbance. Sleep after toil is natural and necessary. The day's work done, Jesus slept (*JTC*, 307–8).

JOHN THE BAPTIST

Preparation of John the Baptist. The man was John, son of Zacharias, soon to be known as the Baptist. He had spent many years in the desert, apart from the abodes of men, years of preparation for his particular mission. He had been a student under the tutelage of divine teachers; and there in the wilderness of Judea the word of the Lord reached him; as in similar environment it had reached Moses and Elijah of old (*JTC*, 121–22).

MINISTRY

Baptism of Jesus Christ. Christ's humble compliance with the will of His Father, by submitting to baptism even though He stood sinless, declares to the world in language more forceful than words that none are exempt from this requirement, and that baptism indeed is a requisite for salvation (*AF*, 130).

Marriage at Cana. The presence of Jesus at the marriage, and His contribution to the successful conduct of the feast, set the seal of His approval upon the matrimonial relationship and upon the propriety of social entertainment. He was neither a recluse nor an ascetic; He moved among men, eating and drinking, as a natural, normal Being (*JTC,* 146).

Purpose of the Law of Moses. At the time of the Exodus the Israelites constituted the few whom the Lord could call His own; and they had to undergo a disciplinary probation—a course of intensive and purifying cultivation, covering four decades in the wilderness—before they were deemed fit to enter the land of their inheritance. They were distinguished as Jehovah-worshipers, and as such stood apart from the more thoroughly apostate and degenerate world.

But even Israel's fields were full of tares; and the Lord mercifully suspended the fulness of the Gospel requirements, which, because of violation, would have been a means of condemnation; and the law of carnal commandments, generalized as the Mosaic Code, was given instead—as a schoolmaster, whose rigid insistence and compelling restraint, whose rod of correction would, in the course of centuries, prepare the covenant though recreant people for the reestablishment of the Gospel—as was effected through the personal ministry of the Redeemer. See Gal. 3:23–26 (*VM,* 33–34).

Law of Moses Honored. Among the afflicted seeking the aid that He alone could give came a leper, who knelt before Him, or bowed with his face to the ground, and humbly professed his faith, saying: "If thou wilt, thou canst make me clean." The petition implied in the words of this poor creature was pathetic; the confidence he expressed is inspiring. The question in his mind was not—Can Jesus heal me? but—Will He heal me? In compassionate mercy Jesus laid His hand upon the sufferer, unclean though he was, both ceremonially and physically, for leprosy is a loathsome affliction, and we know that this man was far advanced in the disease since we are told that he was "full of leprosy." Then the Lord said: "I will: be thou clean." The leper was immediately healed. Jesus instructed him to show himself to the priest, and make the offerings prescribed in the law of Moses for such cases as his.

In this instruction we see that Christ had not come to destroy the law, but, as He affirmed at another time, to fulfil it; and at this stage of His work the fulfillment was incomplete (*JTC,* 188–89).

A New Dispensation. The voice of His Father, to whom He was the Firstborn in the spirit-world, and the Only Begotten in the flesh, was of supreme assurance; yet that voice had been addressed to the three apostles rather than to Jesus, who had already received the Father's acknowledgment and attestation on the occasion of His baptism. The fullest version of the Father's words to Peter, James, and John is that recorded by Matthew: "This is my beloved Son, in whom I am well pleased; hear ye him." Aside from the proclamation of the Son's divine nature, the Father's words were otherwise decisive and portentous. Moses, the promulgator of the law, and Elijah the representative of the prophets and especially distinguished among them as the one who had not died, had been seen ministering unto Jesus and subservient to Him. The fulfillment of the law and the superseding of the prophets by the Messiah was attested in the command—Hear ye *Him.* A new dispensation had been established, that of the gospel, for which the law and the prophets had been but preparatory. The apostles were to be guided neither by Moses nor Elijah, but by *Him,* their Lord, Jesus the Christ (*JTC,* 373–74).

Aaronic Priesthood Operative in the Mosaic Dispensation and Until the Coming of Christ. From the ministry of Moses to that of Christ the Lesser Priesthood alone was operative upon the earth, excepting only the instances of specially delegated authority of the higher order such as is manifest in the ministrations of certain chosen prophets, Isaiah, Jeremiah, Ezekiel and others. It is evident that these prophets, seers, and revelators, were individually and specially commissioned; but it appears that they had not the authority to call and ordain successors, for in their time the Higher Priesthood was not existent on earth in an organized state with duly officered quorums. Not so with the Aaronic or Levitical Priesthood, however, for the courses or quorums of that order were continued until the time of Christ. The last to hold and exercise the authority of the Aaronic Priesthood under the old or Mosaic dispensation was John the Baptist, who was specially commissioned (*HL,* 235).

Authority to Forgive. Whatever may have been the measure of past offense on the part of the man suffering from palsy, Christ recognized his repentance together with the faith that accompanied it, and it was the Lord's rightful prerogative to decide upon the man's fitness to receive remission of his sins and relief from his bodily affliction. The interrogative response of Jesus to the unuttered criticism of the scribes, Pharisees, and doctors, has been interpreted in many ways. He inquired which was easier, to say, "Thy sins be forgiven thee," or to say, "Arise, and take up thy bed, and walk." Is it not a rational explanation that, when spoken authoritatively by Him, the two expressions were of allied meaning? The circumstance should have been a sufficient demonstration to all who heard, that He, the Son of Man, claimed and possessed the right and the power to remit both physical and spiritual penalties, to heal the body of visible disease, and to purge the spirit of the no less real malady of sin. In the presence of people of all classes Jesus thus openly asserted His divinity, and affirmed the same by a miraculous manifestation of power (*JTC*, 192–93).

Raising of Lazarus. The raising of Lazarus stands as the third recorded instance of restoration to life by Jesus. In each the miracle resulted in a resumption of mortal existence, and was in no sense a resurrection from death to immortality. In the raising of the daughter of Jairus, the spirit was recalled to its tenement within the hour of its quitting; the raising of the widow's son is an instance of restoration when the corpse was ready for the grave; the crowning miracle of the three was the calling of a spirit to reenter its body days after death, and when, by natural processes the corpse would be already in the early stages of decomposition. Lazarus was raised from the dead, not simply to assuage the grief of mourning relatives; myriads have had to mourn over death, and so myriads more shall have to do. One of the Lord's purposes was that of demonstrating the actuality of the power of God as shown forth in the works of Jesus the Christ, and Lazarus was the accepted subject of the manifestation; just as the man afflicted with congenital blindness had been chosen to be the one through whom "the works of God should be made manifest."

That the Lord's act of restoring Lazarus to life was of effect in testifying to His Messiahship is explicitly stated. All the circumstances leading up to final culmination in the miracle contributed to its attestation. No question as to the actual death of Lazarus could be raised, for his demise had been witnessed, his body had been prepared and buried in the usual way, and he had lain in the grave four days. At the tomb, when he was called forth, there were many witnesses, some of them prominent Jews, many of whom were unfriendly to Jesus and who would have readily denied the miracle had they been able. God was glorified and the divinity of the Son of Man was vindicated in the result (*JTC*, 495–96).

Jesus Christ Has Power over Elements. So intent were the people on hearing the Lord's words, and so concerned in the miraculous relief resulting from His healing ministrations, that they remained in the wilderness, oblivious to the passing of the hours, until the evening approached. It was the springtime, near the recurrence of the annual Passover festival, the season of grass and flowers. Jesus, realizing that the people were hungry, asked Philip, one of the Twelve, "Whence shall we buy bread, that these may eat?" The purpose of the question was to test the apostle's faith; for the Lord had already determined as to what was to be done. Philip's reply showed surprise at the question, and conveyed his thought that the suggested undertaking was impossible. "Two hundred pennyworth of bread is not sufficient for them, that every one of them may take a little," said he. Andrew added that there was a lad present who had five barley loaves, and two small fishes, "But," said he, "what are they among so many?"

Such is John's account; the other writers state that the apostles reminded Jesus of the lateness of the hour, and urged that He send the people away to seek for themselves food and lodging in the nearest towns. It appears most probable that the conversation between Jesus and Philip occurred earlier in the afternoon; and that as the hours sped, the Twelve became concerned and advised that the multitude be dismissed. The Master's reply to the apostles was: "They need not depart; give ye them to eat." In amazed wonder they replied: "We have here but five loaves and two fishes"; and Andrew's despairing comment is implied again—What are they among so many?

Jesus gave command, and the people seated themselves on the grass in orderly array; they were grouped in fifties and hundreds; and it was found that the multitude numbered about five thousand men, beside women and children. Taking the loaves and the fishes, Jesus looked toward heaven and pronounced a blessing upon the food; then, dividing the provisions, He gave to the apostles severally, and they in turn distributed to the multitude. The substance of both fish and bread increased under the Master's touch; and the multitude feasted there in the desert, until all were satisfied. To the disciples Jesus said: "Gather up the fragments that remain, that nothing be lost"; and twelve baskets were filled with the surplus.

As to the miracle itself, human knowledge is powerless to explain. Though wrought on so great a scale, it is no more nor less inexplicable than any other of the Lord's miraculous works. It was a manifestation of creative power, by which material elements were organized and compounded to serve a present and pressing need. The broken but unused portion exceeded in bulk and weight the whole of the original little store. Our Lord's direction to gather up the fragments was an impressive object-lesson against waste; and it may have been to afford such lesson that an excess was supplied. The fare was simple, yet nourishing, wholesome and satisfying. Barley bread and fish constituted the usual food of the poorer classes of the region (*JTC*, 333–34).

Jesus Christ Did Not Seek Popularity. He urged the people to refrain from spreading His fame; and this He may have done for the reason that at that stage of His work an open rupture with the Jewish hierarchy would have been a serious hindrance; or possibly He desired to leave the rulers, who were plotting against Him, time and opportunity to brew their bitter enmity and fill to the brim the flagons of their determined iniquity. Matthew sees in the Lord's injunctions against publicity a fulfillment of Isaiah's prophecy that the chosen Messiah would not strive nor cry out on the street to attract attention, nor would He use His mighty power to crush even a bruised reed, or to quench even the smoking flax; He would not fail nor be discouraged, but would victoriously establish just judgment upon the earth for the Gentiles, as well as, by implication, for Israel. The figure of the bruised reed and the smoking flax is strikingly expressive of the tender care with which Christ treated even the weakest manifestation of faith and genuine desire to learn the truth, whether exhibited by Jew or Gentile (*JTC*, 266–67).

TEACHINGS

Beatitudes. The opening sentences are rich in blessing, and the first section of the discourse is devoted to an explanation of what constitutes genuine blessedness; the lesson, moreover, was made simple and unambiguous by specific application, each of the blessed being assured of recompense and reward in the enjoyment of conditions directly opposite to those under which he had suffered. The blessings particularized by the Lord on this occasion have been designated in literature of later time as the Beatitudes. The poor in spirit are to be made rich as rightful heirs to the kingdom of heaven; the mourner shall be comforted for he shall see the divine purpose in his grief, and shall again associate with the beloved ones of whom he has been bereft; the meek, who suffer spoliation rather than jeopardize their souls in contention, shall inherit the earth; those that hunger and thirst for the truth shall be fed in rich abundance; they that show mercy shall be judged mercifully; the pure in heart shall be admitted to the very presence of God; the peacemakers, who try to save themselves and their fellows from strife, shall be numbered among the children of God; they that suffer persecution for the sake of righteousness shall inherit the riches of the eternal kingdom. To the disciples the Lord spake directly, saying: "Blessed are ye, when men shall revile you, and persecute you, and shall say all manner of evil against you falsely, for my sake. Rejoice, and be exceeding glad: for great is your reward in heaven: for so persecuted they the prophets which were before you."

It is evident that the specified blessings and the happiness comprised therein are to be realized in their fulness only beyond the grave;

though the joy that comes from the consciousness of right living brings, even in this world, a rich return. An important element in this splendid elucidation of the truly blessed state is the implied distinction between pleasure and happiness. Mere pleasure is at best but fleeting; happiness is abiding, for in the recollection thereof is joy renewed. Supreme happiness is not an earthly attainment; the promised "fulness of joy" lies beyond death and the resurrection. While man exists in this mortal state he needs some of the things of the world; he must have food and clothing and provision for shelter; and besides these bare necessities he may righteously desire the facilities of education, the incidentals of advancing civilization, and the things that are conducive to refinement and culture; yet all of these are but aids to achievement, not the end to attain which man was made mortal.

The Beatitudes are directed to the duties of mortal life as a preparation for a greater existence yet future. In the kingdom of heaven, twice named in this part of the Lord's discourse, are true riches and unfailing happiness to be found. The kingdom of heaven was the all-comprising text of this wonderful sermon; the means of reaching the kingdom and the glories of eternal citizenship therein are the main divisions of the treatise (*JTC*, 230–32).

Sermon on the Mount. The Sermon on the Mount has stood through all the years since its delivery without another to be compared with it. No mortal man has ever since preached a discourse of its kind. The spirit of the address is throughout that of sincerity and action, as opposed to empty profession and neglect. In the closing sentences the Lord showed the uselessness of hearing alone, as contrasted with the efficacy of doing. The man who hears and acts is likened unto the wise builder who set the foundation of his house upon a rock; and in spite of rain and hurricane and flood, the house stood. He that hears and obeys not is likened unto the foolish man who built his house upon the sand; and when rain fell, or winds blew, or floods came, behold it fell, and great was the fall thereof.

Such doctrines as these astonished the people. For His distinctive teachings the Preacher had cited no authority but His own. His address was free from any array of rabbinical precedents; the law was superseded by the gospel: "For he taught them as one having authority, and not as the scribes" (*JTC*, 246).

Jesus Christ Taught by the Father. The first part of His discourse is not recorded, but its scriptural soundness is intimated in the surprise of the Jewish teachers, who asked among themselves: "How knoweth this man letters, having never learned?" He was no graduate of their schools; He had never sat at the feet of their rabbis; He had not been officially accredited by them nor licensed to teach. Whence came His wisdom, before which all their academic attainments were as nothing? Jesus answered their troubled queries, saying: "My doctrine is not mine, but his that sent me. If any man will do his will, he shall know of the doctrine, whether it be of God, or whether I speak of myself." His Teacher, greater even than Himself, was the Eternal Father, whose will He proclaimed. The test proposed to determine the truth of His doctrine was in every way fair, and withal simple; anyone who would earnestly seek to do the will of the Father should know of himself whether Jesus spoke truth or error. The Master proceeded to show that a man who speaks on his own authority alone seeks to aggrandize himself. Jesus did not so; He honored His Teacher, His Father, His God, not Himself; and therefore was He free from the taint of selfish pride or unrighteousness (*JTC,* 400).

Marriage and Divorce. "Is it lawful for a man to put away his wife for every cause?" they asked. Jesus cited the original and eternal law of God in the matter; and indicated the only rational conclusion to be drawn therefrom: "Have ye not read, that he which made them at the beginning made them male and female, and said, For this cause shall a man leave father and mother, and shall cleave to his wife: and they twain shall be one flesh? Wherefore they are no more twain, but one flesh. What therefore God hath joined together, let no man put asunder." God had provided for honorable marriage, and had made the relation between husband and wife paramount even to that of children to parents; the severing of such a union was an invention of man, not a command of God. The Pharisees had a ready rejoinder: "Why did Moses then command to give a writing of divorcement, and to put her away?" Be it remembered that Moses had not commanded divorce, but had required that in case a man should separate from his wife he give her a bill of divorcement. Jesus made this fact plain, saying: "Moses because of the hardness of your hearts suffered you to put away your wives: but from the beginning it was not so."

The higher requirement of the gospel followed: "And I say unto you, Whosoever shall put away his wife, except it be for fornication, and shall marry another, committeth adultery: and whoso marrieth her which is put away doth commit adultery." The Mosaic provision had been but permissive, and was justified only because of existing unrighteousness. Strict compliance with the doctrine enunciated by Jesus Christ is the only means by which a perfect social order can be maintained. It is important to note, however, that in His reply to the casuistical Pharisees, Jesus announced no specific or binding rule as to legal divorces; the putting away of a wife, as contemplated under the Mosaic custom, involved no judicial investigation or action by an established court. In our Lord's day the prevailing laxity in the matter of marital obligation had produced a state of appalling corruption in Israel; and woman, who by the law of God had been made a companion and partner with man, had become his slave. The world's greatest champion of woman and womanhood is Jesus the Christ (*JTC,* 473–75).

NAMES AND TITLES

Jesus Christ—Names and Titles. The divinity of Jesus Christ is indicated by the specific names and titles authoritatively applied to Him. According to man's judgment there may be but little importance attached to names; but in the nomenclature of the Gods every name is a title of power or station. God is righteously zealous of the sanctity of His own name and of names given by His appointment. In the case of children of promise names have been prescribed before birth; this is true of our Lord Jesus and of the Baptist, John, who was sent to prepare the way for the Christ (*JTC,* 35).

Bread of Life. Then, reverting to the symbolism of the bread, He reiterated: "I am the bread of life." In further elucidation He explained that while their fathers did truly eat manna in the wilderness, yet they were dead; whereas the bread of life of which He spake would insure eternal life unto all who partook thereof. That bread, He averred, was His flesh. Against this solemn avowal the Jews complained anew, and disputed among themselves, some asking derisively: "How can this man give us his flesh to eat." Emphasizing the doctrine, Jesus continued: "Verily, verily, I say unto you, Except ye eat the flesh of the Son of man, and drink his blood, ye have no life in you. Whoso eateth my flesh, and drinketh my blood, hath eternal life; and I will raise him up at the last day. For my flesh is meat indeed, and my blood is drink indeed. He that eateth my flesh, and drinketh my blood, dwelleth in me, and I in him. As the living Father hath sent me, and I live by the Father: so he that eateth me, even he shall live by me. This is that bread which came down from heaven: not as your fathers did eat manna, and are dead: he that eateth of this bread shall live forever."

There was little excuse for the Jews pretending to understand that our Lord meant an actual eating and drinking of His material flesh and blood. The utterances to which they objected were far more readily understood by them than they are by us on first reading; for the representation of the law and of truth in general as bread, and the acceptance thereof as a process of eating and drinking, were figures in every-day use by the rabbis of that time. Their failure to comprehend the symbolism of Christ's doctrine was an act of will, not the natural consequence of innocent ignorance. To eat the flesh and drink the blood of Christ was and is to believe in and accept Him as the literal Son of God and Savior of the world, and to obey His commandments. By these means only may the Spirit of God become an abiding part of man's individual being, even as the substance of the food he eats is assimilated with the tissues of his body (*JTC*, 341–42).

Firstborn. His seniority to Abraham plainly referred to the status of each in the antemortal or preexistent state; Jesus was as literally the Firstborn in the spirit-world, as He was the Only Begotten in the flesh. Christ is as truly the Elder Brother of Abraham and Adam as of the last-born child of earth (*JTC*, 412).

I Am. This was an unequivocal and unambiguous declaration of our Lord's eternal Godship. By the awful title I AM He had made Himself known to Moses and thereafter was so known in Israel. As already shown, it is the equivalent of "Yahveh," or "Jahveh," now rendered "Jehovah," and signifies "The Self-existent One," "The Eternal," "The First and the Last" (*JTC*, 411–12).

Jehovah. We claim scriptural authority for the assertion that Jesus Christ was and is God the Creator, the God who revealed Himself to Adam, Enoch, and all the antediluvial patriarchs and prophets down to Noah; the God of Abraham, Isaac and Jacob; the God of Israel as a united people, and the God of Ephraim and Judah after the disruption of the Hebrew nation; the God who made Himself known to the prophets from Moses to Malachi; the God of the Old Testament record; and the God of the Nephites. We affirm that Jesus Christ was and is Jehovah, the Eternal One (*JTC*, 32).

Jesus Christ. When eight days old He was circumcised, as was required of every male born in Israel; and at the same time He received as an earthly bestowal the name that had been prescribed at the annunciation. He was called JESUS, which, being interpreted is Savior; the name was rightfully His for He came to save the people from their sins (*JTC*, 95).

Rabbi. The title Rabbi is equivalent to our distinctive appellations Doctor, Master, or Teacher. By derivation it means Master or my Master, thus connoting dignity and rank associated with politeness of address. A definite explanation of the term is given by John (1:38), and the same meaning attaches by implication to its use as recorded by Matthew (23:8). It was applied as a title of respect to Jesus on several occasions (Matt. 23:7, 8; 26:25, 49; Mark 9:5; 11:21; 14:45; John 1:38, 49; 3:2, 26; 4:31; 6:25; 9:2; 11:8). The title was of comparatively recent usage in the time of Christ, as it appears to have first come into general use during the reign of Herod the Great, though the earlier teachers, of the class without the name of Rabbis, were generally reverenced, and the title was carried back to them by later usage. Rab was an inferior title and Rabban a superior one to Rabbi. Rabboni was expressive of most profound respect, love and honor (see John 20:16) (*JTC*, 71).

Redeemer. So, for the advancement of man from his present fallen and relatively degenerate state to the higher condition of spiritual life, a power above his own must cooperate. Through the operation of the laws obtaining in the higher kingdom man may be reached and lifted; himself he cannot save by his own unaided effort. A Redeemer and Savior of mankind is beyond all question essential to the realization of the plan of the Eternal Father, "to bring to pass the immortality and eternal life of man"; and that Redeemer and Savior is Jesus the Christ, beside whom there is and can be none other (*JTC,* 28).

Son of Man. The distinguishing appellation has been construed by many to indicate our Lord's humble station as a mortal, and to connote that He stood as the type of humanity, holding a particular and unique relationship to the entire human family. There is, however, a more profound significance attaching to the Lord's use of the title "The Son of Man"; and this lies in the fact that He knew His Father to be the one and only supremely exalted Man, whose Son Jesus was both in spirit and in body—the Firstborn among all the spirit-children of the Father, the Only Begotten in the flesh—and therefore, in a sense applicable to Himself alone, He was and is the Son of the "Man of Holiness," Elohim, the Eternal Father. In His distinctive titles of Sonship, Jesus expressed His spiritual and bodily descent from, and His filial submission to, that exalted Father.

As revealed to Enoch the Seer, "Man of Holiness" is one of the names by which God the Eternal Father is known; "and the name of his Only Begotten is the Son of Man, even Jesus Christ." We learn further that the Father of Jesus Christ thus proclaimed Himself to Enoch: "Behold, I am God; Man of Holiness is my name; Man of Counsel is my name; and Endless and Eternal is my name, also." "The Son of Man" is in great measure synonymous with "The Son of God," as a title denoting divinity, glory, and exaltation; for the "Man of Holiness," whose Son Jesus Christ reverently acknowledges Himself to be, is God the Eternal Father (*JTC,* 143–44).

The Word. In the opening lines of the Gospel book written by John the apostle, we read: "In the beginning was the Word, and the Word was with God, and the Word was God. The same was in the beginning with God. All things were made by him; and without him was not anything made that was made. . . . And the Word was made flesh, and dwelt among us, (and we beheld his glory, the glory as of the only begotten of the Father,) full of grace and truth."

The passage is simple, precise and unambiguous. We may reasonably give to the phrase "In the beginning" the same meaning as attaches thereto in the first line of Genesis; and such signification must indicate a time antecedent to the earliest stages of human existence upon the earth. That the Word is Jesus Christ, who was with the Father in that beginning and who was Himself invested with the powers and rank of Godship, and that He came into the world and dwelt among men, are definitely affirmed. These statements are corroborated through a revelation given to Moses, in which he was permitted to see many of the creations of God, and to hear the voice of the Father with respect to the things that had been made: "And by the word of my power, have I created them, which is mine Only Begotten Son, who is full of grace and truth" (*JTC,* 10).

TRUE SHEPHERD

Parable of Lost Sheep. A direct application of the parable appears in the Lord's concise address to the Pharisees and scribes: "I say unto you, that likewise joy shall be in heaven over one sinner that repenteth, more than over ninety and nine just persons, which need no repentance."

Were they the ninety and nine, who, by self-estimation had strayed not, being "just persons, which need no repentance?" Some readers say they catch this note of just sarcasm in the Master's concluding words. In the earlier part of the story, the Lord Himself appears as the solicitous Shepherd, and by plain implication His example is such as the theocratic leaders ought to emulate. Such a conception puts the Pharisees and scribes in the position of shepherds rather than of sheep. Both explications are tenable; and each is of value as portraying the status and duty of professing servants of the Master in all ages (*JTC*, 455).

A True Shepherd of the Sheep. "I am the good shepherd." He then further showed, and with eloquent exactness, the difference between a shepherd and a hireling herder. The one has personal interest in and love for his flock, and knows each sheep by name, the other knows them only as a flock, the value of which is gaged by number; to the hireling they are only as so many or so much. While the shepherd is ready to fight in defense of his own, and if necessary even imperil his life for his sheep, the hireling flees when the wolf approaches, leaving the way open for the ravening beast to scatter, rend, and kill.

Never has been written or spoken a stronger arraignment of false pastors, unauthorized teachers, self-seeking hirelings who teach for pelf and divine for dollars, deceivers who pose as shepherds yet avoid the door and climb over "some other way," prophets in the devil's employ, who to achieve their master's purpose, hesitate not to robe themselves in the garments of assumed sanctity, and appear in sheep's clothing, while inwardly they are ravening wolves (*JTC*, 417–18).

DEATH

Mount of Transfiguration. Of the three synoptists, Luke alone makes even brief mention of the matter upon which Moses and Elijah conversed with the Lord at the Transfiguration. The record states that the visitants, who appeared in glory, "spake of his decease which he should accomplish at Jerusalem" (Luke 9:31). It is significant that the *decease,* which the Lord should *accomplish,* not the *death* that He should *suffer* or *die,* was the subject of that exalted communion. The Greek word of which "decease" appears as the English equivalent in many of the MSS. of the Gospels is one connoting "exodus" or "departure," and the word occurring in other early versions signifies "glory." So also the Greek original of "accomplish," in the account of the Transfiguration, connotes the successful filling out or completion of a specific undertaking, and not distinctively the act of dying. Both the letter of the record and the spirit in which the recorder wrote indicate that Moses and Elijah conversed with their Lord on the glorious consummation of His mission in mortality—a consummation recognized in the law (personified in Moses) and the prophets (represented by Elijah)—and an event of supreme import, determining the fulfillment of both the law and the prophets, and the glorious inauguration of a new and higher order as part of the divine plan. The *decease* that the Savior was then so soon to *accomplish* was the voluntary surrender of His life in fulfillment of a purpose at once exalted and foreordained, not a *death* by which He would passively *die* through conditions beyond His control (*JTC,* 377).

Veil of the Temple. The death of Christ was accompanied by terrifying phenomena. There was a violent earthquake; the rocks of the mighty hills were disrupted, and many graves were torn open. But, most portentous of all in Judaistic minds, the veil of the temple which hung between the Holy Place and the Holy of Holies was rent from top to bottom, and the interior, which none but the high priest had been permitted to see, was thrown open to common gaze. It was the rending of Judaism, the consummation of the Mosaic dispensation, and the inauguration of Christianity under apostolic administration (*JTC,* 662).

RESURRECTION AND ASCENSION

Jesus Christ Foretold His Resurrection. And while He hung in mortal suffering, the scoffers who passed by the cross wagged their heads and taunted the dying Christ with "Ah, thou that destroyest the temple, and buildest it in three days, save thyself, and come down from the cross." Yet His words to the Jews who had demanded the credentials of a sign had no reference to the colossal Temple of Herod, but to the sanctuary of His own body, in which, more literally than in the man-built Holy of Holies, dwelt the ever living Spirit of the Eternal God. "The Father is in me" was His doctrine.

"He spake of the temple of His body," the real tabernacle of the Most High. This reference to the destruction of the temple of His body, and the renewal thereof after three days, is His first recorded prediction relating to His appointed death and resurrection. Even the disciples did not comprehend the profound meaning of His words until after His resurrection from the dead; then they remembered and understood. The priestly Jews were not as dense as they appeared to be, for we find them coming to Pilate while the body of the crucified Christ lay in the tomb, saying: "Sir, we remember that that deceiver said, while he was yet alive, After three days I will rise again." Though we have many records of Christ having said that He would die and on the third day would rise again, the plainest of such declarations were made to the apostles rather than openly to the public. The Jews who waited upon Pilate almost certainly had in mind the utterance of Jesus when they had stood, nonplussed before Him, at the clearing of the temple courts (*JTC*, 156–57).

Jesus Christ the First to Be Resurrected. Christ was the first of all men to emerge from the tomb with spirit and body reunited, a resurrected immortalized Soul. Therefore is He rightly called "the firstfruits of them that slept," as also "the firstborn from the dead," and "the first begotten of the dead." (1 Cor. 15:20; Col. 1:18; Rev. 1:5.) The victory over death thus achieved by the foreordained Redeemer of the race was positively and abundantly foretold. That a literal resurrection shall come to all who have or shall have lived and died on earth is quite as strongly attested in Scripture (*VM*, 279).

Mary Magdalene and the Resurrected Lord. One may wonder why Jesus had forbidden Mary Magdalene to touch Him, and then, so soon after, had permitted other women to hold Him by the feet as they bowed in reverence. We may assume that Mary's emotional approach had been prompted more by a feeling of personal yet holy affection than by an impulse of devotional worship such as the other women evinced. Though the resurrected Christ manifested the same friendly and intimate regard as He had shown in the mortal state toward those with whom He had been closely associated, He was no longer one of them in the literal sense. There was about Him a divine dignity that forbade close personal familiarity. To Mary Magdalene Christ had said: "Touch me not; for I am not yet ascended to my Father." If the second clause was spoken in explanation of the first, we have to infer that no human hand was to be permitted to touch the Lord's resurrected and immortalized body until after He had presented Himself to the Father. It appears reasonable and probable that between Mary's impulsive attempt to touch the Lord, and the action of the other women who held Him by the feet as they bowed in worshipful reverence, Christ did ascend to the Father, and that later He returned to earth to continue His ministry in the resurrected state (*JTC*, 682).

Resurrected Lord Appears to Peter. "The Lord is risen indeed, and hath appeared to Simon." This is the sole mention made by the Gospel-writers of Christ's personal appearance to Simon Peter on that day. The interview between the Lord and His once recreant but now repentant apostle must have been affecting in the extreme. Peter's remorseful penitence over his denial of Christ in the palace of the high priest was deep and pitiful; he may have doubted that ever again would the Master call him His servant; but hope must have been engendered through the message from the tomb brought by the women, in which the Lord sent greetings to the apostles, whom for the first time He designated as His brethren, and from this honorable and affectionate characterization Peter had not been excluded; moreover, the angel's commission to the women had given prominence to Peter by particular mention. To the repentant Peter came the Lord, doubtless with forgiveness and loving assurance. The apostle himself maintains a reverent silence respecting the visitation, but the fact thereof is attested by Paul as one of the definite proofs of the Lord's resurrection (*JTC*, 687–88).

Recorded Appearances of the Savior Jesus Christ between His Resurrection and His Ascension.

1. To Mary Magdalene, near the sepulchre (Mark 16:9, 10; John 20:14).
2. To other women, somewhere between the sepulchre and Jerusalem (Matt. 28:9).
3. To two disciples on the road to Emmaus (Mark 16:12; Luke 24:13).
4. To Peter, in or near Jerusalem (Luke 24:34; 1 Cor. 15:5).
5. To ten of the apostles and others at Jerusalem (Luke 24:36; John 20:19).
6. To the eleven apostles at Jerusalem (Mark 16:14; John 20:26).
7. To the apostles at the Sea of Tiberias, Galilee, (John 21).
8. To the eleven apostles on a mountain in Galilee (Matt. 28:16).
9. To five hundred brethren at once (1 Cor. 15:6); locality not specified, but probably in Galilee.

10. To James (1 Cor. 15:7). Note that no record of this manifestation is made by the Gospel-writers.
11. To the eleven apostles at the time of the ascension, Mount of Olives, near Bethany (Mark 16:19; Luke 24:50, 51) (*JTC,* 699).

Resurrected Lord Foretold Peter's Death. The commission "Feed my sheep" was an assurance of the Lord's confidence, and of the reality of Peter's presidency among the apostles. He had emphatically announced his readiness to follow his Master even to prison and death. Now, the Lord who had died said unto him: "Verily, verily, I say unto thee, When thou wast young, thou girdest thyself, and walkedst whither thou wouldst: but when thou shalt be old, thou shalt stretch forth thy hands, and another shall gird thee, and carry thee whither thou wouldst not." John informs us that the Lord so spake signifying the death by which Peter should find a place among the martyrs; the analogy points to crucifixion, and traditional history is without contradiction as to this being the death by which Peter sealed his testimony of the Christ.

Then said the Lord to Peter, "Follow me." The command had both immediate and future significance. The man followed as Jesus drew apart from the others on the shore; yet a few years and Peter would follow his Lord to the cross. Without doubt Peter comprehended the reference to his martyrdom, as his writings, years later, indicate (*JTC,* 693).

Ascension. Worshipfully and with great joy the apostles returned to Jerusalem, there to await the coming of the Comforter. The Lord's ascension was accomplished; it was as truly a literal departure of a material Being as His resurrection had been an actual return of His spirit to His own corporeal body, theretofore dead. With the world abode and yet abides the glorious promise, that Jesus the Christ, the same Being who ascended from Olivet in His immortalized body of flesh and bones, shall return, descending from the heavens, in similarly material form and substance (*JTC*, 697).

SECOND COMING

God the Father Only Knew the Hour of the Second Coming. The Lord's statement that the time of His advent in glory was unknown to man, and that the angels knew it not, "neither the Son," but that it was known to the Father only, appears plain and unambiguous, notwithstanding many and conflicting commentaries thereon. Jesus repeatedly affirmed that His mission was to do the will of the Father; and it is evident that the Father's will was revealed to Him from time to time. While in the flesh He laid no claim to omniscience; though whatever He willed to know He learned through the medium of communication with the Father. Christ had not asked to know what the Father had not intimated His readiness to reveal, which, in this instance, was the day and hour of the Son's appointed return to earth as a glorified, resurrected Being. We need not hesitate to believe that at the time Jesus delivered to the apostles the discourse under consideration, He was uninformed on the matter; for He so states. In the last interview between Christ and the apostles immediately before His ascension (Acts 1:6, 7) they asked, "Lord, wilt thou at this time restore again the kingdom to Israel? And he said unto them, It is not for you to know the times or the seasons, which the Father hath put in his own power." Nor has the date of the Messianic consummation been since revealed to any man; though even now, the fig tree is rapidly putting forth its leaves, and he who hath eyes to see and a heart to understand knows that the summer of the Lord's purpose is near at hand (*JTC,* 589).

Jesus Christ Did Not Know the Hour of His Second Coming. Questions of supreme import to every one of us are these: (1) When will Christ come? (2) What shall be the purpose and attendant conditions of His coming?

The date of the Lord's advent has never been revealed to man, nor shall it be. Prior to His resurrection Jesus Himself did not know it, as witness His words: "But of that day and that hour knoweth no man, no, not the angels which are in heaven, neither the Son, but the Father." (Mark 13:32) (*VM,* 168–69).

TEACHINGS OF THE CHURCH

Teachings of the Church concerning Jesus Christ. Among the distinguishing features of the teachings of the Church concerning the Savior and Redeemer of the race are these:

First, the Church affirms the unity and continuity of the mission of the Christ in all ages. This, of necessity, involves the actuality, the verity, of His pre-existence and pre-ordination or foreordination in the spirit state.

Second, the fact of His ante-mortal Godship.

Third, the actuality of His birth in the flesh as the natural issue of divine and mortal parentage.

Fourth, the reality of His death and physical resurrection, as a result of which the power of death over mankind shall be eventually overcome.

Fifth, the literalness of the atonement wrought by Him, and the absolute requirement of individual compliance with the laws and requirements of His Gospel as the only means by which salvation may be attained.

Sixth, the restoration of His Priesthood and the re-establishment of His Church in the current age, which is verily the dispensation of the fullness of times.

Seventh, the certainty of His return to earth in the near future with power and great glory to reign in person and in bodily presence as Lord and King (CR, Apr. 1916, 125–26).

BIOGRAPHY

Written Record of Christ. No adequate biography of Jesus as Boy and Man has been or can be written, for the sufficing reason that a fulness of data is lacking. Nevertheless, man never lived of whom more has been said and sung, none to whom is devoted a greater proportion of the world's literature. He is extolled by Christian, Mohammedan and Jew, by skeptic and infidel, by the world's greatest poets, philosophers, statesmen, scientists, and historians. Even the profane sinner in the foul sacrilege of his oath acclaims the divine supremacy of Him whose name he desecrates (*JTC,* 3).

4

THE ATONEMENT
OF JESUS CHRIST

FOREORDAINED

A Sacrifice Foreordained. The offer of the firstborn Son to establish through His own ministry among men the gospel of salvation, and to sacrifice Himself, through labor, humiliation and suffering even unto death, was accepted and made the foreordained plan of man's redemption from death, of his eventual salvation from the effects of sin, and of his possible exaltation through righteous achievement (*JTC*, 18).

Christ Foreordained to Be the Redeemer. A Redeemer was chosen, and that even before the foundation of the world. He, the first-born among all the spirit children of God, was to come to earth, clothed with the attributes of both Godhood and manhood, to teach men the saving principles of the eternal Gospel and so establish on earth the terms and conditions of salvation. In consummation of His mission, Christ gave up His life as a voluntary and vicarious sacrifice for the race. Through the Atonement wrought by Him the power of death has been overcome; for while all men must die, their resurrection is assured. The effect of Christ's Atonement upon the race is twofold:

1. The eventual resurrection of all men, whether righteous or wicked. This constitutes Redemption from the Fall, and, since the Fall came through individual transgression, in all justice relief therefrom must be made universal and unconditional.

2. The providing of a means whereby reparation may be made and forgiveness be obtained for individual sin. This constitutes Salvation, and is made available to all through obedience to the laws and ordinances of the Gospel.

Between redemption from the power of death and salvation in the Kingdom of Heaven there is a vital difference. Man alone cannot save himself; Christ alone cannot save him. The plan of salvation is cooperative. The Atonement effected by the Lord Jesus Christ has opened the way; it is left to every man to enter therein and be saved or to turn aside and forfeit salvation. God will force no man either into heaven or into hell (*VM,* 48–49).

Foreordination of Jesus Christ. As already shown, the plan of the Father to open a way for the redemption of mankind, then to leave all men free to exercise their agency, was adopted by the council in heaven to the rejection of Lucifer's plan of compulsion. Even at that remote period Christ was thus ordained as a mediator for all mankind; in fact, "a covenant was entered into between Him and His Father, in which He agreed to atone for the sins of the world, and He thus, as stated, became the 'Lamb slain from before the foundation of the world.'" Prophets who lived centuries before the time of Christ's birth testified of Him and of the great work He had been ordained to perform. These men of God had been permitted to behold in prophetic vision many of the scenes incident to the Savior's earthly mission, and they solemnly bore record of the manifestations (*AF*, 81).

Ordained by the Father. In that august council of the angels and the Gods, the Being who later was born in flesh as Mary's Son, Jesus, took prominent part, and there was He ordained of the Father to be the Savior of mankind (*JTC*, 9).

Prophets Testify Jesus Christ Was Foreordained. The testimony of scriptures written on both hemispheres, that of records both ancient and modern, the inspired utterances of prophets and apostles, and the words of the Lord Himself, are of one voice in proclaiming the pre-existence of the Christ and His ordination as the chosen Savior and Redeemer of mankind—in the beginning, yea, even before the foundation of the world (*JTC*, 14).

PERFECTION REQUIRED

A Perfect Being. No other man has lived without sin, and therefore wholly free from the domination of Satan. Jesus Christ was the one Being to whom death, the natural wage of sin, was not due. Christ's sinlessness rendered Him eligible as the subject of the atoning sacrifice whereby propitiation could be made for the sins of all men (*SPM*, 129–30).

Jesus Christ Was the Only Acceptable Sacrifice. The Scriptures relieve us from the assumption that any ordinary mortal, by voluntarily giving up his life even as a martyr to the best of causes, could become a ransom for the sins of his fellows and a victor over death. Jesus Christ, though He lived and died as one of the human family, was of unique nature. Never has another such as He walked the earth. Christ was the only Being among all the embodied spirit-children of God suited to and acceptable as the great sacrifice of atonement, in these definite and distinct respects:

1. He was the One chosen and foreordained in the heavens to this specific service.
2. He was and is the Only Begotten of the Father in the body, and therefore the only Being ever born to earth who possessed in their fulness the inherent attributes of both Godhood and manhood.
3. He was and is the one and only sinless Man who has lived in mortality (*VM*, 54).

THE ATONEMENT PROCESS

Voice of God. The realization of the harrowing experiences upon which He was about to enter, and particularly the contemplation of the state of sin, which made His sacrifice imperative, so weighed upon the Savior's mind that He sorrowed deeply. "Now is my soul troubled," He groaned; "and what shall I say?" He exclaimed in anguish. Should He say, "Father, save me from this hour" when as He knew "for this cause" had He come "unto this hour"? To His Father alone could He turn for comforting support, not to ask relief from, but strength to endure, what was to come; and He prayed: "Father, glorify thy name." It was the rising of a mighty Soul to meet a supreme issue, which for the moment had seemed to be overwhelming. To that prayer of renewed surrender to the Father's will, "Then came there a voice from heaven, saying, I have both glorified it, and will glorify it again."

The voice was real; it was no subjective whisper of comfort to the inner consciousness of Jesus, but an external, objective reality. People who were standing by heard the sound, and interpreted it variously; some said it was thunder; others, of better spiritual discernment, said: "An angel spake to him"; and some may have understood the words as had Jesus. Now fully emerged from the passing cloud of enveloping anguish, the Lord turned to the people, saying: "This voice came not because of me, but for your sakes." And then, with the consciousness of assured triumph over sin and death, He exclaimed in accents of divine jubilation, as though the cross and the sepulchre were already of the past: "Now is the judgment of this world: now shall the prince of this world be cast out." Satan, the prince of the world was doomed. "And I," the Lord continued, "if I be lifted up from the earth, will draw all men unto me." John assures us that this last utterance signified the manner of the Lord's death; the people so understood, and they asked an explanation of what seemed to them an inconsistency, in that the scriptures, as they had been taught to interpret the same, declared that the Christ was to abide forever, and now He who claimed to be the Messiah, the Son of Man, averred that He must be lifted up. "Who is this Son of man?" they asked. Mindful as ever not to cast pearls where they would not be appreciated, the Lord refrained from a direct avowal, but admonished them to walk in the light while the light was with them, for darkness would surely follow; and, as He reminded them, "he that walketh in darkness knoweth not whither he goeth." In conclusion the Lord admonished them thus: "While ye have light, believe in the light, that ye may be the children of light" (*JTC*, 520–21).

A FUNDAMENTAL DOCTRINE
OF THE GOSPEL

Fundamental Doctrine. However incomplete may be our comprehension of the scheme of redemption through Christ's vicarious sacrifice in all its parts, we cannot reject it without becoming infidel; for it stands as the fundamental doctrine of all scripture, the very essence of the spirit of prophecy and revelation, the most prominent of all the declarations of God unto man (*AF,* 77).

Meaning of Atonement. The structure of the word in its present form is suggestive of the true meaning; it is literally *at-one-ment,* "denoting reconciliation, or the bringing into agreement of those who have been estranged." And such is the significance of the saving sacrifice of the Redeemer, whereby He expiated the transgression of the fall, through which death came into the world, and provided ready and efficient means for man's attainment of immortality through reconciliation with God (*AF*, 75).

Individual Effort. The individual effect of the Atonement makes it possible for any and every soul to obtain absolution from the effect of personal sins, through the mediation of Christ; but such saving intercession is to be invoked by individual effort as manifested through faith, repentance, and continued works of righteousness. The laws under which individual salvation is obtainable have been prescribed by Christ, whose right it is to say how the blessings made possible by His own sacrifice shall be administered. All men are in need of the Savior's mediation, for all are transgressors. So taught the apostles of old: "For all have sinned, and come short of the glory of God." And again: "If we say that we have no sin, we deceive ourselves, and the truth is not in us." The blessing of redemption from individual sins, while open for all to attain, is nevertheless conditioned on individual effort (*AF*, 89).

Price of Salvation. Thus no man can consistently hope for salvation in the Kingdom of God except through the Atonement of Jesus Christ; and the Atonement is made operative for the remission of sins through individual compliance with the conditions explicitly set forth by "the author of eternal salvation unto all them that obey him." (Heb. 5:9.) Christ's method of saving souls is that of providing definite means, which any one may accept or reject to his own eternal gain or loss.

Universal amnesty for crime may serve to increase crime. God's system of benevolence, which comprises and exceeds all that we call charity, consists in helping sinners to help themselves. Indiscriminate giving fosters pauperism in both the temporal and the spiritual sense. Man alone cannot save himself; and just as truly, Christ alone cannot save him. Obedience to the laws and ordinances of the Gospel is the price of salvation (*VM*, 62).

Purpose of Atonement. The atonement to be wrought by Jesus the Christ was ordained to overcome death and to provide a means of ransom from the power of Satan (*JTC*, 20).

Results of the Atonement Available to All. Thus it is plain that the effect of the atonement, so far as it applies to the victory over temporal or bodily death, includes the entire race. It is equally clear that the release from spiritual death, or banishment from the presence of God, is offered to all; so that if any man lose salvation such loss will be due to himself, and in no way be the inescapable effect of Adam's transgression. That the gift of redemption through Christ is free to all men was specifically taught by the apostles of old (*AF*, 86).

A VOLUNTARY SACRIFICE

Symbolism of a Fig Tree Being Cursed. The blighting of the barren fig tree is regarded by many as unique among the recorded miracles of Christ, from the fact that while all the others were wrought for relief, blessing, and beneficent purposes generally, this one appears as an act of judgment and destructive execution. Nevertheless in this miracle the Lord's purpose is not hidden; and the result, while fatal to a tree, is of lasting blessing to all who would learn and profit by the works of God. If no more has been accomplished by the miracle than the presenting of so impressive an object lesson for the instructions that followed, that smitten tree has proved of greater service to humanity than have all the fig orchards of Bethphage. To the apostles the act was another and an indisputable proof of the Lord's power over nature, His control of natural forces and all material things, His jurisdiction over life and death. He had healed multitudes; the wind and the waves had obeyed His words; on three occasions He had restored the dead to life; it was fitting that He should demonstrate His power to smite and to destroy. In manifesting His command over death, He had mercifully raised a maiden from the couch on which she had died, a young man from the bier on which he was being carried to the grave, another from the sepulchre in which he had been laid away a corpse; but in proof of His power to destroy by a word He chose a barren and worthless tree for His subject. Could any of the Twelve doubt, when, a few days later they saw Him in the hands of vindictive priests and heartless pagans, that did He so will He could smite His enemies by a word, even unto death? Yet not until after His glorious resurrection did even the apostles realize how truly voluntary His sacrifice had been (*JTC,* 525–26).

Jesus Christ—Physical Death a Sacrifice. Christ died, not as other men have died or shall die, because of inability to escape death, but for a special purpose by voluntary surrender. Thus, the atoning sacrifice was no usual death of an ordinary man, but the decease of One who had the power to live. It was a sacrifice, indeed! (*VM,* 56).

Jesus Christ Laid Down His Life. "Therefore doth my Father love me, because I lay down my life, that I might take it again. No man taketh it from me, but I lay it down of myself. I have power to lay it down, and I have power to take it again. This commandment have I received of my Father." The certainty of His death and of His subsequent resurrection are here reiterated. A natural effect of His immortal origin, as the earth-born Son of an immortal Sire, was that He was immune to death except as He surrendered thereto. The life of Jesus the Christ could not be taken save as He willed and allowed. The power to lay down His life was inherent in Himself, as was the power to take up His slain body in an immortalized state (*JTC*, 418).

Mission and Work of the Savior. Isaiah was permitted to read the scroll of futurity as to many distinguishing conditions to attend the Messiah's lowly life and atoning death. In Him the prophet saw One who would be despised and rejected of men, a Man of sorrows, acquainted with grief, One to be wounded and bruised for the transgressions of the race, on whom would be laid the iniquity of us all—a patient and willing Sacrifice, silent under affliction, as a lamb brought to the slaughter. The Lord's dying with sinners, and His burial in the tomb of the wealthy were likewise declared with prophetic certainty (*JTC*, 47).

GETHSEMANE

Suffering in Gethsemane. Christ's agony in the garden is unfathomable by the finite mind, both as to intensity and cause. The thought that He suffered through fear of death is untenable. Death to Him was preliminary to resurrection and triumphal return to the Father from whom He had come, and to a state of glory even beyond what He had before possessed; and, moreover, it was within His power to lay down His life voluntarily. He struggled and groaned under a burden such as no other being who has lived on earth might even conceive as possible. It was not physical pain, nor mental anguish alone, that caused Him to suffer such torture as to produce an extrusion of blood from every pore; but a spiritual agony of soul such as only God was capable of experiencing. No other man, however great his powers of physical or mental endurance, could have suffered so; for his human organism would have succumbed, and syncope would have produced unconsciousness and welcome oblivion. In that hour of anguish Christ met and overcame all the horrors that Satan, "the prince of this world" could inflict. The frightful struggle incident to the temptations immediately following the Lord's baptism was surpassed and overshadowed by this supreme contest with the powers of evil.

In some manner, actual and terribly real though to man incomprehensible, the Savior took upon Himself the burden of the sins of mankind from Adam to the end of the world. Modern revelation assists us to a partial understanding of the awful experience. In March 1830, the glorified Lord, Jesus Christ, thus spake: "For behold, I, God, have suffered these things for all, that they might not suffer if they would repent, but if they would not repent, they must suffer even as I, which suffering caused myself, even God, the greatest of all, to tremble because of pain, and to bleed at every pore, and to suffer both body and spirit: and would that I might not drink the bitter cup and—nevertheless, glory be to the Father, and I partook and finished my preparations unto the children of men."

From the terrible conflict in Gethsemane, Christ emerged a victor (*JTC*, 613–14).

TRIAL

Trial of Jesus Christ. From the account given in the fourth Gospel we infer that the Prisoner was first subjected to an interrogative examination by the high priest in person. That functionary, whether Annas, or Caiaphas is a matter of inference, inquired of Jesus concerning His disciples and His doctrines. Such a preliminary inquiry was utterly unlawful; for the Hebrew code provided that the accusing witnesses in any cause before the court should define their charge against the accused, and that the latter should be protected from any effort to make him testify against himself. The Lord's reply should have been a sufficient protest to the high priest against further illegal procedure. "Jesus answered him, I spake openly to the world; I ever taught in the synagogue, and in the temple, whither the Jews always resort; and in secret have I said nothing. Why askest thou me?—ask them which heard me, what I have said unto them: behold, they know what I said." This was a lawful objection against denying to a prisoner on trial his right to be confronted by his accusers. It was received with open disdain; and one of the officers who stood by, hoping perhaps to curry favor with his superiors, actually struck Jesus a vicious blow, accompanied by the question, "Answerest thou the high priest so?" To this cowardly assault the Lord replied with almost superhuman gentleness: "If I have spoken evil, bear witness of the evil: but if well, why smitest thou me?" Combined with submissiveness, however, this constituted another appeal to the principles of justice; if what Jesus had said was evil, why did not the assailant accuse Him; and if He had spoken well, what right had a police officer to judge, condemn, and punish, and that too in the presence of the high priest? Law and justice had been dethroned that night (*JTC*, 622–23).

CRUCIFIXION

Paschal Lamb Points to Christ. The system of sacrifice expressly enjoined in the Mosaic code was essentially a prototype of the sacrificial death to be accomplished by the Savior on Calvary. The blood of countless altar victims, slain by Israel's priests in the course of prescribed ritual, ran throughout the centuries from Moses to Christ as a prophetic flood in similitude of the blood of the Son of God appointed to be shed as an expiatory sacrifice for the redemption of the race. But, as already shown, the institution of bloody sacrifice as a type of the future death of Jesus Christ dates from the beginning of human history; since the offering of animal sacrifices through the shedding of blood was required of Adam, to whom the significance of the ordinance, as "a similitude of the sacrifice of the Only Begotten of the Father," was expressly defined.

The paschal lamb, slain for every Israelitish household at the annually recurring feast of the Passover, was a particular type of the Lamb of God who in due time would be slain for the sins of the world. The crucifixion of Christ was effected at the Passover season; and the consummation of the supreme Sacrifice, of which the paschal lambs had been but lesser prototypes, led Paul the apostle to affirm in later times: "For even Christ our passover is sacrificed for us" (*JTC*, 45–46).

Simon Carried the Cross. The sentence of death by crucifixion required that the condemned person carry the cross upon which he was to suffer. Jesus started on the way bearing His cross. The terrible strain of the preceding hours, the agony in Gethsemane, the barbarous treatment He had suffered in the palace of the high priest, the humiliation and cruel usage to which He had been subjected before Herod, the frightful scourging under Pilate's order, the brutal treatment by the inhuman soldiery, together with the extreme humiliation and the mental agony of it all, had so weakened His physical organism that He moved but slowly under the burden of the cross. The soldiers, impatient at the delay, peremptorily impressed into service a man whom they met coming into Jerusalem from the country, and him they compelled to carry the cross of Jesus. No Roman or Jew would have voluntarily incurred the ignominy of bearing such a gruesome burden; for every detail connected with the carrying out of a sentence of crucifixion was regarded as degrading. The man so forced to walk in the footsteps of Jesus, bearing the cross upon which the Savior of the world was to consummate His glorious mission, was Simon, a native of Cyrene. From Mark's statement that Simon was the father of Alexander and Rufus we infer that the two sons were known to the evangelist's readers as members of the early Church, and there is some indication that the household of Simon the Cyrenian came to be numbered with the believers (*JTC*, 652–53).

113

Agony of Gethsemane Returned. Jesus was nailed to the cross during the forenoon of that fateful Friday, probably between nine and ten o'clock. At noontide the light of the sun was obscured, and black darkness spread over the whole land. The terrifying gloom continued for a period of three hours. This remarkable phenomenon has received no satisfactory explanation from science. It could not have been due to a solar eclipse, as has been suggested in ignorance, for the time was that of full moon; indeed the Passover season was determined by the first occurrence of full moon after the spring equinox. The darkness was brought about by miraculous operation of natural laws directed by divine power. It was a fitting sign of the earth's deep mourning over the impending death of her Creator. Of the mortal agony through which the Lord passed while upon the cross the Gospel-scribes are reverently reticent.

At the ninth hour, or about three in the afternoon, a loud voice, surpassing the most anguished cry of physical suffering issued from the central cross, rending the dreadful darkness. It was the voice of the Christ: *"Eloi, Eloi, lama sabachthani? which is, being interpreted, My God, my God, why hast thou forsaken me?"* What mind of man can fathom the significance of that awful cry? It seems, that in addition to the fearful suffering incident to crucifixion, the agony of Gethsemane had recurred, intensified beyond human power to endure. In that bitterest hour the dying Christ was alone, alone in most terrible reality. That the supreme sacrifice of the Son might be consummated in all its fulness, the Father seems to have withdrawn the support of His immediate Presence, leaving to the Savior of men the glory of complete victory over the forces of sin and death (*JTC,* 660–61).

Crucifixion. We know however that our Lord was nailed to the cross by spikes driven through the hands and feet, as was the Roman method, and not bound only by cords as was the custom in inflicting this form of punishment among some other nations. Death by crucifixion was at once the most lingering and most painful of all forms of execution. The victim lived in ever increasing torture, generally for many hours, sometimes for days. The spikes so cruelly driven through hands and feet penetrated and crushed sensitive nerves and quivering tendons, yet inflicted no mortal wound. The welcome relief of death came through the exhaustion caused by intense and unremitting pain, through localized inflammation and congestion of organs incident to the strained and unnatural posture of the body.

As the crucifiers proceeded with their awful task, not unlikely with roughness and taunts, for killing was their trade and to scenes of anguish they had grown callous through long familiarity, the agonized Sufferer, void of resentment but full of pity for their heartlessness and capacity for cruelty, voiced the first of the seven utterances delivered from the cross. In the spirit of God-like mercy He prayed: *"Father, forgive them; for they know not what they do."* Let us not attempt to fix the limits of the Lord's mercy; that it would be extended to all who in any degree could justly come under the blessed boon thereof ought to be a sufficing fact. There is significance in the form in which this merciful benediction was expressed. Had the Lord said, "I forgive you," His gracious pardon may have been understood to be but a remission of the cruel offense against Himself as One tortured under unrighteous condemnation; but the invocation of the Father's forgiveness was a plea for those who had brought anguish and death to the Father's Well Beloved Son, the Savior and Redeemer of the world (*JTC,* 655–56).

Mocking of the Son of God. The soldiers whose duty it was to guard the crosses, until loitering death would relieve the crucified of their increasing anguish, jested among themselves, and derided the Christ, pledging Him in their cups of sour wine in tragic mockery. Looking at the title affixed above the Sufferer's head, they bellowed forth the devil-inspired challenge: "If thou be the king of the Jews, save thyself." The morbid multitude, and the passers-by "railed on him, wagging their heads, and saying, Ah, thou that destroyest the temple, and buildest it in three days, save thyself, and come down from the cross." But worst of all, the chief priests and the scribes, the elders of the people, the un-venerable Sanhedrists, became ringleaders of the inhuman mob as they gloatingly exulted and cried aloud: "He saved others; himself he can-not save. If he be the King of Israel, let him now come down from the cross, and we will believe him. He trusted in God; let him deliver him now, if he will have him: for he said, I am the Son of God." Though uttered in ribald mockery, the declaration of the rulers in Israel stands as an attestation that Christ had saved others, and as an intended iron-ical but a literally true proclamation that He was the King of Israel. The two malefactors, each hanging from his cross, joined in the general derision, and "cast the same in his teeth." One of them, in the despera-tion incident to approaching death, echoed the taunts of the priests and people: "If thou be Christ, save thyself and us."

The dominant note in all the railings and revilings, the ribaldry and mockery, with which the patient and submissive Christ was assailed while He hung, "lifted up" as He had said He would be, was that awful "If" hurled at Him by the devil's emissaries in the time of mortal agony; as in the season of the temptations immediately after His baptism it had been most insidiously pressed upon Him by the devil himself. That "If" was Satan's last shaft, keenly barbed and doubly envenomed, and it sped as with the fierce hiss of a viper. Was it possible in this the final and most dreadful stage of Christ's mission, to make Him doubt His divine Sonship, or, failing such, to taunt or anger the dying Savior into the use of His superhuman powers for personal relief or as an act of vengeance upon His tormentors? To achieve such a victory was Satan's desperate purpose. The shaft failed. Through taunts and derision, through blasphemous challenge and diabolical goading, the agonized Christ was silent (*JTC,* 657–59).

Power over Physical Death. What other man has lived with power to withstand death, over whom death could not prevail except through his own submission? Yet Jesus Christ could not be slain until His "hour had come," and that, the hour in which He voluntarily surrendered His life, and permitted His own decease through an act of will. Born of a mortal mother He inherited the capacity to die; begotten by an immortal Sire He possessed as a heritage the power to withstand death indefinitely. He literally gave up His life; to this effect is His own affirmation: "Therefore doth my Father love me, because I lay down my life, that I might take it again. No man taketh it from me, but I lay it down of myself. I have power to lay it down, and I have power to take it again." And further: "For as the Father hath life in himself; so hath he given to the Son to have life in himself." Only such a One could conquer death; in none but Jesus the Christ was realized this requisite condition of a Redeemer of the world (*JTC,* 22).

The Atonement Accepted by the Father. Fully realizing that He was no longer forsaken, but that His atoning sacrifice had been accepted by the Father, and that His mission in the flesh had been carried to glorious consummation, He exclaimed in a loud voice of holy triumph: *"It is finished."* In reverence, resignation, and relief, He addressed the Father saying: *"Father, into thy hands I commend my spirit."* He bowed His head, and voluntarily gave up His life.

Jesus the Christ was dead. His life had not been taken from Him except as He had willed to permit. Sweet and welcome as would have been the relief of death in any of the earlier stages of His suffering from Gethsemane to the cross, He lived until all things were accomplished as had been appointed (*JTC,* 661–62).

Consummation of the Mission of Jesus Christ. The shout of divine exultation from the cross, "It is finished," signified the consummation of the Lord's mission in mortality (*JTC,* 671).

VICARIOUS SACRIFICE

A Vicarious Sacrifice. The atonement was plainly to be a vicarious sacrifice, voluntary and love-inspired on the Savior's part, universal in its application to mankind so far as men shall accept the means of deliverance thus placed within their reach. For such a mission only one who was without sin could be eligible (*JTC,* 21).

The Greatest Event in History. The most significant sacrifice of all, the greatest work ever wrought amongst mankind, the pivotal event in human history, the supreme achievement which was at once the most glorious consummation and the most blessed beginning, is the Atonement of Christ; and this was pre-eminently a vicarious offering. No one who believes that Jesus died for man can doubt the validity and efficacy of vicarious ministration. He gave His life as a fore-ordained sacrifice, voluntarily offered and duly accepted as a propitiation for broken law, and the means by which salvation was made possible unto man.

"For behold, I, God, have suffered these things for all, that they might not suffer if they would repent, but if they would not repent, they must suffer even as I, which suffering caused myself, even God, the greatest of all, to tremble because of pain, and to bleed at every pore, and to suffer both body and spirit: and would that I might not drink the bitter cup and shrink—nevertheless, glory be to the Father, and I partook and finished my preparations unto the children of men."

The vicarious effect of the atonement of Christ is twofold; it has wrought a universal redemption of all men from the mortal death incident to the transgression of Adam; and it has provided a means of propitiation for individual sin whereby the sinner may attain salvation through obedience. It is by His mortal life and sacrificial death in behalf of others,—and those others, all who have lived or shall live,—that Jesus the Christ earned His title, Savior and Redeemer of mankind (*HL*, 78–79).

LAW OF JUSTICE

Atonement Effected According to Law. We have learned but little of the eternal laws operative in the heavens; but that God's purposes are accomplished through and by law is beyond question. There can be no irregularity, inconsistency, arbitrariness or caprice in His doings, for such would mean injustice. Therefore, the Atonement must have been effected in accordance with law. The self-sacrificing life, the indescribable agony, and the voluntary death of One who had life in Himself with power to halt His torturers at any stage, and whom none could slay until He permitted, must have constituted compliance with the eternal law of justice, propitiation and expiation by which victory over sin and death could be and has been achieved. Through the mortal life and sacrificial death of our Lord Jesus Christ the demands of justice have been fully met, and the way is opened for the lawful ministration of mercy so far as the effects of the Fall are concerned (*VM,* 58–59).

ALL WILL BE RESURRECTED

All Will Be Resurrected. So shall it be with every one of God's spirit-children who has been born in flesh; he shall be resurrected in flesh; for, through the infinite Atonement, physical death is but a temporary separation of spirit from body (*VM,* 282).

5

MORTAL PROBATION

AGENCY

Agency, a Gift from God. "The Father of souls has endowed His children with the divine birthright of free agency; He does not and will not control them by arbitrary force; He impels no man toward sin; He compels none to righteousness. Unto man has been given freedom to act for himself; and, associated with this independence, is the fact of strict responsibility and the assurance of individual accountability. In the judgment with which we shall be judged, all the conditions and circumstances of our lives shall be considered. The inborn tendencies due to heredity, the effect of environment whether conducive to good or evil, the wholesome teachings of youth, or the absence of good instruction—these and all other contributory elements must be taken into account in the rendering of a just verdict as to the soul's guilt or innocence. Nevertheless, the divine wisdom makes plain what will be the result with given conditions operating on known natures and dispositions of men, while every individual is free to choose good or evil within the limits of the many conditions existing and operative" (*JTC*, 29).

Mortal Man Free to Choose. The Church teaches as a strictly scriptural doctrine, that man has inherited among the inalienable rights conferred upon him by his divine Father, freedom to choose the good or the evil in life, to obey or disobey the Lord's commands, as he may elect. This right cannot be guarded with more jealous care than is bestowed upon it by God Himself; for in all His dealings with man He has left the mortal creature free to choose and to act, without compulsion or restraint beyond the influences of paternal counsel and direction. True, He has given commandments and has established statutes, with promises of blessings for compliance and penalties for infraction; but in the choice of these, men are untrammeled. In this respect, man is no less free than are the angels except as he has fettered himself with the bonds of sin and forfeited his power of will and force of soul. The individual has as full a measure of capability to violate the laws of health, the requirements of nature, and the commandments of God in matters both temporal and spiritual, as he has to obey all such; in the one case he brings upon himself the penalties that belong to the broken law; as in the other he inherits the specific blessings and the added freedom that attend a law-abiding life. Obedience to law is the habit of the free man; the transgressor fears the law, for he brings upon himself deprivation and restraint, not because of the law, which would have protected him in his freedom, but because of his antagonism to law (*AF*, 52–53).

Free to Choose. The doctrines of the Church are explicit in defining the relationship between the mortal probation and the future state, and in teaching individual accountability and the free agency of man. The Church affirms that in view of the responsibility under which every man rests, as the director of his own course, he must be and is free to choose in all things, from the life that leads to the celestial home to the career that is but the introduction to the miseries of perdition. Freedom to worship, or to refuse to worship, is a God-given right, and every soul must abide the result of his choice (*AF,* 410–11).

Man Subject to Good and Evil. A knowledge of good and evil is essential to the advancement that God has made possible for His children to achieve; and this knowledge can be best gained by actual experience, with the contrasts of good and its opposite plainly discernible. Therefore has man been placed upon earth subject to the influence of good and wicked powers, with a knowledge of the conditions surrounding him, and the heaven-born right to choose for himself. The words of the prophet Lehi are explicit: "Wherefore, the Lord God gave unto man that he should act for himself." . . . When the plans for creating and peopling the earth were under discussion in heaven, Lucifer sought to destroy the free agency of man by obtaining power to force the human family to do his will, promising the Father that by such means he would redeem all mankind so that not one of them should be lost. This proposition was rejected, while the original purpose of the Father—to use persuasive influences of wholesome precept and sacrificing example with the inhabitants of the earth, then to leave them free to choose for themselves—was agreed upon; and the one to be known as the Only Begotten Son was chosen as the chief instrument in carrying the purpose into effect (*AF*, 53–55).

PURPOSE OF MORTALITY

A Test of Obedience. The test of obedience constitutes the very purpose of our being upon earth—the object in view in the creation of the earth as an abode for man, the great object that the Lord had in peopling the earth. Do you remember his words to Abraham after the decree had been made plain that there should be formed an earth upon which those then unembodied spirits should dwell? The explanation was in part given: "And we will prove them herewith to see if they will do all things whatsoever the Lord their God shall command them." That is the sum total of the test of the examination under which every mortal has to pass in this great university of life. The Israel of old were required to pass that test, and promises were made unto them provided they passed it successfully (CR, Oct. 1919, 93–94).

Accountability. Our condition in the world to come will be strictly a result of the life we lead in this probation, as, by the light of revealed truth regarding the preexistent state, we perceive our present condition to be determined by the fidelity with which we kept our first estate. The scriptures declare that man shall reap the natural harvest of his works in life, be such good or evil; in the effective language with which the Father encourages and warns his frail children, every one will be rewarded or punished according to his works (*AF*, 404–5).

Adam and Eve Deserve Our Gratitude. It has become a common practise with mankind to heap reproaches upon the progenitors of the family, and to picture the supposedly blessed state in which we would be living but for the fall; whereas our first parents are entitled to our deepest gratitude for their legacy to posterity—the means of winning title to glory, exaltation, and eternal lives. But for the opportunity thus given, the spirits of God's offspring would have remained forever in a state of innocent childhood, sinless through no effort of their own; negatively saved, not from sin, but from the opportunity of meeting sin; incapable of winning the honors of victory because prevented from taking part in the conflict. As it is, they are heirs to the birthright of Adam's descendants—mortality, with its immeasurable possibilities and its God-given freedom of action. From Father Adam we have inherited all the ills to which flesh is heir; but such are necessarily incident to a knowledge of good and evil, by the proper use of which knowledge man may become even as the Gods (*AF,* 70).

Importance of the Physical Body. We have been told, as many of us know, and knew before, that this life is a necessary part in the course of progression designed by our Father. We have been taught, again, to look upon these bodies of ours as gifts from God. We Latter-day Saints do not regard the body as something to be condemned, something to be abhorred, and something to be subdued in the sense in which that expression is oft-times heard in the world. We regard as the sign of our royal birthright, that we have bodies upon the earth. We recognize the fact that those who kept not their first estate, in the primeval existence, were denied that inestimable blessing, the taking of mortal bodies. We believe that these bodies are to be well cared for, that they are to be looked upon as something belonging to the Lord, and that each may be made, in very truth, the temple of the Holy Ghost, the place into which the Spirit of God shall enter and where He shall delight to dwell, if He shall find there cleanliness and order and purity and uprightness of thought and conduct (CR, Oct. 1913, 117).

Proper Use of the Procreative Power. The earliest recorded commandment to the newly embodied pair provided for the procreation of their kind; for unto them the Lord said: "Be fruitful, and multiply, and replenish the earth." That the wedded state thus inaugurated was to be the permanent order of life amongst Adam's posterity is attested by the further Scripture: "Therefore shall a man leave his father and his mother, and shall cleave unto his wife: and they shall be one flesh." (Gen. 2:24.)

Inasmuch as the union of the sexes is the only way by which the perpetuity of the race is possible, such union is essentially as beneficent as it is necessary. Lawful, that is to say righteous, association of the sexes, is an uplifting and ennobling function to the participants, and the heritage of earth-life to preexistent spirits who are thereby advanced to the mortal state. Conversely, all sexual union outside the bonds of legitimacy is debasing and pernicious, not only to the guilty parties themselves, but to children who are thus ill-born, and to organized society in general. . . . Without the power of perpetuating his kind man is in part bereft of his glory; for small is the possibility of achievement within the limited range of an individual life. Grand as may seem to be the attainments of a man who is really great as gaged by the best standards of human estimation, the culmination of his glorious heritage lies in his leaving offspring from his own body to carry forward the worthy efforts of their sire. And as with the man, so with the woman. We regard children literally as gifts from God, committed to our parental care, for whose support, protection, and training in righteousness we shall be held to a strict accounting, remembering the solemn admonition and profound affirmation of the Christ: "Take heed that ye despise not one of these little ones; for I say unto you, That in heaven their angels do always behold the face of my Father which is in heaven." (Matt. 18:10.) (*VM*, 213–15).

Mortality Is an Opportunity to Ascend Back to God. It has been shown that mortality is divinely provided as a means of schooling and test, whereby the spirit offspring of God may develop their powers and demonstrate their characters. Every one of us has been advanced from the unembodied or preexistent state to our present condition, in which the individual spirit is temporarily united with a body of flesh and bones. Yet this promotion to the mortal state is regarded by many as a degradation; and we are prone to bewail the fallen condition of the race as an unmitigated calamity. The Scriptures make plain the glorious truth that man may rise far above the plane upon which he existed before his birth in the flesh. We have stooped that we may conquer; we have been permitted to descend only that we may attain greater heights (*VM*, 47–48).

Mortality Is Part of Eternal Progression. Our life in the flesh is but one stage in the course of the soul's eternal progress, a link connecting the eternities past with the eternities yet to come. The purpose of our mortal probation is that of education, training, trial, and test, whereby we demonstrate whether we will obey the commandments of the Lord our God and so lay hold on the boundless opportunities of advancement in the eternal worlds, or elect to do evil and forfeit the boon of citizenship in the Kingdom of Heaven.

The condition upon which mankind may have place in that Kingdom is compliance with the requirements laid down by Jesus Christ the Redeemer and Savior of the world, whose name is "the only name which shall be given under heaven, whereby salvation shall come unto the children of men." (Pearl of Great Price, p. 33.) (*VM*, 230).

Mortality Necessitates Help from God. The mortal probation is provided as an opportunity for advancement; but so great are the difficulties and the dangers, so strong is the influence of evil in the world, and so weak is man in resistance thereto, that without the aid of a power above that of humanity no soul would find its way back to God from whom it came. The need of a Redeemer lies in the inability of man to raise himself from the temporal to the spiritual plane, from the lower kingdom to the higher. . . . So, for the advancement of man from his present fallen and relatively degenerate state to the higher condition of spiritual life, a power above his own must cooperate. Through the operation of the laws obtaining in the higher kingdom man may be reached and lifted; himself he cannot save by his own unaided effort. A Redeemer and Savior of mankind is beyond all question essential to the realization of the plan of the Eternal Father, "to bring to pass the immortality and eternal life of man"; and that

Redeemer and Savior is Jesus the Christ, beside whom there is and can be none other (*JTC*, 26–28).

Righteous Also Suffer. We know the Lord does permit these calamities to come upon those who, according to our means of judgment and powers of analysis, may not have deserved the fate, but death, remember, is not finality. It is that which follows death with which we should have concern. Many are allowed to die in tempest and earthquake, whose death is but a passage into the blessed realms, because they are deserving of blessings; while unto others death does come as a judgment; and the Lord knows who fall because of their sins and who are permitted to fall because of their righteousness.

We have an instance in point concerning the connection of affliction and distress with individual culpability. You remember the Lord and his apostles once came to a blind beggar upon the street near the temple gates; "And his disciples asked him, saying, Master, who did sin, this man, or his parents, that he was born blind?"

Incidentally let us note that those who asked that question had an understanding of premortal existence, for surely the man could not have sinned in the flesh and brought upon him blindness at birth as a result. But the explanation given by the Lord is the important point for us to consider: "Jesus answered, Neither hath this man sinned, nor his parents: but that the works of God should be made manifest in him." The Lord's purposes were worked out in the case, for the man was healed, and the instance stands as a testimony for or against those who have become acquainted with the circumstance.

Incident to a period of cruel intolerance in religious matters among the aboriginal people of this continent, we read that evil-hearted persecutors put to death many women and children by burning, thinking that by this means they could terrify the rest into a denial of their faith. The Prophets Alma and Amulek were forced to witness the awful scenes. Though themselves in bonds they were brought there to witness the agony of the victims; and Amulek with zeal and righteous indignation desired to invoke the power of God to save those innocent sufferers: "But Alma said unto him: The Spirit constraineth me that I must not stretch forth mine hand: for behold the Lord receiveth them up unto himself, in glory; and he doth suffer that they may do this thing, or that the people may do this thing unto them, according to the hardness of their hearts, that the judgments which he shall exercise upon them in his wrath may be just; and the blood of the innocent shall stand as a witness against them, yea, and cry mightily against them at the last day." (Alma 14:11) (CR, Oct. 1923, 52).

Soul of Man. We have been told, as many of us know, and knew before, that this life is a necessary part in the course of progression designed by our Father. We have been taught, again, to look upon these bodies of ours as gifts from God. We Latter-day Saints do not regard the body as something to be condemned, something to be abhorred, and something to be subdued in the sense in which that expression is oft-times heard in the world. We regard as the sign of our royal birthright, that we have bodies upon the earth. We recognize the fact that those who kept not their first estate, in the primeval existence, were denied that inestimable blessing, the taking of mortal bodies. We believe that these bodies are to be well cared for, that they are to be looked upon as something belonging to the Lord, and that each may be made, in very truth, the temple of the Holy Ghost, the place into which the Spirit of God shall enter and where He shall delight to dwell, if He shall find there cleanliness and order and purity and uprightness of thought and conduct.

It is peculiar to the theology of the Latter-day Saints that we regard the body as an essential part of the soul. Read your dictionaries, the lexicons, and encyclopedias, and you will find that nowhere, outside of the Church of Jesus Christ, is the solemn and eternal truth taught that the soul of man is the body and the spirit combined. It is quite the rule to regard the soul as that incorporeal part of men, that immortal part which existed before the body was framed and which shall continue to exist after that body has gone to decay; nevertheless, that is not the soul; that is only a part of the soul; that is the spirit-man, the form in which every individual of us, and every individual human being, existed before called to take tabernacle in the flesh. It has been declared in the solemn word of revelation, that the spirit and the body constitute the soul of man; and, therefore, we should look upon this body as something that shall endure in the resurrected state, beyond the grave, something to be kept pure and holy. Be not afraid of soiling its hands; be not afraid of scars that may come to it if won in earnest effort, or in honest fight, but beware of scars that disfigure, that have come to you in places where you ought not have gone, that have befallen you in unworthy undertakings; beware of the wounds of battles in which you have been fighting on the wrong side (CR, Oct. 1913, 117).

We Become More like God through Obedience and Service. One may draw a lesson if he will, from the association of our Lord's words with the occurrence of Caesar's image on the coin. It was that effigy with its accompanying superscription that gave special point to His memorable instruction, "Render therefore unto Caesar the things which are Caesar's." This was followed by the further injunction: "and unto God the things that are God's." Every human soul is stamped with the image and superscription of God, however blurred and indistinct the line may have become through the corrosion or attrition of sin; and as unto Caesar should be rendered the coins upon which his effigy appeared, so unto God should be given the souls that bear His image. Render unto the world the stamped pieces that are made legally current by the insignia of worldly powers, and give unto God and His service, yourselves—the divine mintage of His eternal realm (*JTC*, 546–47).

WISE STEWARDS

Beware of Covetousness. This combined admonition and profound statement of truth was emphasized by the *Parable of the Foolish Rich Man*. Thus runs the story: "The ground of a certain rich man brought forth plentifully: And he thought within himself, saying, What shall I do, because I have no room where to bestow my fruits? And he said, This will I do: I will pull down my barns, and build greater; and there will I bestow all my fruits and my goods. And I will say to my soul, Soul, thou hast much goods laid up for many years; take thine ease, eat, drink, and be merry. But God said unto him, Thou fool, this night thy soul shall be required of thee: then whose shall those things be, which thou hast provided? So is he that layeth up treasure for himself, and is not rich toward God."

The man's abundance had been accumulated through labor and thrift; neglected or poorly-tilled fields do not yield plentifully. He is not represented as one in possession of wealth not rightfully his own. His plans for the proper care of his fruits and goods were not of themselves evil, though he might have considered better ways of distributing his surplus, as for the relief of the needy. His sin was twofold; first, he regarded his great store chiefly as the means of securing personal ease and sensuous indulgence; secondly, in his material prosperity he failed to acknowledge God, and even counted the years as his own. In the hour of his selfish jubilation he was smitten. Whether the voice of God came to him as a fearsome presentiment of impending death, or by angel messenger, or how otherwise, we are not informed; but the voice spoke his doom: "Thou fool, this night thy soul shall be required of thee." He had used his time and his powers of body and mind to sow, reap and garner—all for himself. And what came of it all? Whose should be the wealth, to amass which he had jeopardized his soul? Had he been other than a fool he might have realized as Solomon had done, the vanity of hoarding wealth for another, and he perhaps of uncertain character, to possess (*JTC*, 439–40).

SIN

Growth Hindered by Sin. What is the nature of sin? To this question the Apostle John replies: "Sin is the transgression of the law." In the original language of the Biblical records, many words occur for which our single term sin is used, all, however, conveying the common idea of opposition to the divine will. As God is the embodiment of perfection, such opposition is rebellion against the principles of advancement and adherence to the practises that lead to degradation. Sin is any condition, whether omission of things required or in commission of acts forbidden, that tends to prevent or hinder the development of the human soul. As a righteous course leads to eternal life, so sin tends toward the darkness of the second death. Sin was introduced to the world by Satan; yet it is by divine permission that mankind are brought in contact with sin, the contrast between evil and good thus being learned by experience (*AF*, 57–58).

Parable of Two Sons. Although this excellent parable was addressed to the chief priests, scribes, and elders, who had come in hostile spirit to demand of Christ the credentials of His authority, its lesson is of universal application. The two sons are yet alive in every human community—the one openly boastful of his sin, the other a hypocritical pretender. Jesus did not commend the rough refusal of the first son of whom the father made a righteous demand for service; it was his subsequent repentance attended by works that made him superior to his brother who had made fair promise but had kept it not. There are many today who boast that they make no profession of religion, nor pretense of godly life. Their frankness will not mitigate their sins; it simply shows that a certain species of hypocrisy is not prominent among their numerous offenses; but that a man is innocent of one vice, say that of drunkenness, in no wise diminishes his measure of guilt if he be a liar, a thief, an adulterer, or a murderer. Both the sons in the parable were grievous sinners; but the one turned from his evil ways, which theretofore he had followed with flagrant openness, while the other continued in dark deeds of sin, which he sought to cover by a cloak of hypocrisy. Let no man think that because he becomes intoxicated at the public bar he is any the less a drunkard than is he who swallows the "beverage of hell" in comparative privacy, though the latter be both drunkard and hypocrite. For these sins, as for all others, genuine repentance is the only saving antidote (*JTC*, 541).

Sin May Cause Disease. In many instances, however, disease is the direct result of individual sin (*JTC*, 192).

Sign Seekers. Have you never pondered over that remark of the Savior to those who came seeking a sign at his hand, when there were signs all about them? They had seen the sick healed, the lame made to walk, the deaf made to hear, the blind made to see, the dead raised to life, and still they came asking for a sign; and he answered them as be-fitted their hypocrisy:

"An evil and adulterous generation seeketh after a sign."

I ask, have you ever considered the connection between the awful sin of adultery and that godlessness that made those curiosity-seekers come asking for a sign? The word "adultery" and the word "idolatry" were originally one, that is, they sprang from the same root, and mean essentially the condition of being false to a solemn covenant.

The Lord compared himself—though in terms of rebuke—to the Israelites of old, as their husband. "I am married unto you," he said; and further, in effect: "O recreant Judah, backsliding Israel. I am married unto you. I love you as a husband loves his wife, and yet you go after strange gods and desert me, with whom you have made covenant" (CR, Oct. 1930, 71).

Sin Restricts Mortal Man. In the course of certain laboratory investigations I had need of a primary electric current of considerable power. My assistant prepared a voltaic battery consisting of a dozen cells of simple type. He followed the usual procedure, but, as I discovered later, gave inadequate attention to the details—those seeming trifles that make or mar perfection.

Each cell consisted of a cylindrical jar, containing an acid liquid in which were immersed a pair of plates, one of carbon, the other of zinc. The cells were connected "in series," so that the strength of the battery was the sum of the power developed by the twelve individual units. The working efficiency, or available and usable strength, was the total force developed less the resistance opposed by the cells themselves. The condition is comparable to that of income in the case of an individual or a company; the gross income includes all receipts, from which must be subtracted all costs, if we would determine the net income or actual profit. Or, by another simile, the condition presented by this battery was like that of a mechanical engine, the available efficiency of which is the total energy developed less the effect of friction and all other losses due to imperfect operation.

I was disappointed in the behavior of the battery; its working efficiency was far below what ought to be developed by twelve such units under normal conditions. A casual inspection showed that the cells were not working alike; some of them exhibited intense activity, and in all such the contained liquid was bubbling like boiling water, owing to the escape of liberated gases. The jar was a scene of fuss and fury; yet from such a cell there flowed a current so feeble as to be detectable only with difficulty. The energy developed within those foaming and fuming cells was practically used up in overcoming their own internal resistance, with no surplus power for outside service. I found some cells to be almost inert—with no observable action within, and from such, of course, no current was given out; these cells were practically dead. Certain others were working quietly, with little visible evidence of action aside from the gentle and regular escape of gas bubbles; nevertheless, from the quiet intensity of these, there issued a current potent to transmit messages from continent to continent beneath thousands of miles of ocean turmoil. By diluting the liquid in some jars and intensifying it in others, by replacing a few poorly amalgamated zincs with better ones, and by other modifying adjustments, I succeeded in restraining the wasteful energy of the abnormally active cells, and in arousing to action the dormant ones. The battery was brought into more harmonious operation—just as the restive members of a twelve-horse team might be quieted to steady action, the unwilling ones stimulated, and both brought into unison with their normal and really serviceable fellows.

However, after all such adjustments had been made, the battery was still unsatisfactory. Its operation was weak, irregular, uncertain, and wholly unsuited to the electrolysis required by the work in progress. At length, having become convinced that the fault was a radical one, that some defect was present which no ordinary patching-up process would remedy, I took the battery apart and subjected each cell to an individual examination. One after another passed the test and proved itself to be in measurably perfect condition, until eight had been thus disposed of; the ninth was seriously at fault. This cell was set aside, and the remaining three were tested; all of these were good. Plainly then, the inefficiency of the battery was chargeable to that one unit, number nine; and this, as I remembered, had been among the worst of the abnormally active cells. The eleven good units were connected up; and from the battery thus assembled there issued a current fairly adequate for my needs, and ample to operate an electric receiver or to fire a blast on the opposite side of the globe.

At the first opportunity of convenience I gave closer attention to the rejected unit. There was little difficulty in determining the true cause of the trouble. The cell was in a state of short-circuit; it had short-circuited itself. Through its unnatural intensity of action, as a result of its foaming and fuming, the acid had destroyed the insulation of some parts; and the current that should have been sent forth for service was wholly used up in destructive corrosion within the jar. The cell had violated the law of right action—*it had corrupted itself.* In its defective state it was not only worthless as a working unit, an unproductive member in the community of cells, but was worse than worthless in that it interposed an effective resistance in the operation of the other clean and serviceable units.

Do you wish to know what I did with the unclean cell? I did not destroy it, nor throw it aside as beyond all repair; there was a possibility of its restoration to some measure of usefulness. I searched its innermost parts, and with knife and file and rasp removed the corroded incrustment. I baptized it in a cleansing bath, then set it up again and tried it out in practical employ. Gradually it developed energy until it came to work well—almost as well as the other cells. Yet to this day I watch that unit with special care; I do not trust it as fully as I trusted before it had befouled itself.

I have called this little anecdote of the defective battery a parable; the story, however, is one of actual occurrence. To me there is profound suggestiveness in the incidents related. Even as I wrought in the laboratory, while hands and mind were busy in the work that engaged my close attention, the under-current of thought—the inner consciousness—was making comparison and application.

How like unto those voltaic cells are we! There are men who are loud and demonstrative, even offensive in their abnormal activity; like unto madmen in their uncontrol. Yet what do they accomplish in effective labor? Their energy is wholly consumed in overcoming the internal resistance of their defective selves. There are others who do but sleep and dream; they are slothful, dormant, and, as judged by the standard of utility, dead.

And again, there are men who labor so quietly as scarcely to reveal the fact that they are hard at work; in their utmost intensity there is no evidence of fussy demonstration or wasteful activity; yet such is their devoted earnestness that they influence the thoughts and efforts of the race.

How like a sinner was the unclean cell! Its unfitness was the direct effect of internal disorder, self-corruption, such defection as in man we call sin, which is essentially the violation of law. In association with others who are clean, able, and willing, the sinner is as an obstruction to the current; the efficiency of the whole is lessened if not entirely neutralized, by a single defective unit.

If you would have your personal prayers reach the Divine destination to which they are addressed, see to it that they are transmitted by a current of pure sincerity, free from the resistance of unrepented sin (*PJT,* 7–11).

Hypocrisy. Men are prone to judge their fellows and to praise or censure without due consideration of fact or circumstance. On prejudiced or unsupported judgment the Master set His disapproval. "Judge not, that ye be not judged," He admonished, for, according to one's own standard of judging others, shall he himself be judged. The man who is always ready to correct his brother's faults, to remove the mote from his neighbor's eye so that that neighbor may see things as the interested and interfering friend would have him see, was denounced as a hypocrite. What was the speck in his neighbor's vision to the obscuring beam in his own eye? Have the centuries between the days of Christ and our own time made us less eager to cure the defective vision of those who cannot or will not assume our point of view, and see things as we see them? (*JTC,* 244).

The Justice of God. According to the technical definition of sin it consists in the violation of law, and in this strict sense sin may be committed inadvertently or in ignorance. It is plain, however, from the scriptural doctrine of human responsibility and the unerring justice of God, that in his transgressions as in his righteous deeds man will be judged according to his ability to comprehend and obey law. To him who has never been made acquainted with a higher law the requirements of that law do not apply in their fulness. For sins committed without knowledge—that is, for laws violated in ignorance—a propitiation has been provided in the atonement wrought through the sacrifice of the Savior; and sinners of this class do not stand condemned, but shall be given opportunity yet to learn and to accept or reject the principles of the Gospel (*AF,* 58).

Justice of God Is Fair to All of His Children. Who shall question the justice of God, which denies salvation to all who will not comply with the prescribed conditions on which alone it is declared obtainable? Christ is "the author of eternal salvation unto all them that obey him," and God "will render to every man according to his deeds: to them who by patient continuance in well doing seek for glory and honor and immortality, eternal life: but unto them that are contentious, and do not obey the truth, but obey unrighteousness, indignation and wrath, tribulation and anguish, upon every soul of man that doeth evil" (*JTC,* 26).

PROFANITY

Profanity Common in the World. To take the name of God in vain, therefore, is to use that name lightly, to use it emptily, to use it without effect, so far as the intent is concerned—but nevertheless, with awful effect upon the profane user. We are apt to think that this has reference to the speaking of the name of God only, and in that particular respect the commandment is sufficiently weighty and important to us.

Profanity is all too common in the world—profanity of speech (CR, Oct. 1931, 50).

Profanity More Than the Spoken Word. But beyond this there is profanity of action which is of greater import than the spoken word, even as the prayer of the heart is greater than the prayer of the lips. Profanity in this sense is any manifestation of disrespect or irreverence for the name of God: blasphemy consists in attributing to Deity any unworthy act or motive, or in claiming for one's self the distinguishing attributes of Deity.

I listen with horror to profane swearing. One can not escape it wholly, go where one will; that is to say, as one has to meet diverse associations one is sure to encounter it. Of profanity I have not yet heard one word of defense. It is wholly demoralizing, wholly base, to say nothing of the sacrilege and blasphemy ofttimes associated in the linking of the name of Deity with our perverse expressions (CR, Oct. 1931, 50).

Misuse of God's Name. By way of summary:

1. We may take the name of God in vain by profane speech.
2. We take it in vain when we swear falsely, not being true to our oaths and promises.
3. We take it in vain in a blasphemous sense when we presume to speak in that name without authority.
4. And we take his name in vain whenever we wilfully do aught that is in defiance of his commandments,

since we have taken his name upon ourselves. (CR, October 1931, p. 53)

Blasphemy. Who were to be accursed? Those who preached any other gospel than that which he had preached unto them, for the gospel he had preached unto them was not of men; it had been given by revelation; and he preached it, as he had a right to do, in the name of the Lord Jesus Christ. Now he was referring to those who were on the inside, people who were going about amongst the Saints, many of whom, perhaps all of whom, claimed some standing with them, preaching a false doctrine and setting up a false gospel, and upon them he pronounced the anathema of cursing for presenting their own conceptions and their own views as the revealed word of God. Were such not deserving of a curse? Was it not deception of the most serious kind—preaching as the doctrines of Christ what was nothing more than the theories, the precepts and the commandments of men? (CR, April 1924, 67).

Preaching without Authority. If you wish to preach these things as the precepts of men, all well and good. Let those who will, listen to them; but to preach such and affirm that they are the doctrines of Jesus Christ, unless they are in harmony with the doctrines of Jesus Christ, is blasphemy (CR, Apr. 1924, 67).

LAW OF NATURE

Miracles in Harmony with Natural Law. Miracles are commonly regarded as occurrences in opposition to the laws of nature. Such a conception is plainly erroneous, for the laws of nature are inviolable. However, as human understanding of these laws is at best but imperfect, events strictly in accordance with natural law may appear contrary thereto. The entire constitution of nature is founded on system and order; the laws of nature, however, are graded as are the laws of man. The operation of a higher law in any particular case does not destroy the actuality of an inferior one. For example, society has enacted a law forbidding any man appropriating the property of another; yet oftentimes officers of the law forcibly seize the possessions of their fellowmen against whom judgments may have been rendered; and such acts are done to satisfy, not to violate justice. Jehovah commanded, "Thou shalt not kill," and mankind has reenacted the law, prescribing penalties for violation thereof. Yet sacred history testifies, that, in certain cases, the Lawgiver Himself has directly commanded that justice be vindicated by the taking of human life. The judge who passes the extreme sentence upon a convicted murderer, and the executioner who carries the mandate into effect act not in opposition to "Thou shalt not kill" but actually in support of this decree.

With some of the principles upon which the powers of nature operate we are in a degree acquainted; and in contemplating them we are no longer surprised, though deeper reflection may show that even the commonest phenomena are but little understood. But any event beyond the ordinary is regarded by the less thoughtful as miraculous, supernatural, if not indeed unnatural. When the prophet Elisha caused the ax to float in the river, he brought to his service a power superior to that of gravity. Without doubt the iron was heavier than the water; yet by the operation of this higher force it was supported, suspended, or otherwise sustained at the surface, as if it were held there by a human hand or rendered sufficiently buoyant by attached floaters.

Wine ordinarily consists of about four-fifths water, the rest being a variety of chemical compounds the elements of which are abundantly present in the air and soil. The ordinary method—what we term the natural method—of bringing these elements into proper combination is by planting the grape, then cultivating the vine till the fruit is ready to yield its juices in the press. But by a power not within purely human reach, Jesus Christ at the marriage in Cana brought those elements together, and effected a chemical transmutation within the waterpots resulting in the production of wine. So, too, when the multitudes were fed, under His priestly touch and authoritative blessing the bread and fish substance increased as if months had been covered by their growth according to what we consider the natural order. In the healing of the leprous, the palsied, and the infirm, the disordered bodily parts were brought again into their normal and healthful state; the impurities operating as poisons in the tissues were removed by means more rapid and effectual than those which depend upon the action of medicine (*AF*, 220–22).

EARTH AND MAN

Population of the Earth Is Set. But we are not left to mere inference on a basis of analogy; the scriptures plainly teach that the spirits of mankind are known and numbered unto God before their earthly advent. In his farewell administration to Israel Moses sang: "Remember the days of old. . . . When the Most High divided to the nations their inheritance, when he separated the sons of Adam, he set the bounds of the people according to the number of the children of Israel." From this we learn that the earth was allotted to the nations, according to the number of the children of Israel; it is evident therefore that the number was known prior to the existence of the Israelitish nation in the flesh; this is most easily explained on the basis of previous existence in which the spirits of the future nation were known.

No chance is possible, therefore, in the number or extent of the temporal creations of God. The population of the earth is fixed according to the number of spirits appointed to take tabernacles of flesh upon this planet; when these have all come forth in the order and time appointed, then, and not till then, shall the end come (*AF,* 193–94).

Relationship between Earth and Man. The earth was created primarily for the carrying out of the divine purposes respecting man. The astronomer regards it as one of the stellar units; the geologist looks upon it as the field for his investigation; but beyond such conceptions we regard it as one of the many spheres created with definite purpose, in which the destiny of the human race is the chief element and was the principal concern of the Creator, in bringing it into existence. We read, as the Lord revealed unto his friend and servant, Abraham, that before the earth was framed the Creator and those immediately associated with him looked out into space and said: We will take of these materials, and we will make an earth whereon these unembodied spirits may dwell; and we will prove them herewith, to see if they will do whatsoever the Lord their God shall command them.

Now, that being the purpose for which this world was created, we can readily understand that there is a very close relationship between earth and man. We read that when the transgression in Eden was passed upon by the voice of judgment the Lord said unto Adam: "Cursed is the ground for thy sake; . . . Thorns also and thistles shall it bring forth to thee; . . . In the sweat of thy face shalt thou eat bread."

This seemingly dire pronouncement would be nothing but fiction did it not mean that a great change came upon the earth itself under the curse; and the Scriptures reveal a very significant relationship between the development of earth processes and that of mankind. Indeed the earth has been personified. Righteous Enoch, we are told, regarded it as a being conscious and sentient, for we read:

"And it came to pass that Enoch looked, upon the earth: and he heard a voice from the bowels thereof, saying: Wo, wo is me, the mother of men; I am pained, I am weary, because of the wickedness of my children. When shall I rest, and be cleansed from the filthiness which is gone forth out of me? When will my Creator sanctify me that I may rest, and righteousness for a season abide upon my face?" (Moses 7:48)

Following further revelation unto this prophet and seer, concerning the then future development of the human race and the purposes of God concerning such, he cried out in anguish to the Lord: "When shall the earth rest?" It was then shown unto him that the resurrected Christ would return to the earth in a dispensation to be known as the last, the dispensation of fulness and restitution; and that he, the Lord, would inaugurate the millennial reign of peace. "And the day shall come that the earth shall rest, but before that day the heavens shall be darkened, and a veil of darkness shall cover the earth; and the heavens shall shake, and also the earth: and great tribulations shall be among the children of men, but my people will I preserve." Has it not been made known unto us that we may sanctify the earth or defile it according to our acts? There is a close connection between the righteousness or sinfulness of mankind and the occurrence of natural phenomena, benign or malignant as we regard them, good or bad, preserving or destroying as the case may be. Now the gross materialist may say there is no relationship between the righteousness of man and earthquakes, or between man's probity and floods. But there is! . . . As was foreseen, aye, and foretold, by the Christ himself and by his prophets who lived before his mortal birth and by those who lived after, in the earlier ages. and by the prophets of the present dispensation, great destruction has come and shall come upon the earth because of the sins of the human race (CR, Oct. 1923, 48–49, 51).

6

SATAN IS AN ENEMY
TO GOD AND MAN

PRE-EARTH

Fall of Lucifer. And there was war in heaven; Michael and his angels fought against the dragon; and the dragon fought and his angels, And prevailed not; neither was their place found any more in heaven." (See Rev. 12:7–9.)

John the Revelator beheld in vision this scene of primeval conflict between the hosts of unembodied spirits. Plainly this battle antedated the beginning of human history, for the dragon or Satan had not then been expelled from heaven, and at the time of his first recorded activity among mortals he was a fallen being.

In this antemortal contest the forces were unequally divided; Satan drew to his standard only a third of the spirit children of God (Rev. 12:4; Doctrine and Covenants 29:36–38 and 76:25–27), while the majority either fought with Michael or refrained from active opposition, and so accomplished the purpose of their "first estate." The angels who followed Satan "kept not their first estate" (Jude 6) and so forfeited the glorious possibilities of an advanced or "second estate." (Pearl of Great Price, p. 66.) The victory was won by Michael and his angels; and Satan, theretofore a "son of the morning," was cast out of heaven, yea "he was cast out into the earth, and his angels were cast out with him." (Rev. 12:9.)

About eight centuries prior to John's time, the principal facts of these momentous occurrences were revealed to Isaiah the prophet, who lamented with inspired pathos the fall of so great a one as Lucifer, and specified selfish ambition as the cause. Read Isaiah 14:12–15.

The question at issue in the war in heaven is of first importance to human-kind. From the record of Isaiah we learn that Lucifer, then of exalted rank among the spirits, sought to aggrandize himself without regard to the rights and agency of others. He aspired to the unrighteous powers of absolute autocracy. The principle for which Michael, the archangel contended, and which Lucifer sought to nullify, comprised the individual liberties or the free agency of the spirit hosts destined to be embodied in the flesh. The whole matter is set forth in a revelation given to Moses and repeated through Joseph Smith, the first prophet of the present dispensation:

"And I, the Lord God, spake unto Moses, saying: That Satan, whom thou hast commanded in the name of mine Only Begotten, is the same which was from the beginning, and he came before me, saying—Behold, here am I, send me, I will be thy son, and I will redeem all mankind, that one soul shall not be lost, and surely I will do it; wherefore give me thine honor. But, behold, my Beloved Son, which was my Beloved and Chosen from the beginning, said unto me—Father, thy will be done, and the glory be thine forever. Wherefore, because that Satan rebelled against me, and sought to destroy the agency of man, which I, the Lord God, had given him, and also, that I should give unto him mine own power; by the power of mine Only Begotten, I caused that he should be cast down. And he became Satan, yea, even the devil, the father of all lies, to deceive and to blind men, and to lead them captive at his will, even as many as would not hearken unto my voice." (Pearl of Great Price, pp. 15–16.)

Thus it is shown that before this earth was tenanted by man, Christ and Satan together with the hosts of the spirit offspring of God existed as intelligent individuals, with ability and power of choice, and freedom to follow the leaders whom they elected to obey. In that innumerable concourse of spirit intelligences, the Father's plan, whereby His children would be advanced to their second estate, was submitted and doubtless discussed.

Satan's plan of compulsion whereby all would be forcibly guided through mortality, bereft of freedom to act and agency to choose, so circumscribed that forfeiture of salvation would be impossible and not one soul could be lost, was rejected; and the humble offer of Jesus the Firstborn—to live among men as their Exemplar, observing the sanctity of man's agency while teaching men to use aright that Divine heritage—was accepted. The decision brought war, which resulted in the vanquishment of Lucifer and his angels, and they were cast out, deprived of the boundless privileges incident to the mortal or second estate (*VM*, 225–27).

Reality of Satan. But there is a personage known as Satan. Before he was cast out from heaven he was called Lucifer. [See D&C 76:26] He is just as truly a personage as are you or I am though he is not embodied. He is in that un-embodied state in which we existed prior to our birth into the flesh. And we read, as the Revelator tells us, [See Rev 12:1–9] and as Jude attests [See Jude 1:6], that he was cast out from heaven because of his rebellion, and all his angels or followers were cast out with him; numbering a third of the spirit-hosts of that particular class in heaven. So they were many, and they are many (CR, Apr. 1931, 30).

Satan Cast Out before the Earth Was Inhabited by Man. The devils are many, and their chieftain is Satan, who though unembodied is as truly an individual being as is any one of us. He is the personage who in the primeval world bore the exalted title of Lucifer, a son of the morning, and who with his rebellious horde was cast out, prior to the peopling of the earth. (See Rev. 12:7–9; also Doctrine and Covenants 29:36–38, and 76:25–27; and Isa. 14:12–15.) (*VM, 332*).

SATAN AND HIS FOLLOWERS

Evil Spirits Denied Mortal Bodies. In the synagog, on one of these occasions, was a man who was a victim of possession, and subject to the ravages of an evil spirit, or, as the text so forcefully states, one who "had a spirit of an unclean devil." It is significant that this wicked spirit, which had gained such power over the man as to control his actions and utterances, was terrified before our Lord and cried out with a loud voice, though pleadingly: "Let us alone; what have we to do with thee, thou Jesus of Nazareth? art thou come to destroy us? I know thee who thou art; the Holy One of God." Jesus rebuked the unclean spirit, commanding him to be silent, and to leave the man; the demon obeyed the Master, and after throwing the victim into violent though harmless paroxysm, left him. Such a miracle caused the beholders to wonder the more, and they exclaimed: "What a word is this! for with authority and power he commandeth the unclean spirits, and they come out. And the fame of him went out into every place of the country round about."

In the evening of the same day, when the sun had set, and therefore after the Sabbath had passed, the people flocked about Him, bringing their afflicted friends and kindred; and these Jesus healed of their divers maladies whether of body or of mind. Among those so relieved were many who had been possessed of devils, and these cried out, testifying perforce of the Master's divine authority: "Thou art Christ the Son of God."

On these as on other occasions, we find evil spirits voicing through the mouths of their victims their knowledge that Jesus was the Christ; and in all such instances the Lord silenced them with a word; for He wanted no such testimony as theirs to attest the fact of His Godship. Those spirits were of the devil's following, members of the rebellious and defeated hosts that had been cast down through the power of the very Being whose authority and power they now acknowledged in their demoniac frenzy. Together with Satan himself, their vanquished chief, they remained unembodied, for to all of them the privileges of the second or mortal estate had been denied; their remembrance of the scenes that had culminated in their expulsion from heaven was quickened by the presence of the Christ, though He stood in a body of flesh (*JTC*, 181–82).

Evil Spirits Recognized the Son of God. Christ was once followed by a multitude made up of people from Idumaea and Jerusalem, from Tyre and Sidon; among them were many who were possessed of evil spirits, and these, when they saw Him, fell down in the attitude of worship, exclaiming: "Thou art the Son of God." Was there ever mortal believer who confessed more unreservedly a knowledge of God and His Son Jesus Christ than did these servants of Satan? Satan knows God and Christ; remembers, perchance, somewhat concerning the position which he himself once occupied as a Son of the Morning; yet with all such knowledge he is Satan still. Neither belief nor its superior, actual knowledge, is efficient to save; for neither of these is faith. If belief is a product of the mind, faith is of the heart; belief is founded on reason, faith largely on intuition (*AF*, 98).

Gradation among Evil Spirits. The Savior's statement concerning the evil spirit that the apostles were unable to subdue—"Howbeit this kind goeth not out but by prayer and fasting"—indicates gradation in the malignity and evil power of demons, and gradation also in the results of varying degrees of faith (*JTC*, 395).

Type of Being Satan Is. On the best authority, that of the Lord Jesus Christ, we learn something of the character of this fallen son of the morning, the antagonist of righteousness, and the enemy of God and man. In denouncing the false beliefs and evil practices of certain unregenerate Jews, Christ spoke in these definite and forceful terms:

"Ye are of your father the devil, and the lusts of your father ye will do. He was a murderer from the beginning, and abode not in the truth, because there is no truth in him. When he speaketh a lie, he speaketh of his own: for he is a liar, and the father of it. And because I tell you the truth, ye believe me not." (John 8:44–45.)

A liar and a murderer from the beginning! He it was who beguiled the mother of the race, and that by the most dangerous of all falsehoods, the half-truth, in the use of which he is a past master.

He it was who taught the awful secret of murder to the fratricide, Cain, baiting the hook of infamous temptation with the lie, that, by slaying his brother, Cain would come into possession of Abel's flocks, and have much gain beside. (See Pearl of Great Price, pp. 22 and 23.)

He it was who deceived Israel, by inducing them to revolt against the theo-democracy under which they had prospered, and to clamor for a king. Under kingly rule the nation was brought into vassalage and obscurity.

Primordially he and his angels were "cast out into the earth," and here they have since been, going up and down in the world, seeking whom they may deceive.

He is the author of sophistry and degrading skepticism, and of the whole foul mass of the philosophy and science "falsely so called," by which mankind are led to doubt the word of God, to becloud the Scriptures with vain imaginings and private interpretations, and to narcotize the mind with the poison of human invention as a substitute for revealed truth.

He is an adept at compounding mixtures of truth and falsehood, with just enough of the one to inspire a dangerous confidence, and of the other a toxic portion.

Beware of his prescriptions, his tonics and medicaments. Remember that water may be crystal clear, and yet hold in solution the deadliest of poisons.

He it is who has deceived peoples, tribes, and races, into servile submission to self-constituted rulers, and made of the masses slaves of autocrats, rather than to assert and maintain their rights as free men, whatever the effort and sacrifice be.

He it is who seeks to lead men captive at his will, to destroy their power of agency and choice, to dupe them into bartering their birthright of freedom for the nauseating pottage of present expediency.

He it is who has cajoled men into the unscriptural conception that there are ways, many and variable, by which salvation is attainable, other than the one and only way provided by the Savior of souls.

He is the arch-deceiver, the master sophist, the prime dissembler, the prince of hypocrites.

Concerning the devil's plan of subverting the rights of man, and of those who support it, Moroni, the last of the Nephite prophets, wrote:

"Whoso buildeth it up, seeketh to overthrow the freedom of all lands, nations, and countries; and it bringeth to pass the destruction of all people, for it is built up by the devil, who is the father of all lies; even that same liar who beguiled our first parents; yea, even that same liar who hath caused man to commit murder from the beginning; who hath hardened the hearts of men, that they have murdered the

prophets, and stoned them, and cast them out from the beginning."
(Book of Mormon, Ether 8:25.)

Though great be Satan's power, deliverance therefrom is provided
through compliance with the Gospel of Jesus Christ, at whose advent,
now near at hand, the promised millennium of peace shall be inaugurated, a blessed feature of which is that the devil shall be rendered
impotent to further subjugate the souls of men, and "that he should deceive the nations no more, till the thousand years should be fulfilled."
(Rev. 20:3.) (*VM,* 332–34).

FALSE REVELATION

Spurious Revelations and Deceptions. The Lord manifested himself
to Moses, and talked to the man face to face. Moses records the fact,
and adds that he could not have looked upon the Lord with his physical eyes, but that the glory of the Lord was upon him, and he was able
to see with his spiritual eyes.

Then came Satan, the audacious, the father of lies, and represented
himself as being the son of God in the distinctive sense. Moses was
able to discern and perceive.

"And it came to pass that Moses looked upon Satan and said: Who
art thou? For behold, I am a son of God, in the similitude of his Only
Begotten; and where is thy glory, that I should worship thee?

"For behold, I could not look upon God, except his glory should
come upon me, and I were strengthened before him. But I can look
upon thee in the natural man. Is it not so surely?"

Oh, that we all had such power of discernment. That is a gift of the Spirit, to which we are entitled and we will have it as we live for it. With that gift we shall be free, to a great extent, from the deception that otherwise might lead us astray.

As the Lord gives revelations, so does Satan, each in his way. As the Lord has revelators upon the earth, so has Satan, and he is operating upon those men by his power, and they are receiving revelations, manifestations, that are just as truly of the devil as was his manifestation to Moses, to which I have referred.

We need the power of discernment. We need the inspiration of the Lord, that we may know the spirits with whom we have to deal, and recognize those who are speaking and acting under the influence of heaven, and those who are the emissaries of hell. Many have been led away in this Church. Go back to 1830. In September of that year, a few months only after the Church had been organized, Satan was at work, and men were receiving revelations which were put forth to offset those that were given to the Church through the Lord's chosen revelator, the Prophet Joseph Smith. He had been instrumental in translating the ancient records, and he had been given the aid of the Urim and Thummim. Hiram Page found a peculiar stone, and used that, as the devil seems to have influenced him, until the Lord had to speak and declare that that which Hiram Page had given unto the people was not of him and that when he had revelations to give to the Church he would give them through the man who was sustained as the revelator at the head of the Church, and not through somebody else. Read D&C, section 28.

Nevertheless the Lord makes plain in the scriptures of these days that his wondrous gifts, the gifts of the Spirit, can be possessed by those who live for them and they will be given severally, according as the Lord will, and he wills to give them unto those who will use them rightly, and not unto those who would dishonor them.

The Lord does not work miracles to satisfy idle curiosity or to gratify the lust of the evil-doer. When you hear, if hear you should, of men who are receiving revelations concerning the conduct of this Church, and those men are not such as you have sustained by the uplifted hand before the Lord as your representatives with the Lord, and as his prophets and revelators unto you, you may know that those men are not speaking by the power of God.

Now, do not be deceived. If men come to you and tell you that they have received manifestations and revelations telling of great developments that are to come, beware! So live that you may have the power of discernment. When they tell you that it has been made known to them that great wealth is to be taken out of the hills, under their direction; that they are to bring it forth with the prime purpose of using that wealth for the building up of the Church, for the erection of a great temple, toward which eventuality the eyes of the Latter-day Saints are turned, you may know that they are not of God. No temple will ever be built as the result of the gifts of a rich man, or of a few rich men. In building temples the Lord requires a specific kind of money. It must be sanctified money. It must be the money of sacrifice, and he needs the pennies of the faithful poor as much as the gold pieces of the rich.

We may all have part in building the great temple to which reference is often made, as we have all had the privilege of taking part in building the temples that have already been erected.

Satan has tried to appear as an angel of light in earlier dispensations.

He is doing so today. John the Revelator warned the people of this very day in which we live. He wrote for our warning of what would take place. He saw evil powers, and he calls them the spirits of devils, working miracles and deceiving the people. It was so in olden time. While the Lord was speaking through Isaiah and the other great prophets of pre-meridian time, Satan was at work with his witches and wizards, with his soothsayers, giving spurious messages and trying to lead the people astray.

When the Christ came in person manifesting his inherent power over men and evil spirits, when he cast out unclean spirits that were afflicting men, there arose many who undertook to exorcise the demons, and to imitate the work of Christ so far as was possible. And when the Gospel was again brought to earth, and the Priesthood restored in this, the last dispensation, there was a great revival and increase in the manifestations called spiritualistic phenomena, in the effort to put something forth that looked like the original and the genuine, and so lead people astray.

Oh, ye Latter-day Saints, ye men of mighty testimony, ye women of wondrous assurance, shall you, shall we, forget what the Lord has given us by way of certain knowledge, and be led away by false lights, by those who are receiving spurious revelations, as they call them, for guidance? (CR, Apr. 1931, 28–30).

TEMPTATION

Serpent in the Garden of Eden. The serpent, having served the purposes of Satan, was made a subject of divine displeasure, being doomed to crawl forever in the dust, and to suffer from the enmity which it was decreed should be placed in the hearts of Eve's children (*AF,* 68).

Complacency. Sin is conducive to lethargy in things spiritual; the Gospel inspires to life and activity. Contentment with the things of this world, so long as they go to suit us, with no thought of what shall follow, is the devil's lullaby. In the moment of supreme complacency when we are expressing by word, act, thought, or through sheer inaction, the stultifying soliloquy "Soul, take thine ease," may come the summoning decree: "Thou fool, this night thy soul shall be required of thee." Read Luke 12:16–21 (*VM,* 316).

Pleasure versus True Happiness. "The present is an age of pleasure-seeking, and men are losing their sanity in the mad rush for sensations that do but excite and disappoint. In this day of counterfeits, adulterations, and base imitations, the devil is busier than he has ever been in the course of human history, in the manufacture of pleasures, both old and new; and these he offers for sale in most attractive fashion, falsely labeled, *Happiness.* In this soul-destroying craft he is without a peer; he has had centuries of experience and practice, and by his skill he controls the market. He has learned the tricks of the trade, and knows well how to catch the eye and arouse the desire of his customers. He puts up the stuff in bright-colored packages, tied with tinsel string and tassel; and crowds flock to his bargain counters, hustling and crushing one another in their frenzy to buy.

"Follow one of the purchasers as he goes off gloatingly with his gaudy packet, and watch him as he opens it. What finds he inside the gilded wrapping? He has expected fragrant happiness, but uncovers only an inferior brand of pleasure, the stench of which is nauseating.

"Happiness includes all that is really desirable and of true worth in pleasure, and much beside. Happiness is genuine gold, pleasure but gilded brass, which corrodes in the hand, and is soon converted into poisonous verdigris. Happiness is as the genuine diamond, which, rough or polished, shines with its own inimitable luster; pleasure is as the paste imitation that glows only when artificially embellished. Happiness is as the ruby, red as the heart's blood, hard and enduring; pleasure, as stained glass, soft, brittle, and of but transitory beauty.

"Happiness is true food, wholesome, nutritious and sweet; it builds up the body and generates energy for action, physical, mental and spiritual; pleasure is but a deceiving stimulant which, like spirituous drink, makes one think he is strong when in reality enfeebled; makes him fancy he is well when in fact stricken with deadly malady.

"Happiness leaves no bad after-taste, it is followed by no depressing reaction; it calls for no repentance, brings no regret, entails no remorse; pleasure too often makes necessary repentance, contrition, and suffering; and, if indulged to the extreme, it brings degradation and destruction.

"True happiness is lived over and over again in memory, always with a renewal of the original good; a moment of unholy pleasure may leave a barbed sting, which, like a thorn in the flesh, is an ever-present source of anguish.

"Happiness is not akin with levity, nor is it one with light-minded mirth. It springs from the deeper fountains of the soul, and is not infrequently accompanied by tears. Have you never been so happy that you have had to weep? I have" (*JTC*, 247–48).

Cannot Blame Satan for All Evil. In the same way many of us blame Satan for a great deal for which he is not responsible—poor devil. If Satan and his hosts were bound today and no longer able to work personally upon the earth, evil would go on for a long time, because he has very able representatives in the flesh. When I traveled in distant Russia, years ago, I learned of a peculiar conception among the moujiks, or peasants, in that land. They say that there is a household sprite, an unseen little imp that dwells in every house and that is always trying to cause trouble; and if a girl, through carelessness, drops a dish and breaks it, the mother shakes her head and says, "That was the sprite." If the man forgets himself and gets drunk, and in his drunkenness wreaks barbarity, they say, "Ah, poor fellow; he is under the influence of the sprite; he could not help it;" and so for every little detail of life they find an excuse and blame that little unseen imp for their own acts of evil or carelessness (CR, Oct. 1914, 104).

Jesus Christ Tempted. Hungry as Jesus was, there was a temptation in Satan's words even greater than that embodied in the suggestion that He provide food for His famishing body—the temptation to put to proof the possible doubt implied in the tempter's "If." The Eternal Father had proclaimed Jesus as His Son; the devil tried to make the Son doubt that divine relationship. Why not prove the Father's interest in His Son at this moment of dire necessity? Was it proper that the Son of God should go hungry? Had the Father so soon forgotten as to leave

His Beloved Son thus to suffer? Was it not reasonable that Jesus, faint from long abstinence, should provide for Himself, and particularly so since He could provide, and that by a word of command, *if* the voice heard at His baptism was that of the Eternal Father. *If* thou be in reality the Son of God, demonstrate thy power, and at the same time satisfy thy hunger—such was the purport of the diabolical suggestion. To have yielded would have been to manifest positive doubt of the Father's acknowledgment (*JTC*, 129).

Jesus Christ Knows How to Succor His People. But why proceed with labored reasoning, which can lead to but one conclusion, when our Lord's own words and other scriptures confirm the fact? Shortly before His betrayal, when admonishing the Twelve to humility, He said: "Ye are they which have continued with me in my temptations." While here we find no exclusive reference to the temptations immediately following His baptism, the exposition is plain that He had endured temptations, and by implication, these had continued throughout the period of His ministry. The writer of the epistle to the Hebrews expressly taught that Christ was peccable, in that He was tempted "in all points" as are the rest of mankind. Consider the unambiguous declaration: "Seeing then that we have a great high priest, that is passed into the heavens, Jesus the Son of God, let us hold fast our profession. For we have not an high priest which cannot be touched with the feeling of our infirmities; but was in all points tempted like as we are, yet without sin." And further: "Though he were a Son, yet learned he obedience by the things which he suffered" (*JTC*, 135).

Constant War with Satan. That Christ was subject to temptation during the period of His association with the apostles He expressly affirmed. That His temptations extended even to the agony in Gethsemane will appear as we proceed with this study. It is not given to the rest of us, nor was it given to Jesus, to meet the foe, to fight and overcome in a single encounter, once for all time. The strife between the immortal spirit and the flesh, between the offspring of God on the one hand, the world and the devil on the other, is persistent through life (*JTC,* 133).

Peter, James, and John in Gethsemane. Returning to them in an agony of soul Jesus found them sleeping; and addressing Peter, who so short a time before had loudly proclaimed his readiness to follow the Lord even to prison and death, Jesus exclaimed: "What, could ye not watch with me one hour? Watch and pray, that ye enter not into temptation"; but in tenderness added, "the spirit indeed is willing, but the flesh is weak." The admonition to the apostles to pray at that time lest they be led into temptation may have been prompted by the exigencies of the hour, under which, if left to themselves, they would be tempted to prematurely desert their Lord (*JTC,* 611–12).

Imitator. But the admonishment is: "Touch not the evil gift, nor the unclean thing." What is meant by that? Satan from the first has been a great imitator; he is an experienced strategist. Never has the Lord set his hand to do a specific thing for the good of his people upon the earth, of outstanding feature, but that Satan has attempted to imitate it in some degree (CR, Apr. 1931, 27).

Satan Counterfeits. You know this is a day of imitations, a day of adulteration and counterfeits, a day when shoddy is palmed off for all-wool cloth, and gilded brass passes too often current for genuine gold; aye, a day when glass paste does duty as diamonds of the first water. Of all the imitators, of all the counterfeiters, Satan is the chief, for he has had the greatest experience and the longest training and he is a skillful salesman: he not only knows how to manufacture his spurious goods, but how to put them upon the market. And it is wonderfully attractive—the way in which he does up those little packages in bright-colored paper, tied with tinsel string to attract: and we are very apt to pay the price asked before we open the package. And do you know of all the counterfeits and of all the imitations that the devil has put forth on sale, I know of none that is more dangerous than his spurious brands of liberty and freedom, such as are being offered on every hand (CR, Oct. 1912, 127).

SPIRIT PRISON

Prisoners of Satan. In the decisive issues of war there are victors and vanquished; the casualties comprise killed, wounded, and prisoners. Generally, capture by the enemy is the form of individual calamity most dreaded by the gallant soldier who knows he is fighting for the right, and particularly so if the foe be ruthless or treacherous.

In the battle of life as a whole, analogous conditions and categories obtain. The slain may have fallen in honor; for the disabled there is hope of recovery; but the fate of the captured is one of apprehension or dread certainty, ofttimes of horror.

When one is taken prisoner as the result of venturesome curiosity, reckless exposure, or disobedience to orders he must bear the blame as well as the suffering consequent on capture. Many are prisoners because thoughtlessly, wilfully, or defiantly, they have trespassed upon the devil's ground, without warrant of duty or justifiable excuse. The soldier's part is to keep within the lines until ordered forward in attack to dislodge the foe.

Hosts of capable souls have heedlessly put themselves into the enemy's power by yielding to the treacherous invitation to fraternize with sin. Such a one is made welcome in the camp of the foe, and, at first a visitor, he sooner or later awakens to the fact that he is a prisoner, and withal a deserter from the ranks of patriotism and honor (*VM, 335*).

Eternal Punishment. True, the Scriptures speak of endless punishment, and depict everlasting burnings, eternal damnation, and the sufferings incident to unquenchable fire, as features of the judgment reserved for the wicked. But none of these awful possibilities are anywhere in Scripture declared to be the unending fate of the individual sinner.

Blessing or punishment ordained of God is eternal, for He is eternal, and eternal are all His ways. His is a system of endless and eternal punishment, for it will always exist as the place or condition provided for the rebellious and disobedient; but the penalty as visited upon the individual will terminate when through repentance and expiation the necessary reform has been effected and the uttermost farthing paid (*VM,* 255).

Hell Has an Entrance and Exit. During this hundred years many other great truths not known before, have been declared to the people, and one of the greatest is that to hell there is an exit as well as an entrance. Hell is no place to which a vindictive judge sends prisoners to suffer and to be punished principally for his glory; but it is a place prepared for the teaching, the disciplining of those who failed to learn here upon the earth what they should have learned. True, we read of everlasting punishment, unending suffering, eternal damnation. That is a direful expression; but in his mercy the Lord has made plain what those words mean. "Eternal punishment," he says, is God's punishment, for he is eternal; and that condition or state or possibility will ever exist for the sinner who deserves and really needs such condemnation; but this does not mean that the individual sufferer or sinner is to be eternally and everlastingly made to endure and suffer. No man will be kept in hell longer than is necessary to bring him to a fitness for something better. When he reaches that stage the prison doors will open and there will be rejoicing among the hosts who welcome him into a better state. The Lord has not abated in the least what he has said in earlier dispensations concerning the operation of his law and his gospel, but he has made clear unto us his goodness and mercy through it all, for it is his glory and his work to bring about the immortality and eternal life of man (CR, Apr. 1930, 97).

Demands of Justice Must Be Met. It is blasphemous to thus attribute caprice and vindictiveness to the divine nature. In the justice of God no soul shall be condemned under any law that has not been made known unto him. True, eternal punishment has been decreed as the lot of the wicked; but the meaning of this expression has been given by the Lord Himself: eternal punishment is God's punishment; endless punishment is God's punishment, for "Endless" and "Eternal" are among His names, and the words are descriptive of His attributes. No soul shall be kept in prison or continued in torment beyond the time requisite to work the needed reformation and to vindicate justice, for which ends alone punishment is imposed (*AF,* 146–47).

Punished according to the Sin. As rewards for righteous deeds are proportionate to deserving acts, so the punishment prescribed for sin is made adequate to the offense. But, be it remembered, both rewards and punishments are natural consequences. Punishment is inflicted upon the sinner for disciplinary and reformatory purposes and in accordance with justice. There is nothing of vindictiveness or of desire to cause suffering manifest in the divine nature; on the contrary, our Father is cognizant of every pang, and permits such to afflict for beneficent purposes only. God's mercy is declared in the retributive pains that He allows, as in the blessings of peace that issue from Him. It is scarcely profitable to speculate as to the exact nature of the spiritual suffering imposed as punishment for sin. Comparison with physical pain, such as the tortures of fire in a sulphurous lake, serve to show that the human mind is incapable of comprehending the extent of these penalties. The sufferings entailed by the fate of condemnation are more to be feared than are any possible inflictions of physical torture; the mind, the spirit, the whole soul is doomed to suffer, and the torment is known by none in the flesh (*AF,* 59).

Spirits in Prison. Upon all who reject the word of God in this life will fall the penalties provided; but after the debt has been paid the prison doors shall be opened, and the spirits once confined in suffering, then chastened and clean, shall come forth to partake of the glory provided for their class (*AF,* 148).

SONS OF PERDITION

Unpardonable Sin. Then, the demonstration being complete, and the absurdity of His opponents' assumption proved, Christ directed their thoughts to the heinous sin of condemning the power and authority by which Satan was overcome. He had proved to them on the basis of their own proposition that He, having subdued Satan, was the embodiment of the Spirit of God, and that through Him the kingdom of God was brought to them. They rejected the Spirit of God, and sought to destroy the Christ through whom that Spirit was made manifest. What blasphemy could be greater? Speaking as one having authority, with the solemn affirmation "I say unto you," He continued: "All manner of sin and blasphemy shall be forgiven unto men: but the blasphemy against the Holy Ghost shall not be forgiven unto men. And whosoever speaketh a word against the Son of man, it shall be forgiven him: but whosoever speaketh against the Holy Ghost, it shall not be forgiven him, neither in this world, neither in the world to come."

Who among men can word a more solemn and awful warning against the danger of committing the dread unpardonable sin? Jesus was merciful in His assurance that words spoken against Himself as a Man, might be forgiven; but to speak against the authority He possessed, and particularly to ascribe that power and authority to Satan, was very near to blasphemy against the Holy Ghost, for which sin there could be no forgiveness (*JTC*, 268–69).

Sons of Perdition. Consider the word of the Lord regarding those whose sin is the unpardonable one, whose transgression has carried them beyond the present horizon of possible redemption; those who have sunk so low in their wickedness as to have lost the power and even the desire to attempt reformation. Sons of Perdition they are called. These are they who, having learned the power of God afterward renounce it; those who sin wilfully in the light of knowledge; those who open their hearts to the Holy Spirit and then put the Lord to a mockery and a shame by denying it; and those who commit murder wherein they shed innocent blood; these are they of whom the Savior has declared that it would be better for them had they never been born. These are to share the punishment of the devil and his angels—punishment so terrible that the knowledge is withheld from all except those who are consigned to this doom, though a temporary view of the picture is permitted to some. These sinners are the only ones over whom the second death hath power: "Yea, verily, the only ones who shall not be redeemed in the due time of the Lord" (*AF*, 60).

Betrayal of Judas. On earlier occasions they had made futile attempts to get Jesus into their hands; and they were naturally dubious as to the outcome of their later machinations. At this juncture they were encouraged and gladdened in their wicked plots by the appearance of an unexpected ally. Judas Iscariot, one of the Twelve, sought an audience with these rulers of the Jews, and infamously offered to betray his Lord into their hands. Under the impulse of diabolic avarice, which, however, was probably but a secondary element in the real cause of his perfidious treachery, he bargained to sell his Master for money, and chaffered with the priestly purchasers over the price of the Savior's blood. "What will ye give me?" he asked; "and they covenanted with him for thirty pieces of silver." This amount, approximately seventeen dollars in our money, but of many times greater purchasing power with the Jews in that day than now with us, was the price fixed by the law as that of a slave; it was also the foreseen sum of the blood-money to be paid for the Lord's betrayal. That the silver was actually paid to Judas, either at this first interview or at some later meeting between the traitor and the priests, is demonstrated by after events.

He had pledged himself to the blackest deed of treachery of which man is capable, and from that hour he sought the opportunity of superseding his infamous promise by its more villainous fulfilment. We are yet to be afflicted by other glimpses of the evil-hearted Iscariot in the course of this dread chronicle of tragedy and perdition; for the present let it be said that before Judas sold Christ to the Jews, he had sold himself to the devil; he had become Satan's serf, and did his master's bidding (*JTC*, 591–92).

Fall of Judas. Today we speak of a traitor as a "Judas" or an "Iscariot." The man who made the combined name infamous has been for ages a subject of discussion among theologians and philosophers, and in later times the light of psychological analysis has been turned upon him. German philosophers were among the earliest to assert that the man had been judged in unrighteousness, and that his real character was of brighter tint than that in which it had been painted. Indeed some critics hold that of all the Twelve Judas was the one most thoroughly convinced of our Lord's divinity in the flesh; and these apologists attempt to explain the betrayal as a deliberate and well-intended move to force Jesus into a position of difficulty from which He could escape only by the exercise of His powers of Godship, which, up to that time, He had never used in His own behalf.

We are not the invested judges of Judas nor of any other; but we are competent to frame and hold opinions as to the actions of any. In the light of the revealed word it appears that Judas Iscariot had given himself up to the cause of Satan while ostensibly serving the Christ in an exalted capacity. Such a surrender to evil powers could be accomplished only through sin. The nature and extent of the man's transgressions through the years are not told us. He had received the testimony that Jesus was the Son of God; and in the full light of that conviction he turned against his Lord, and betrayed Him to death. Modern revelation is no less explicit than ancient in declaring that the path of sin is that of spiritual darkness leading to certain destruction. If the man who is guilty of adultery, even in his heart only, shall, unless he repents, surely forfeit the companionship of the Spirit of God, and "shall deny the faith," and so the voice of God hath affirmed (see Doc. and Cov. 63:16), we cannot doubt that any and all forms of deadly sin shall poison the soul and, if not forsaken through true repentance, shall bring that soul to condemnation. For his trained and skillful servants, Satan will provide opportunities of service commensurate with their evil ability. Whatever the opinion of modern critics as to the good character of Judas, we have the testimony of John, who for nearly three years had been in close companionship with him, that the man was a thief (12:6); and Jesus referred to him as a devil (6:70), and as "the son of perdition" (17:12). See in this connection Doc. and Cov. 76:41–48.

That the evil proclivities of Judas Iscariot were known to Christ is evidenced by the Lord's direct statement that among the Twelve was one who was a devil; (John 6:70; compare 13:27; Luke 22:3); and furthermore that this knowledge was His when the Twelve were selected is suggested by the words of Jesus: "I know whom I have chosen," coupled with the explanation that in the choice He had made would the scriptures be fulfilled. As the sacrificial death of the Lamb of God was foreknown and foretold so the circumstances of the betrayal were foreseen. It would be contrary to both the letter and spirit of the revealed word to say that the wretched Iscariot was in the least degree deprived of freedom or agency in the course he followed to so execrable an end. His was the opportunity and privilege common to the Twelve, to live in the light of the Lord's immediate presence, and to receive from the source divine the revelation of God's purposes.

Judas Iscariot was no victim of circumstances, no insensate tool guided by a superhuman power, except as he by personal volition gave himself up to Satan, and accepted a wage in the devil's employ. Had Judas been true to the right, other means than his perfidy would have operated to bring the Lamb to the slaughter. His ordination to the apostleship placed him in possession of opportunity and privilege above that of the uncalled and unordained; and with such blessed possibility of achievement in the service of God came corresponding capability to fall. A trusted and exalted officer of the government can commit acts of treachery and treason such as are impossible to the citizen who has never learned the secrets of State. Advancement implies increased accountability, even more literally so in the affairs of God's kingdom than in the institutions of men. . . . Concerning the fate of the "sons of perdition," the Lord has given a partial but awful account through a revelation dated February 16, 1832: "Thus saith the Lord, concerning all those who know my power, and have been made partakers thereof, and suffered themselves, through the power of the devil, to be overcome, and to deny the truth and defy my power—They are they who are the sons of perdition, of whom I say that it had been better for them never to have been born, For they are vessels of wrath, doomed to suffer the wrath of God, with the devil and his angels in eternity; Concerning whom I have said there is no forgiveness in this world nor in the world to come, Having denied the Holy Spirit after having received it, and having denied the Only Begotten Son of the Father—having crucified him unto themselves and put him to an open shame. These are they who shall go away into the lake of fire and brimstone, with the devil and his angels, And the only ones on whom the second death shall have any power. . . . Wherefore, he saves all except them: they shall go away into everlasting punishment, which is endless punishment, which is eternal punishment, to reign with the devil and his angels in eternity, where their worm dieth not, and the fire is not quenched, which is their torment; And the end thereof, neither the place thereof, nor their torment, no man knows. Neither was it revealed, neither is, neither will be revealed unto man, except to them who are made partakers thereof: Nevertheless I, the Lord, show it by vision unto many, but straightway shut it up again; Wherefore the end, the width, the height, the depth, and the misery thereof, they under-stand not, neither any man except them who are ordained unto this condemnation.'"—Doc. and Cov. 76:31–37, 44–48 (*JTC*, 604).

SATAN BOUND

Satan Knows His Time Is Short. Satan knows how little time is left before that day which is spoken of as being both great and blessed, and likewise terrible, which shall characterize the coming of the Lord in his glory to take his place as ruler of this earth. With him shall come concourses of angels, the blessed ones, and many upon the earth at that time shall meet him and his goodly company, and be numbered among them. Verily, that day is near at hand. The evil one knows it, and knows his time is short, and therefore, amidst our rejoicing over the improvement that is manifest among the Latter-day Saints, we must beware of the evil powers that are at work, that we may not be led away, that our children may not be led away, but that they may be firm and true to the faith which the Lord has implanted in their hearts—the faith of their fathers (CR, Oct. 1921, 188).

Satan Bound during the Millennium. In glorious vision John, the apostle and revelator, foresaw Christ's personal reign, during which Satan is to be bound:

"And I saw thrones, and they sat upon them, and judgment was given unto them: and I saw the souls of them that were beheaded for the witness of Jesus and for the word of God, and which had not wor-shiped the beast, neither his image, neither had received his mark upon their foreheads, or in their hands; and they lived and reigned with Christ a thousand years. But the rest of the dead lived not again until the thousand years were finished." (Rev. 20:4, 5; see also verse 2.)

The Millennium is to be a Sabbatical era, when the earth shall rest; and men, relieved from the tyranny of Satan, shall, if they will, live in righteousness and peace. Man, to whom was given dominion over the earth and its creatures, shall rule by love, for enmity between him and the brute creation shall cease, and the ferocity and venom of the beasts shall be done away. So hath the Lord avowed through the prophet Isaiah. (See Isa., ch. 65.)

We are definitely assured that the Millennium is to be inaugurated by the advent of Christ, and that Satan's power over men shall be restrained (*VM*, 171–72).

7

THE DISPENSATION OF THE
FULNESS OF TIMES

APOSTASY PRECEDED RESTORATION

Apostasy and the Need for Reformation. We accept as fact the belief common to Christendom that the Church of Christ was established under our Lord's personal direction and that during the early period of apostolic administration the Church was blessed with rapid growth and marvelous development. A question of profound importance confronts us: Has the Church of Jesus Christ maintained an organized existence upon the earth from the apostolic age to the present?

We affirm that with the passing of the apostolic period the Church drifted into a condition of apostasy, whereby succession in the Holy Priesthood was broken; and that the Church as an earthly organization operating under Divine direction and having authority to officiate in spiritual ordinances ceased to exist among men.

We affirm that this great apostasy, whereby the world was enshrouded in spiritual darkness, was foretold by the Savior Himself while He lived as a Man among men, and by His prophets both before and after the period of His life in mortality.

The apostolic ministry continued in the Primitive Church for about sixty years after the death of Christ, or nearly to the end of the first century of the Christian Era. For some time thereafter the Church existed as a unified body, officered by men duly invested by ordination in the Holy Priesthood, though, even during the lifetime of some of the Apostles, the leaven of apostasy and disintegration had been working. Indeed, hardly had the Gospel seed been sown before the enemy of all righteousness had started assiduously to sow tares in the field; and so intimate was the growth of the two that any forcible attempt to extirpate the tares would have imperiled the wheat. The evidences of spiritual decline were observed with anguish by the Apostles who, however, recognized the fulfilment of earlier prophecy in the declension, and added their own inspired testimony to the effect that even a greater falling away was imminent.

The apostasy progressed rapidly, in consequence of a cooperation of disrupting forces without and within the Church. The dreadful persecution to which the early Christians were subjected drove great numbers of Christians to renounce their allegiance to Christianity, thus causing a widespread apostasy from the Church. But far more destructive was the contagion of evil that spread within the body, manifesting its effects mainly in the following developments:

(1) The corrupting of the simple principles of the Gospel of Christ by admixture with the so-called philosophical systems of the times.

(2) Unauthorized additions to the rites of the Church, and the introduction of vital changes in essential ordinances.

(3) Unauthorized changes in Church organization and government.

The result of the degeneracy so produced was to bring about an actual apostasy of the entire Church (*VM,* 106–8).

Ministry of John. The final ministry of John marked the close of the apostolic administration in the Primitive Church. His fellow apostles had gone to their rest, most of them having entered through the gates of martyrdom, and although it was his special privilege to tarry in the flesh until the Lord's advent in glory, he was not to continue his service as an acknowledged minister, known to and accepted by the Church. Even while many of the apostles lived and labored, the seed of apostasy had taken root in the Church and had grown with the rankness of pernicious weeds. This condition had been predicted, both by Old Testament prophets and by the Lord Jesus. The apostles also spake in plain prediction of the growth of the apostasy all too grievously apparent to them as then in progress. Personal manifestations of the Lord Jesus to mortals appear to have ceased with the passing of the apostles of old, and were not again witnessed until the dawn of the Dispensation of the Fulness of Times (*JTC,* 717–18).

COLUMBUS

Columbus. Many who had suffered because of their religious beliefs separated themselves; some of them fled from England to Holland. They came to be known specifically as Separatists. Then, following that man of God—Columbus—for he was carrying out a divine

THE DISPENSATION OF THE FULNESS OF TIMES

purpose, the discoverer of the western world, came those other Gentiles of whom we read; and they were brought to this land and here they found the remnant of Lehi's posterity who had formerly been established upon this continent (CR, Oct. 1919, 96).

Mission of Columbus Appointed by God. Lehi and his people were Hebrews; all other nations are designated in the Book of Mormon as Gentiles. As later parts of the record make plain, "the promised land" is the continent of America. The "man among the Gentiles," who was to come across the many waters and discover the descendants of Nephi's brethren upon whom the wrath of God had fallen, was Christopher Columbus whose mission was as surely foreappointed as was that of any prophet (*VM*, 190–91).

AMERICA THE PROMISED LAND

Cradle of Civilization. There is no authentic record of the human race having inhabited the eastern hemisphere until after the flood. The western continent, called now the New World, comprises indeed the oldest inhabited regions of earth. The West not the East is the "cradle of nations" (*AF*, 475).

Meaning of Eden. In the Hebrew tongue, from which our word Eden is taken, this term signifies something particularly delightful—a place of pleasantness; the place is also called "the garden of the Lord." One particular spot in the land of Eden was prepared by the Lord as a garden; this was situated eastward in Eden (*AF*, 474).

Garden of Eden. For the reception of the first man the Creator had especially prepared a choice region of earth, and had embellished it with natural beauties to gladden the heart of its possessor (*AF,* 63–64).

A Land Choice above All Other Lands. In line with the excellent precedent set by my brethren, who have given you scripture after scripture, I desire to add another and I pray you read it more deliberately and more studiously than you may be able to listen to it in the brief time that I can give to its consideration. You may easily remember it. It is the first chapter of the Second Book of Nephi. Lehi, the prophet, stricken with years, trembling in limb and knowing that his days in the flesh had been numbered and that he was soon to follow the way of his fathers, spoke unto his posterity who had then become numerous, respecting this particular land, the land of promise, the land of Zion, and he said unto them:

Notwithstanding our afflictions, we have obtained a land of promise, a land which is choice above all other lands; a land which the Lord God hath covenanted with me should be a land for the inheritance of my seed. Yea, the Lord hath covenanted this land unto me, and to my children for ever; and also all those who should be led out of other countries by the hand of the Lord.

Mark you, I pray, the prophet knew that it was not to be a selfish inheritance, it was not to be kept forever solely for the habitation of his lineal descendants. It was to be for all those who were then to be led out from other countries by the hand of the Lord.

Wherefore, I, Lehi, prophesy according to the workings of the

Spirit which is in me, that there shall none come into this land, save they shall be brought by the hand of the Lord.

Wherefore, this land is consecrated unto him whom he shall bring. And if it so be that they shall serve him according to the commandments which he hath given, it shall be a land of liberty unto them; wherefore, they shall never be brought down into captivity; if so, it shall be because of iniquity; for if iniquity shall abound, cursed shall be the land for their sakes; but unto the righteous it shall be blessed for ever.

And behold, it is wisdom that this land should be kept as yet from the knowledge of other nations; for behold, many nations would overrun the land, that there would be no place for an inheritance (CR, Oct. 1919, 97–98).

Inheritance of Israel. In the economy of God, America, which is veritably the land of Zion, was aforetime consecrated as the home of a free and independent nation. It is the divinely assured inheritance of the "House of Israel"; and people of all nationalities who will abide by the laws of righteousness, which embody the principles of true liberty, may become by adoption members of the House of Israel. For a wise purpose this promised land, the American continent, was long kept from the knowledge of men; and the hand of the Lord has been potent in directing its discovery and in the establishment of the nation of promise and destiny thereon. Nephite prophets reiterated this solemn assurance, and proclaimed as the will and purpose of God that the government of the land should be a government of the people and not the tyranny of kings (*VM,* 191–92).

THE UNITED STATES CONSTITUTION

The Constitution Is a Pattern. The Constitution of this land is the pattern after which the organic laws of other nations shall be framed, and thus has been already fulfilled in part the prophecy that out of Zion shall go forth the law (CR, Oct. 1919, 98).

The Declaration of Independence and the Constitution. We hold that the Declaration of Independence and the Constitution of the United States are inspired documents, veritable scriptures of the nation, framed by men under Divine direction, men specifically empowered and raised up for this high mission; and that these charters of liberty constitute a pattern after which the governments of the nations shall be shaped. Thus shall be fulfilled, in part at least, the prophecy of the ancient revelator, that out of this land, which in solemn truth is the land of Zion, shall go forth the law of the Lord unto the world at large. In the majesty of her high destiny our Nation has taken a stand as the champion of freedom and human rights. Her enduring greatness is conditioned only by the righteousness of her people, who, if they will but serve the God of the land—the God of Heaven and earth—shall never be subject to alien domination (*VM*, 198).

Democracy. From American soil, which of all was first to be prepared for the cultivation of representative government by the people, the seed of democracy shall be carried to every other land, until all men are free, in accordance with Divine intent (*VM*, 195).

THE FIRST VISION

First Vision. Joseph Smith has given us his solemn testimony that in the early spring of 1820, while engaged in solitary prayer, to which he had been impelled by scriptural admonition (James 1:5), he was visited by the Eternal Father and His Son Jesus Christ, and that the Father, pointing to the Christ, spake, saying: "This is my beloved Son, hear Him."

In this wise was ushered in the Dispensation of the Fulness of Times, foretold by the Apostle of old (Eph. 1:10) (*VM,* 43).

Greatest Theophany. The Church today affirms to the world that in A.D. 1820 there was manifested to Joseph Smith a theophany such as never before had been vouchsafed to man (*SPM,* 156).

First Vision Ushered in the Final Dispensation. In this wise was ushered in the Dispensation of the Fulness of Times. The darkness of the long night of apostasy was dispelled; the glory of the heavens once more illumined the world; the silence of centuries was broken; the voice of God was heard again upon the earth. In the spring of A.D. 1820 there was one mortal, a boy not quite fifteen years old, who knew as well as that he lived, that the current human conception of Deity as an incorporeal essence of something possessing neither definite shape nor tangible substance was as devoid of truth in respect to both the Father and the Son as its statement in formulated creeds was incomprehensible. The boy Joseph knew that both the Eternal Father and His glorified Son, Jesus Christ, were in form and stature, perfect Men; and that in Their physical likeness mankind had been created in the flesh. He knew further that the Father and the Son were individual Personages, each distinct from the other—a truth fully attested by the Lord Jesus during His mortal existence, but which had been obscured if not buried by the sophistries of human unbelief. He realized that the unity of the Godhead was a oneness of perfection in purpose, plan, and action, as the scriptures declare it to be, and not an impossible union of personalities, as generations of false teachers had tried to impress. This resplendent theophany confirmed the fact of a universal apostasy, with the inevitable corollary—that the Church of Christ was nowhere existent upon the earth. It effectively dissipated the delusion that direct revelation from the heavens had forever ceased; and affirmatively proved the actuality of personal communication between God and mortals (*JTC*, 763–64).

Joseph Smith Saw God the Father. The centuries passed and by and by a light appeared; a glorious illumination broke forth; and the word of God was heard again, for God the Eternal Father—I speak it without reservation or modification—that Being after whom we have been formed in physical, mental and spiritual image, did appear upon the earth unto the lad Joseph Smith (CR, Oct. 1922, 70).

Joseph Smith Knew of Man's Relationship to God. In the spring of 1820, there lived one person who knew that the word of the Creator, "Let us make man in our own image, after our likeness," had a meaning more than figurative. Joseph Smith, the youthful prophet and revelator of the nineteenth century, knew that the Eternal Father and the Beloved Son, Jesus Christ, were in form and stature like unto perfect men; and that the human family was in very truth of divine origin (*SPM,* 13).

EVENTS OF THE RESTORATION

Preparation for the Establishment of the Church. Time and timeliness are very important in the affairs of men, and no less in the ever unfolding purposes of the Lord our God. He does things in his own due time, and that is always the right time. In the establishment of this nation, of which we have heard much, he chose the time, after due preparation had been made. I believe that had an attempt been made by men to establish a democracy, such as this, a hundred or fifty or twenty years earlier, it would have been a failure.

There is a time for seeding and there is a time for harvest. Many of us become impatient and desire to reap the harvests of the fields and the orchards even before the harvests of the snows have been garnered in the storage recesses of these everlasting hills.

There was a time for the establishment of this Church. It was the Lord's time. Great and numerous events had been leading up to it, and at the appointed time it was established, never again to be thrown down (CR, Apr. 1933, 107–8).

Restoration of the Melchizedek Priesthood. A short time after this event, Peter, James, and John appeared to Joseph Smith and Oliver Cowdery, and ordained the two to the higher or Melchizedek Priesthood, bestowing upon them the keys of the apostleship, which these heavenly messengers had held and exercised in the former Gospel

187

dispensation. This order of Priesthood holds authority over all the offices in the Church, and includes power to administer in spiritual things; consequently all the authorities and powers necessary to the establishment and development of the Church were by this visitation restored to earth (*AF*, 188).

Church Permanently Established. In its early days the Church received the word of the Lord avouching the perpetuity of the organization. While no individual was promised that he should not fall away, and though the forfeiture of the Holy Spirit's companionship was specified as the sure and incalculable loss to all who wilfully persisted in sin, the blessed assurance was given that the Church of Jesus Christ was established for the last time, never to be destroyed, nor again driven from the earth through apostasy. Men may come and men may go, but the Church shall go on forever (*VM*, 16–17).

Origin of the Church. The Church of Jesus Christ stands, in a particular sense, alone. Not even a hostile commentator or an unfavorable critic has ever yet ventured to put forth the assertion that this Church has any relationship of origin and development with any other church or denomination on the face of the earth. We are not regarded as an offshoot of any mother church. Churches generally treat us for what we are, a body of religionists standing alone in the world.

That does not mean that we shall refuse to lend our ready cooperation with other religionists or religious bodies in any movement for the general good, in any civic or patriotic duty; but it does mean that, so far as the essential characteristics of our organization are concerned, this Church has no counterpart amongst the sects and denominations of the day (CR, Apr. 1920, 100).

Restoration of the Gospel. But, many have asked, had we not the Gospel? The Holy Bible, which is the scriptural repository of the Gospel record, has been among men from the time of its earliest compilation; why then the necessity of a restoration? Yes, we had the Bible; but the Gospel is something other and greater than a book.

The Holy Scriptures, invaluable and sacred though they be, profess to be only the letter of the Gospel. Is it reasonable to assume that the mere possession of a Bible, or even a perfect memorization of its contents, could give to man the authority to administer the ordinances prescribed therein? It is quite as plausible to say that if one owns a copy of the statutes of his state or nation and learns therefrom the duties of sheriff, judge, governor or president, the knowledge thus acquired would be authority for him to administer in the respective offices. Statutes are not self-operative.

The Holy Scriptures define and prescribe certain administrative ordinances, such as water baptism and the laying on of hands for the bestowal of the Holy Ghost, which ordinances, unless the Lord Christ spoke fable and falsehood, are indispensable to individual salvation. But the right and authority to administer those essential and saving ordinances cannot be arrogated to one's self by ever so intensive a study of the scriptural record (*VM*, 112).

Gospel Restored. Following the apostolic administration apostasy again darkened the world; and now, in the current or last dispensation, the Gospel has been restored anew with all its ancient authority, power, and blessings. The Church of Jesus Christ of Latter-day Saints proclaims these glad tidings to the world. This Gospel is new only in the fact of its restoration to earth according to prophecy. It is the Gospel of Jesus Christ, which was preached to and by Adam, Enoch, Noah, Abraham and a host of other men of God who ministered anciently; it is the Gospel that was taught by the Savior Himself and by His Apostles; it is the Eternal Gospel brought again to earth in preparation for the advent of the Lord Jesus Christ (*VM*, 295–96).

Dispensation of the Fulness of Times. The Church of Jesus Christ of Latter-day Saints proclaims the present as the dispensation of the fulness of times, in which shall be gathered and re-established all the saving principles and essential ordinances of earlier dispensations, and during which the great plan of universal redemption shall be fully revealed (*HL*, 92–93).

The Church of Jesus Christ Was Restored. The Primitive Church was of comparatively short duration. The world fell into spiritual darkness, and a restoration of power and commission from the Heavens became necessary to the reestablishment of the Church with its ancient blessings and privileges. The Church of Jesus Christ of Latter-day Saints proclaims the imperative need of "the same organization that existed in the Primitive Church," and solemnly avers that through the ministration of heavenly beings the Church of Jesus Christ is restored to earth, for the salvation of mankind both living and dead (*VM*, 106).

FULFILLMENT OF PROPHECY

The Church of Jesus Christ Has Been Restored. The Church of Jesus Christ of Latter-day Saints is unique in that it solemnly affirms to the world that the new dispensation, foretold in prophecy as a characteristic of the last days precedent to the second advent of Christ, is established, and that the Holy Priesthood, with all its ancient authority and power, has been restored to earth (*VM,* 27).

Prophets Foretold the Restoration. We proclaim the restoration which the prophets of old said should follow the apostasy. The Church of Jesus Christ has been established upon the earth anew, through the instrumentality of Joseph Smith the Prophet and his immediate associates in the ministry. It is the Church of Jesus Christ brought to earth again, established anew as had been predicted, I repeat; and its mission is the preparation of the earth for the great consummation, the coming of the Lord Jesus Christ (CR, Oct. 1922, 71).

JOSEPH SMITH WAS A PROPHET

Evidence Joseph Smith Was a Prophet. The evidence of divine authority in the work established by Joseph Smith, and of the justification of the claims made by and for the man, may be summarized as follows:

1. Ancient prophecy has been fulfilled in the restoration of the Gospel and the reestablishment of the Church upon the earth through his instrumentality.

2. He received by direct ordination and appointment, at the hands of those who held the power in former dispensations, authority to minister in the various ordinances of the Holy Priesthood.

3. His possession of the power of true prophecy, and of other spiritual gifts, is shown by the results of his ministry.

4. The doctrines he proclaimed are true and scriptural (*AF,* 16).

Joseph Smith Had the Spirit of Prophecy. In the days of ancient Israel an effective method of testing the claims of a professed prophet was prescribed. "When a prophet speaketh in the name of the Lord, if the thing follow not, nor come to pass, that is the thing which the Lord hath not spoken, but the prophet hath spoken it presumptuously: thou shalt not be afraid of him." Conversely, if the words of the prophet are verified by fulfilment there is at least proof presumptive of his divine calling. Of the many predictions uttered by Joseph Smith and already fulfilled or awaiting the set time of their realization, a few citations will suffice.

One of the earliest prophecies delivered through him, which, while not his independent utterance but that of the angel Moroni was nevertheless given to the world by Joseph Smith, had specific reference to the Book of Mormon, of which the angel said: "The knowledge that this record contains will go to every nation, and kindred, and tongue, and people, under the whole heaven." This declaration was made four years before the work of translation was begun, and fourteen years before the elders of the Church began their missionary labor in foreign lands. Since that time the Book of Mormon has been published in many languages and the work of its world-wide distribution is still in progress.

In August, 1842, while the Church was suffering persecution in Illinois, and when the western part of what is now the United States of America was but little known and so only as the territory of an alien nation, Joseph Smith prophesied "that the saints would continue to suffer much affliction, and would be driven to the Rocky Mountains," and that while many then professing allegiance to the Church would apostatize, and others, faithful to their testimony, would meet the martyr's fate, some would live to "assist in making settlements and build cities and see the saints become a mighty people in the midst of the Rocky Mountains." The literal fulfilment of this prediction, uttered in 1842, and it may be added, foreshadowed by an earlier prophecy in 1831, the one five, the other sixteen years before the migration of the Church to the west, is attested by the common history of the settlement and development of this once forbidding region. Even skeptics and pronounced opponents of the Church proclaim the miracle of the establishment of a great commonwealth in the valleys of the Rocky Mountains.

A remarkable prediction regarding national affairs was uttered by Joseph Smith, December 25, 1832; it was soon thereafter promulgated among the members of the Church and was preached by the elders, but did not appear in print until 1851. The revelation reads in part as follows: "Verily, thus saith the Lord concerning the wars that will shortly come to pass, beginning at the rebellion of South Carolina, which will eventually terminate in the death and misery of many souls; And the time will come that war will be poured out upon all nations, beginning at this place. For behold, the Southern States shall be divided against the Northern States, and the Southern States will call on other nations, even the nation of Great Britain. . . . And it shall come to pass, after many days, slaves shall rise up against their masters, who shall be marshaled and disciplined for war."

Every student of United States history is acquainted with the facts establishing a complete fulfilment of this astounding prophecy. In 1861, more than twenty-eight years after the foregoing prediction was recorded, and ten years after its publication in England, the Civil War broke out, beginning in South Carolina (*AF*, 23–25).

THE CHURCH IN ISOLATION IN UTAH

Persecution of the Saints in Missouri. I stated that professional men, and even college professors raised their voices in commiseration of the "Mormon" situation and in reprehension of the "Mormon" oppressors. Prof. Turner of Illinois College wrote:

"Who began the quarrel? Was it the 'Mormons?' Is it not notorious on the contrary that they were hunted like wild beasts from county to county before they made any resistance? Did they ever, as a body, refuse obedience to the laws, when called upon to do so, until driven to desperation by repeated threats and assaults by the mob? Did the state ever make one decent effort to defend them as fellow-citizens in their rights or to redress their wrongs? Let the conduct of its governors and attorneys and the fate of their final petitions answer! Have any who plundered and openly insulted the 'Mormons' ever been brought to the punishment due to their crimes? Let boasting murderers of begging and helpless infancy answer! Has the state ever remunerated even those known to be innocent for the loss of either their property or their arms? Did either the pulpit or the press through the state raise a note of remonstrance or alarm? Let the clergymen who abetted and the editors who encouraged the mob answer!"

As a sample of the press comments against the brutality of the Missourians, consider a paragraph from the Quincy *Argus,* March 16, 1839:

"We have no language sufficiently strong for the expression of our indignation and shame at the recent transaction in a sister state, and that state, Missouri, a state of which we had long been proud, alike for her men and history, but now so fallen that we could wish her star stricken from the bright constellation of the Union. We say we know of no language sufficiently strong for the expression of our shame and abhorrence of her recent conduct. She has written her own character in letters of blood, and stained it by acts of merciless cruelty and brutality that the waters of ages cannot efface. It will be observed that an organized mob, aided by many of the civil and military officers of Missouri, with Gov. Boggs at their head, have been the prominent actors in this business, incited too, it appears, against the 'Mormons' by political hatred, and by the additional motives of plunder and revenge. They have but too well put in execution their threats of extermination and expulsion, and fully wreaked their vengeance on a body of industrious and enterprising men, who had never wronged nor wished to wrong them, but on the contrary had ever comported themselves as good and honest citizens, living under the same laws, and having the same right with themselves to the sacred immunities of life, liberty and property" (*SPM*, 40–42).

Temporary Isolation of Latter-day Saints. Now, hastening over centuries, we come to the time when an important segregation took place upon this continent. After the Church had been established through the instrumentality of the prophet Joseph Smith, the Lord led his people out, and others came from beyond the seas to join them. Because of persecution they were driven, literally driven, beyond the frontiers of what was then the United States. They came here as a body, settled in this part of the desert, their inspired leader utterly putting aside every suggestion that they should go on to the green pastures and the fat fields about the coast. Can you imagine what the result would be today had Brigham Young listened to the advice of those men, wise in their own knowledge? There never would have been, except the Lord had brought it about in another way, a unit such as this Church presents. Before the pioneers and those who came immediately after them could have been trained in the ways of God, their lands would have been invaded and they would again have become one with the people of the world. But the Lord kept them in this uninviting place, of which other people were mostly afraid until they, with whom were our worthy sires and mothers and grandparents, had been sufficiently trained to know that they had something in common which the rest of the world had not. But that physical segregation, isolation, separation was of comparatively short duration. When the Lord thought that the Latter-day Saints had learned the lesson, then he permitted others to come. It was not his intention to shut his people up within the walls of a building or within these valleys of the eternal hills, keeping them perpetually aloof from all the temptations of the world, for they had to be tried. In due time means of steam transportation were established and multitudes came and have since been coming by the hosts every year, mingling with this people who are the covenant people of the last days. But in spite of this termination of physical separation, the people are a unit wherever you find them throughout the world. They are recognized by their distinctive characteristics (CR, Apr. 1919, 96).

Tribute to Brigham Young, Who Led the Saints to Utah. When Brigham Young passed from earth, he was mourned of the people as deeply as was Moses of Israel. And had he not proved himself a Moses, aye and a Joshua, too? He led the people into the land of holy promise, and had divided unto them their inheritances. He was a man with clear title as one of the small brotherhood we call great. As carpenter, farmer, pioneer, capitalist, financier, preacher, apostle, prophet—in everything, he was a leader among men. Even those who opposed him in politics and in religion respected him for his talents, his magnanimity, his liberality, and his manliness; and years after his demise, men who had refused him honor while alive brought their mites and their gold to erect a monument of stone and bronze to the memory of this man who needs it not (*SPM*, 99–100).

Latter-day Saints Uphold the Constitution. It was just when the Overland Telegraph wire from the east was approaching the end of the wire that was coming from the west, for you know it was within the boundaries of this state that those two ends were joined and the nerve of steel that connected the east with the west was made complete. It was just at that time that the great unpleasantness was at its height between the North and the South, when brother was rising against brother, and it was rumored that Utah had seceded from the Union, or, as represented by some, Utah was to become a separate and independent government, the seat of a separate power, and that in addition to a North and a South, which had already been declared, there was to be a West also. You know the first message that was sent through that metallic nerve, went from the West to Washington, from Brigham Young to the President of the United States and this was the purport of the message, "Utah has not seceded but is firm for the Constitution and laws of our country." That declaration has never been changed; it is as true in its application today as it was when it was flashed as the initial message across the overland telegraph wire. We stand for the Constitution and do not believe in any false notions of advancement and enlightenment and progressivism such as seeks to undermine that foundation of our liberties, for as a document we know that it was inspired and we believe that the men who framed it were raised up, as truly as was ever prophet raised up in Israel in ancient or modern times, to frame that instrument and thereby provide for the fulfilment of prophetic utterances regarding the freedom and the liberty that should prevail in this choice land (CR, Oct. 1912, 128–29).

PLURAL MARRIAGE

Plural Marriage. But perhaps I am suspected of having forgotten or of having intentionally omitted reference to what popular belief once considered the chief feature of "Mormonism," the cornerstone of the structure, the secret of its influence over its members, and of its attractiveness to its proselytes, viz., the peculiarity of the "Mormon" institution of marriage. The Latter-day Saints were long regarded as a polygamous people. That plural marriage has been practised by a limited proportion of the people, under sanction of Church ordinance, has never been denied. But that plural marriage is a vital tenet of The Church is not true. What the Latter-day Saints call celestial marriage is characteristic of the Church, and is in very general practise; but of celestial marriage, plurality of wives was an incident, never an essential. Yet the two have often been confused in the popular mind (*SPM,* 100–101).

TEMPLES

Latter-day Temples. The present is the age of greatest import in all history, embodying as it does the fruition of the past and the living seed of the yet greater future. The present is the dispensation of fulness, for which the dispensations of bygone centuries have been but preliminary and preparatory. The saving and sanctifying labor incident to modern Temples surpasses that of the Temples of earlier times as the light of the full day exceeds the twilight of the dawn.

The authority of administration in the Temples of Solomon, Zerubbabel, and Herod, was that of the Lesser or Aaronic Priesthood; for the Higher or Melchisedek Priesthood, otherwise known as the Holy Priesthood after the order of the Son of God, had been taken from Israel with Moses. The temples of the present are administered under the greater authority (*HL,* 233–34).

JUDGMENTS

Elements Part of the Predicted Judgments. Even now, if the nations will turn unto the Lord it shall be unto them as it was unto Nineveh—they shall be spared; but if they will not, then the Lord will permit the predicted judgments to come upon them until they are brought to a realization of the fact that they do depend upon the Lord God of heaven and of earth. The forces of nature are co-operating and are permitted to wreak destruction and the end is not yet. Latter-day Saints, remember the admonition of the Lord: "Stand ye in holy places," and we cannot do that unless we are holy. "Stand ye in holy places, and be not moved," but await the working out of the Lord's purposes, the while living lives of righteousness and crying repentance unto the people of the world (CR, Oct. 1923, 54).

God Passes Judgment As He Sees Fit. The execution of judgment is not always made to follow the acts of men immediately; good deeds may not be at once rewarded, nor evil be peremptorily punished; and this is according to divine wisdom, for were it otherwise the test of individual character and the trial of human faith, for which purposes this mortal probation was primarily ordained, would be greatly lessened; as the certainty of immediate pleasure or pain would largely determine human acts to secure the one and avoid the other. Judgment, therefore, is postponed, that every one may prove himself, the good man increasing in righteousness, and the evil-doer having opportunity for repentance and reparation. On rare occasions, speedy judgment of a temporal nature has been executed, the physical results of worldly blessing for good, and calamity for evil deeds following swiftly upon the acts. Whether such retribution entirely satisfies the claims of justice, or a further visitation of judgment is to take place beyond this life matters not. Such acts are exceptional in the divine administration (*AF,* 56).

Plagues. Have you not read of the pestilences, including perhaps strange diseases, that are to sweep the earth? They are among the judgments that were foretold for these days. We had a taste of such back in 1918–19, when the great influenza carried, according to the established records, over sixteen millions of people to their graves. . . .

We have heard of these ills—calamities we call them though they may be blessings to the race in disguise—that are characteristic of these days. They have been predicted, and some people are apt to place responsibility if not blame for all these upon the Lord, and to envision him as a God of vengeance. He is a God of love, and it is necessary that some of these experiences shall come upon mankind, that they may be better prepared for what the Lord has in store for them by way of blessing (CR, Apr. 1933, 109).

ZION

Zion Located in America. Zion is to be established on this continent, and as the word of modern revelation avers, in the western part of the United States (See Doctrine and Covenants 45:64–71; 57:1–5.) The time of the blessed consummation is conditioned by the fitness of the people. Hither shall come the hosts of scattered Israel, and the Lost

Tribes from their long obscurity. Here shall yet be built the City of the Lord, Zion, the New Jerusalem, which in time shall be made one with the "Holy City," which the Revelator saw "coming down from God, out of heaven, prepared as a bride adorned for her husband." (Rev. 21:2.) (*VM,* 166).

The Elect Will Be Gathered to Zion. Great events are to mark the latter days; the elect are to be gathered from the four quarters of the earth to a place prepared for them; the tabernacle of the Lord is to be established there, and the place "shall be called Zion, a New Jerusalem." Then Enoch and his people are to return to earth and meet the gathered elect in the holy place (*AF,* 351).

Zion and the New Jerusalem Are the Same Place. We have seen that the names Zion and New Jerusalem are used interchangeably; and, furthermore, that righteous people as well as sanctified places are called Zion; for, by the Lord's special word, Zion to Him means "the pure in heart." The Church in this day teaches that the New Jerusalem seen by John and by the prophet Ether, as descending from the heavens in glory, is the return of exalted Enoch and his righteous people; and that the people or Zion of Enoch, and the modern Zion, or the gathered saints on the western continent, will become one people (*AF,* 351–52).

Ten Tribes Will Come to Zion. From the express and repeated declaration, that in their exodus from the north the Ten Tribes are to be led to Zion, there to receive honor at the hands of those who are of

Ephraim, who necessarily are to have previously gathered there, it is plain that Zion is to be first established (*AF,* 341).

World Capitals. Two gathering centers are distinctively mentioned, and the maintenance of a separate autonomy for the ancient kingdoms of Judah and Israel is repeatedly affirmed in Scripture, with Jerusalem and Zion as the respective capitals. In the light of modern revelation by which many ancient passages are illumined and made clear, we hold that the Jerusalem of Judea is to be rebuilt by the reassembled house of Judah, and that Zion is to be built up on the American continent by the gathered hosts of Israel, other than the Jews. When such shall have been accomplished, Christ shall personally rule in the earth, and then shall be realized the glad fulfilment: "For out of Zion shall go forth the law, and the word of the Lord from Jerusalem." (Isa. 2:3; see also Joel 3:16; Zeph. 3:14.) (*VM,* 162).

RESTORATION OF THE LOST TRIBES

History of the Lost Tribes. Immediately following the death of Solomon, about 975 B.C. according to the most generally accepted chronology, the nation was disrupted by revolt. The tribe of Judah, part of the tribe of Benjamin, and small remnants of a few other tribes remained true to the royal succession, and accepted Rehoboam, son of Solomon, as their king; while the rest, usually spoken of as the Ten Tribes, broke their allegiance to the house of David, and made Jeroboam, an Ephraimite, their king. The Ten Tribes retained the title Kingdom of Israel though also known as Ephraim. Rehoboam and his adherents were distinctively called the Kingdom of Judah. For about two hundred and fifty years the two kingdoms maintained their separate autonomy; then, about 722 or 721 B.C., the independent status of the Kingdom of Israel was destroyed, and the captive people were transported to Assyria by Shalmanezer and others. Subsequently they disappeared so completely as to be called the Lost Tribes (*JTC,* 59).

Lost Tribes in a Body. From the scriptural passages already considered, it is plain that, while many of those belonging to the Ten Tribes were diffused among the nations, a sufficient number to justify the retention of the original name were led away as a body and are now in existence in some place where the Lord has hidden them. To them the resurrected Christ went to minister after His visit to the Nephites, as before stated. Their return constitutes a very important part of the gathering, characteristic of the dispensation of the fulness of times (*AF,* 340–41).

Lost Tribes Will Return. Prophecies that have not yet been fulfilled are by many of us made the subjects of hypothesis and theory and strained interpretation. We read that one of the characteristic signs to precede the second advent of Christ shall be the bringing forth of the tribes that have been lost to history, led away where men have not yet found them, and we are told that they shall be brought forth with a strong hand by the power of God and shall come unto Zion and receive their blessings at the hands of Ephraim. But some people say that prediction is to be explained in this way: A gathering is in progress, and has been in progress from the early days of this Church; and thus the "Lost Tribes" are now being gathered; but that we are not to look for the return of any body of people now unknown as to their whereabouts. True, the gathering is in progress, this is a gathering dispensation; but the prophecy stands that the tribes shall be brought forth from their hiding place bringing their scriptures with them, which scriptures shall become one with the scriptures of the Jews, the holy Bible, and with the scriptures of the Nephites, the Book of Mormon, and with the scriptures of the Latter-day Saints as embodied in the volumes of modern revelation (CR, Apr. 1916, 130).

Records of the Lost Tribes. Nevertheless, I have found elders in Israel who would tell me that the predictions relating to the Lost Tribes are to be explained in this figurative manner—that the gathering of those tribes is already well advanced and that there is no hiding place whereto God has led them, from which they shall come forth, led by their prophets to receive their blessings here at the hands of gathered Ephraim, the gathered portions that have been scattered among the nations. Yea, let God be true, and doubt we not his word, though it makes the opinions of men appear to be lies. The tribes shall come; they are not lost unto the Lord; they shall be brought forth as hath been predicted; and I say unto you there are those now living—aye, some here present—who shall live to read the records of the Lost Tribes of Israel, which shall be made one with the record of the Jews, or the Holy Bible, and the record of the Nephites, or the Book of Mormon, even as the Lord hath predicted; and those records, which the tribes lost to man but yet to be found again shall bring, shall tell of the visit

of the resurrected Christ to them, after He had manifested Himself to
the Nephites upon this continent (CR, Oct. 1917, 76).

THE SECOND COMING
AND THE MILLENNIUM

A Warning to All People Being Sent Forth. A distinctive characteristic of the revelations given in the present dispensation, regarding the
second coming of our Lord, is the emphatic and oft-repeated declaration that the event is near at hand. The call is, "Prepare ye, prepare
ye, for that which is to come; for the Lord is nigh." Instead of the cry
of one man in the wilderness of Judea, the voice of thousands is heard
authoritatively warning the nations and inviting them to repent and
flee to Zion for safety. The fig-tree is rapidly putting forth its leaves;
the signs in heaven and earth are increasing; the great and dreadful day
of the Lord is near (*AF,* 362).

Events That Precede the Second Coming. The date of the future
advent of Christ has never been revealed to man. To the inquiring
apostles who labored with the Master, He said: "But of that day and
hour knoweth no man, no, not the angels of heaven, but my Father
only." In the present age, a similar declaration has been made by the
Father: "I, the Lord God, have spoken it, but the hour and the day no
man knoweth, neither the angels in heaven, nor shall they know until
he comes." Only through watchfulness and prayer may the signs of
the times be correctly interpreted and the imminence of the Lord's appearing be apprehended. To the unwatchful and the wicked the event

will be as sudden and unexpected as the coming of a thief in the night. But we are not left without definite information as to precedent signs. Biblical prophecies bearing upon this subject we have heretofore considered. As later scriptures affirm: "Before the great day of the Lord shall come, Jacob shall flourish in the wilderness, and the Lamanites shall blossom as the rose. Zion shall flourish upon the hills and rejoice upon the mountains, and shall be assembled together unto the place which I have appointed." War shall become so general that every man who will not take arms against his neighbor must of necessity flee to the land of Zion for safety. Ephraim shall assemble in Zion on the western continent, and Judah shall be again established in the east; and the cities of Zion and Jerusalem shall be the capitals of the world empire, over which Messiah shall reign in undisputed authority. The Lost Tribes shall be brought forth from the place where God has hidden them through the centuries and receive their long deferred blessings at the hands of Ephraim. The people of Israel shall be restored from their scattered condition (*JTC*, 785–86).

The Day of the Second Coming Has Not Been Revealed. The Lord warned them against men who would set dates, and that warning has never been abrogated, but, on the contrary, has been repeated and emphasized. I say unto you, beware of the men who undertake to set the year and the day in which the Christ shall come, for that has not been revealed unto man (CR, Apr. 1918, 162).

The Second Coming Is Near. In the light of such scriptural affirmations we may dismiss as empty conjecture all alleged determinations as to the precise time of the Lord's appearing. Nevertheless, the specified signs and conditions by which is shown the imminence of the event are definite, and from these we know that the great day of the Lord is very near. So near is the consummation that the intervening period is called "today"; and on the morrow mankind shall rejoice or tremble at the presence of the Lord. (See Doctrine and Covenants 64:23–25.)

Christ's advent shall be made with the accompaniment of power and great glory. While in suddenness and unexpectedness to the unobserving it shall be comparable to the coming of a thief in the night, it shall be a manifestation of surpassing glory to all the world: "For as the lightning cometh out of the east, and shineth even unto the west; so shall also the coming of the Son of man be." (Matt. 24:27.)

With the Lord's appearing a general resurrection of the righteous dead shall be effected, and many then in the flesh shall be changed from the mortal to the immortal state without the intervening experience of prolonged disembodiment or the sleep of the grave. (See 1 Thess. 4:14–17.) (*VM*, 169–70).

Second Coming, Day of Glory and a Day of Terror. The scriptures abound in declarations and reiterations, in repeated and solemn affirmations of the great fact that the day of the Lord's coming will be a day of glory and a day of terror—of glory and recompense unto those who are living righteously, and a day of terror unto the proud and unto all who do wickedly (CR, Apr. 1916, 128).

The Saints Participate in the Second Coming. When the Messiah comes to rule and reign, He will be accompanied by the hosts of the righteous who have already passed through the change of death; and the righteous who are yet in the flesh shall be caught up to meet Him, and shall descend with Him as partakers of His glory. Then shall the Kingdom of God on earth be made one with the Kingdom of Heaven. Then shall be realized the glorious fulfilment of the prayer taught by the Christ, and voiced by men through the ages past, Thy Kingdom come (*VM*, 175).

The Millennium the Earth's Sabbath. It is evident, then, that in speaking of the Millennium we have to consider a definite period, with important events marking its beginning and its close, and conditions of unusual blessedness extending throughout. It will be a sabbatical era—a thousand years of peace. Enmity between man and beast shall cease; the fierceness and venom of the brute creation shall be done away, and love shall rule (*AF*, 369).

Summary of the Millennium. The inauguration of Christ's reign on earth is to be the beginning of a period that shall be distinct in many important particulars from all precedent and subsequent time; and the Lord shall reign with His people a thousand years. The government of individuals, communities and nations throughout this Millennium is to be that of a perfect theocracy, with Jesus the Christ as Lord and King. The more wicked part of the race shall have been destroyed; and during the period Satan shall be bound "that he should deceive the nations no more, till the thousand years should be fulfilled"; while the just shall share with Christ in rightful rule and dominion. The righteous dead shall have come forth from their graves, while the wicked shall remain unresurrected until the thousand years be past. Men yet in the flesh shall mingle with immortalized beings; children shall grow to maturity and then die in peace or be changed to immortality "in the twinkling of an eye." There shall be surcease of enmity between man and beast; the venom of serpents and the ferocity of the brute creation shall be done away, and love shall be the dominant power of control (*JTC*, 790).

8

CHURCH GOVERNMENT

THE NAME OF THE CHURCH

Full Name of the Church. When this restored church was organized in 1830, ninety-two years ago yesterday, it was named the Church of Jesus Christ; but afterward, by special revelation through the Prophet Joseph Smith, the Lord himself gave the extended name and said: "For thus shall my Church be called in the last days, even the Church of Jesus Christ of Latter-day Saints." Many of us content ourselves with the assumption that this addition was made to avoid confusion with the Church of Jesus Christ as it had existed in earlier days, the primitive Church as we call it; and I agree with that as being a good purpose well served. Nevertheless, to me there is a deeper meaning. This is in one sense, and that an all-comprehending sense, the Church of Jesus Christ. It was organized by his commandment. Its doctrines are his doctrines. The salvation it preaches is the salvation which he made possible; but as an organization among men, as a body of human beings it

is likewise the Church of the Latter-day Saints, and to this body constituting the organization is committed certain authority and to such are
given certain privileges coupled with commensurate responsibilities.
It is a self-perpetuating organization, all its affairs being carried on by
men who are duly called under the inspiration or by direct revelation
from the Lord who stands at its head (CR, Apr. 1922, 70–71).

Explanation of the Term Mormon. Permit me to explain that the
term "Mormon," with its several derivatives, is no part of the name of
the Church with which it is usually associated. It was first applied to
the Church as a convenient nickname, and had reference to an early
publication, *The Book of Mormon;* but the appellative is now so generally current that the Church and people answer readily to its call. The
proper designation of the so-called "Mormon" Church is *The Church of
Jesus Christ of Latter-day Saints.* The philosophy of its religious system
is largely expressed in its name" (*SPM,* 112).

"Mormon Church" a Nickname. The members of that Church are
often spoken of as "Mormons," and the Church has come to be known
more generally as the "Mormon Church" than by its proper name and
distinguishing title, the Church of Jesus Christ of Latter-day Saints.
We as a people do not maintain any strong protest against the application of the term "Mormon" and its several derivatives; though
we deplore the fact that misunderstanding may arise in the minds of
inquirers and investigators respecting the significance of that name,
which originally was used as a nickname in its application to the
Church. You may call us Mormons if you will; remember, however, as

you must—must, if you will have respect unto the truth—that this is not the church of Mormon. Mormon was a man, a very worthy man and a very great man in his day when he lived in the flesh, and a very great personage since that time; but he was a man among men, and while his name is very properly applied to the abridgement of certain early records, which abridgement he made and supplemented by many writings of his own, now published under the name of the Book of Mormon, the Church is not his church, nor is it the church of Peter or James or John, nor is it the church of Joseph Smith, nor of Brigham Young, nor of Joseph F. Smith, nor the church of the present authorities of the body. It is the Church of Jesus Christ and it is the only Church upon the face of the earth affirming divine authorization for the use of the name of the Savior of mankind as part of its distinctive designation (CR, Apr. 1916, 125).

"Mormon Church" a Pseudonym. They call us "Mormons." The Church to which we belong is known as the "Mormon Church." The gospel which is committed to the Church is called "Mormonism." These names, pseudonyms as they are, have been fastened upon us. We do not resent the titles, but we must not forget that they are false names, as thus applied. Nicknames they were; and where the Church of Jesus Christ of Latter-day Saints is known in the world to one by its proper name, it has been heard of by hundreds as the "Mormon Church." The possibility of error, misunderstanding, false conception, through this application of the term "Mormon" should not be forgotten. The Lutheran Church is named after a great man, and those who chose to follow his banner called themselves "Lutherans." So in

many other instances have sects and denominations been named after men; but this is not the Church of Mormon, nor the Church of Joseph Smith, nor of Brigham Young, nor of any other man save only that Man who was the Son of the Living God, He who was and is Jesus the Christ (CR, Apr. 1922, 70).

True Name of the Church. The "Mormon" people do not resent the misnomer by which they are commonly known, and which has been put upon them by popular usage. They deplore, however, the possible misunderstanding that the Church to which they belong professes to be the church of Mormon. It should be known that Mormon was a man, a very distinguished and a very able man it is true, an eminent prophet and historian according to the record bearing his name, but a man nevertheless. The "Mormon" Church affirms itself to be in no sense the church of Mormon, nor the church of Joseph Smith, nor of Brigham Young, nor of any man other than the Savior and Redeemer of the race. The true name of this Church, the designation by which it is officially known is *The Church of Jesus Christ of Latter-day Saints* (*VM,* 23).

GOVERNMENT OF THE CHURCH

Apostles Foreordained. On the following day Jesus set out for Galilee, possibly accompanied by some or all of his newly-made disciples; and on the way He found a man named Philip, in whom He recognized another choice son of Israel. Unto Philip He said: "Follow me." It was customary with rabbis and other teachers of that time to strive for popularity that many might be drawn to them to sit at their feet and be known as their disciples. Jesus, however, selected His own immediate associates; and, as He found them and discerned in them the spirits who, in their preexistent state had been chosen for the earthly mission of the apostleship, He summoned them. They were the servants; He was the Master (*JTC,* 140–41).

Apostle. The Holy Apostleship is an office and calling belonging to the Higher or Melchizedek Priesthood, at once exalted and specific, comprising as a distinguishing function that of personal and special witness to the divinity of Jesus Christ as the one and only Redeemer and Savior of mankind. The apostleship is an individual bestowal, and as such is conferred only through ordination (*JTC,* 227).

Apostle a Sacred Term. By derivation the word 'apostle' is the English equivalent of the Greek *apostolos,* indicating a messenger, an ambassador, or literally 'one who is sent.' It signifies that he who is rightly so called, speaks and acts not of himself, but as the representative of a higher power whence his commission issued; and in this sense the title is that of a servant, rather than that of a superior. Even the Christ, however, is called an Apostle with reference to His ministry in the flesh (Hebrews 3:1), and this appellation is justified by His repeated declaration that He came to earth to do not His own will but that of the Father by whom *He was sent.*

Though an apostle is thus seen to be essentially an envoy, or ambassador, his authority is great, as is also the responsibility associated therewith, for he speaks in the name of a power greater than his own—the name of Him whose special witness he is. When one of the Twelve is sent to minister in any stake, mission or other division of the Church, or to labor in regions where no Church organization has been effected, he acts as the representative of the First Presidency, and has the right to use his authority in doing whatever is requisite for the furtherance of the work of God. His duty is to preach the Gospel, administer the ordinances thereof, and set in order the affairs of the Church, wherever he is sent. So great is the sanctity of this special calling, that the title 'Apostle' should not be used lightly as the common or ordinary form of address applied to living men called to this office. The quorum or council of the Twelve Apostles as existent in the Church to-day may better be spoken of as the 'Quorum of the Twelve,' the 'Council of the Twelve,' or simply as the 'Twelve,' than as the 'Twelve Apostles,' except as particular occasion may warrant the use of the more sacred term. It is advised that the title 'Apostle' be not applied as a prefix to the name of any member of the Council of the Twelve; but that such a one be addressed or spoken of as 'Brother———,' or 'Elder———,' and when necessary or desirable, as in announcing his presence in a public assembly, an explanatory clause may be added, thus, 'Elder———, one of the Council of the Twelve'" (*JTC*, 229).

Need of a Prophet. It is a privilege of the Holy Priesthood to commune with the heavens, and to learn the immediate will of the Lord; this communion may be effected through the medium of dreams and visions, by Urim and Thummim, through the visitation of angels, or by the higher endowment of face to face communication with the Lord. The inspired utterances of men who speak by the power of the

Holy Ghost are scripture unto the people. In specific terms the promise was made in olden times that the Lord would recognize the medium of prophecy through which to make His will and purposes known unto man: "Surely the Lord God will do nothing, but he revealeth his secret unto his servants the prophets." Not all men may attain the position of special revelators: "The secret of the Lord is with them that fear him; and he will show them his covenant." Such men are oracles of truth, privileged counselors, friends of God. (*AF,* 298–99).

Prophets Are Vindicated. Thus the scriptures of both hemispheres and in all ages of ante-meridian time bore solemn testimony to the certainty of Messiah's advent; thus the holy prophets of old voiced the word of revelation predicting the coming of the world's King and Lord, through whom alone is salvation provided, and redemption from death made sure. It is a characteristic of prophets sent of God that they possess and proclaim a personal assurance of the Christ, "for the testimony of Jesus is the spirit of prophecy." Not a word of inspired prophecy relating to the great event has been found void. The literal fulfilment of the predictions is ample attestation of their origin in divine revelation, and proof conclusive of the divinity of Him whose coming was so abundantly foretold (*JTC,* 52–53).

Offices in the Priesthood and Their Duties. The office of *Deacon* is the first or lowest in the Aaronic Priesthood. The duties of this calling are primarily of a temporal nature, pertaining to the care of houses of worship, the comfort of the worshipers, and ministration to the members of the Church as the bishop may direct. In all things, however, the deacon may be called to assist the teacher in his labors. Twelve deacons form a quorum; such a body is to be presided over by a president and counselors selected from among their number.

Teachers are local officers, whose function it is to mingle with the saints, exhorting them to their duties, and strengthening the Church by their constant ministry; they are to see that there is no iniquity in the Church; that the members do not cherish ill feelings toward one another, but observe the law of God respecting Church duties. They may take the lead of meetings when no priest or higher officer is present. Both teachers and deacons may preach the word of God when properly directed so to do; but they have not the power to independently officiate in any spiritual ordinances, such as baptizing, administering the sacrament, or laying on of hands. Twenty-four teachers constitute a quorum, including a president and two counselors.

Priests are appointed to preach, teach, expound the scripture, to baptize, to administer the sacrament, to visit the homes of the members, exhorting them to diligence. When properly directed, the priest may ordain deacons, teachers, and other priests; and he may be called upon to assist the elder in his work. A quorum of priests comprises forty-eight members, and is under the personal presidency of a bishop.

Elders are empowered to officiate in any or all duties connected with lower callings in the Priesthood; and in addition, they may ordain other elders, confirm as members of the Church candidates who have been properly baptized, and confer upon them the Holy Ghost. Elders have authority to bless children in the Church, and to take charge of meetings, conducting the same as they are led by the Holy Ghost. The elder may officiate in the stead of the high priest when the latter is not present. Ninety-six elders form a quorum; three of these constitute the presidency of the body.

Seventies are primarily traveling elders, especially ordained to promulgate the Gospel among the nations of the earth, "unto the Gentiles first, and also unto the Jews." They are to act under the direction of the apostles in this specific labor. A full quorum comprises seventy members, including seven presidents.

High Priests are ordained with power to officiate, when set apart or otherwise authoritatively directed, in all the ordinances and blessings of the Church. They may travel as do the seventies, carrying the Gospel to the nations; but they are not especially charged with this duty; their particular calling being that of standing presidency and service. The high priests of any stake of the Church may be organized into a quorum, and this without limit as to number; over such a quorum, three of the members preside as president and counselors.

Patriarchs or Evangelists are charged with the duty of blessing the members of the Church; of course they have authority to officiate also in other ordinances. There is one "Patriarch to the Church," known officially as the Presiding Patriarch, with general jurisdiction throughout the whole organization; he holds the keys of the patriarchal office, and unto him the promise is given "that whoever he blesses shall be blessed, and whoever he curses shall be cursed, that whatsoever he shall bind on earth shall be bound in heaven, and whatsoever he shall loose on earth shall be loosed in heaven."

Concerning the patriarchal authority the Lord has said: "The order of this priesthood was confirmed to be handed down from father to son, and rightly belongs to the literal descendants of the chosen seed to whom the promises were made. This order was instituted in the days of Adam, and came down by lineage." But, besides this office of general patriarchal power, there are a number of local patriarchs appointed in the branches of the Church, all subject to counsel and instruction from the Presiding Patriarch as he is directed by the First Presidency or the Council of the Twelve, yet possessing the same privileges and authority within their districts as belong to the Presiding Patriarch throughout the Church. "It is the duty of the Twelve, in all large branches of the church, to ordain evangelical ministers, as they shall be designated unto them by revelation" (*AF,* 206–8).

Church Officers Called by Revelation. Revelation is essential to the Church, not only for the proper calling and ordination of its ministers but also that the officers so chosen may be guided in their administrations—to teach with authority the doctrines of salvation, to admonish, to encourage, and if necessary to reprove the people, and to declare unto them by prophecy the purposes and will of God respecting the Church, present and future (*AF,* 304).

Presiding Bishopric. The Presiding Bishopric, as at present constituted, comprises the Presiding Bishop of the Church and two counselors. This body holds jurisdiction over the duties of other bishops in the Church, and of all activities and organizations pertaining to the Aaronic Priesthood. The oldest living representative among the sons of Aaron is entitled to this office of presidency, provided he be in all respects worthy and qualified; however, he must be designated and ordained by the First Presidency of the Church. If such a literal

descendant of Aaron be found and ordained, he may act without counselors except when he sits in judgment in a trial of one of the Presidents
of the High Priesthood, in which case he is to be assisted by twelve
High Priests. But in the absence of any direct descendant of Aaron
properly qualified, a High Priest of the Melchizedek Priesthood may
be called and set apart by the First Presidency of the Church to the office of Presiding Bishop; he is to be assisted by two other High Priests
properly ordained and set apart as his counselors (*AF*, 211).

THE IMPORTANCE OF THE CHURCH

Foundation of the Church. The philosophical foundation of
"Mormonism" is constructed upon the following outline of facts and
premises:

1. The eternal existence of a living personal God; and
    the preexistence and eternal duration of mankind as
    His literal offspring.
2. The placing of man upon the earth as an embodied
    spirit to undergo the experiences of an intermediate
    probation.
3. The transgression and fall of the first parents of
    the race, by which man became mortal, or in other
    words was doomed to suffer a separation of spirit
    and body through death.
4. The absolute need of a Redeemer, empowered to
    overcome death, and thereby provide for a reunion

of the spirits and bodies of mankind through a material resurrection from death to immortality.

5. The providing of a definite plan of salvation, by obedience to which man may obtain remission of his sins, and be enabled to advance by effort and righteous achievement throughout eternity.

6. The establishment of the Church of Jesus Christ in the "meridian of time," by the personal ministry and atoning death of the foreordained Redeemer and Savior of mankind, and the proclamation of His saving Gospel through the ministry of the Holy Priesthood during the apostolic period and for a season thereafter.

7. The general "falling away" from the Gospel of Jesus Christ, by which the world degenerated into a state of apostasy, and the Holy Priesthood ceased to be operative in the organization of sects and churches designed and effected by the authority of man.

8. The restoration of the Gospel in the current age, the reestablishment of the Church of Jesus Christ by the bestowal of the Holy Priesthood through Divine revelation.

9. The appointed mission of the restored Church of Jesus Christ to preach the Gospel and administer in the ordinances thereof amongst all nations, in preparation for the near advent of our Savior Jesus Christ, who shall reign on earth as Lord and King (*SPM,* 112–14).

Church Blessed with Gifts. The distinguishing feature of a miraculous manifestation of the Holy Spirit, as contrasted with a wonder wrought through other agencies, lies in the fact that the former is always done in the name of Jesus Christ, and has for its object the fostering of faith and the furthering of Divine purposes.

The Church of Jesus Christ of Latter-day Saints rejoices in the possession of the several gifts and graces with which the Church of old was endowed; and within her pale signs do follow them that believe. Come and see (*VM,* 120).

Sometimes Church Discipline Is Necessary. Extreme measures were to be adopted only after all gentler means had failed. Should the man persist in his obstinacy, the case was to be brought before the Church, and in the event of his neglect or refusal to heed the decision of the Church, he was to be deprived of fellowship, thereby becoming in his relationship to his former associates "as an heathen man and a publican." In such state of non-membership he would be a fit subject for missionary effort; but, until he became repentant and manifested willingness to make amends, he could claim no rights or privileges of communion in the Church. Continued association with the unrepentant sinner may involve the spread of his disaffection, and the contamination of others through his sin. Justice is not to be dethroned by Mercy (*JTC,* 391–92).

Lost Recovered. Between this parable and that of the lost sheep there are certain notable differences, though the lesson in each is in general the same. The sheep had strayed by its own volition; the coin had been dropped, and so was lost as a result of inattention or culpable carelessness on the part of its owner. The woman, discovering her loss institutes a diligent search; she sweeps the house, and perhaps learns of dirty corners, dusty recesses, cobwebby nooks, to which she had been oblivious in her self-complacency as an outwardly clean and conventional housewife. Her search is rewarded by the recovery of the lost piece, and is incidentally beneficial in the cleansing of her house. Her joy is like that of the shepherd wending his way homeward with the sheep upon his shoulders—once lost but now regained.

The woman who by lack of care lost the precious piece may be taken to represent the theocracy of the time, and the Church as an institution in any dispensational period; then the pieces of silver, every one a genuine coin of the realm, bearing the image of the great King, are the souls committed to the care of the Church; and the lost piece symbolizes the souls that are neglected and, for a time at least, lost sight of, by the authorized ministers of the Gospel of Christ (*JTC*, 456).

Mission of the Church. In preparing the world for the coming of the Lord there is a duty laid upon the Church as an organization, and upon every member of the Church individually; and that duty or obligation is to carry the word to our neighbors, to all with whom we may come in contact. Remember the mission of the Church is not wholly and solely to convert men to the acceptance of its principles and to bring them into membership. The duty laid upon us is also that of warning the world of the judgments that are to come. Can you doubt that the present dread scenes of conflict and slaughter on land and sea, in the air and beneath the water, are insignificant as signs of the times? (CR, Apr. 1917, 67).

Scriptural Usage of the Kingdom of God. In the Gospel according to Matthew the phrase "kingdom of heaven" repeatedly occurs; while in the writings of the other evangelists and throughout the epistles, the corresponding expression is "kingdom of God," "kingdom of Christ," or simply "kingdom." In many instances these designations are used with the same meaning, though a distinction is apparent in others. The several scriptural usages of the terms comprise:

1. A signification practically identical with that of "The Church of Jesus Christ."
2. The designation of the literal kingdom, material and spiritual, over which Christ the Lord shall rule by personal ministration in days yet future.

Under the first conception, the "kingdom" of scriptural mention has been already established as an organization among men, and is today in a state of war against sin, with its powers and resources mobilized in defense of freedom of worship and for the salvation of the race. Plainly, when we speak of the Church as the Kingdom we refer to an institution already extant on the earth, not one that is yet to come.

The Church of Jesus Christ asserts no right of control in the government of nations; and its jurisdiction in temporal affairs is limited to matters of organization and discipline within itself, such as are essential to the maintenance and perpetuity of any community body.

The Kingdom of God and the Church of Christ are virtually

synonymous terms. We do not pray that this organization shall come; for it is now existent. We pray and strive for its growth and development, for the spread of its saving principles, and for their acceptance by all mankind. But the Kingdom of Heaven is greater than the Church as the latter exists today, and when fully established will be seen to be a development thereof. Its advent is yet to be prayed for (*VM,* 173–74).

Kingdom of God / Kingdom of Heaven. Do you believe that the kingdom of heaven has been already set up upon the earth? I do not. I know that the kingdom of God has been established upon the earth, but the kingdom of God is a preparation for the kingdom of heaven, which is yet to come. The expressions "Kingdom of God" and "Kingdom of Heaven" are ofttimes used synonymously and interchangeably in our imperfect English translation of the Holy Bible, particularly in the Gospel according to Matthew, where the expression "Kingdom of Heaven" is most commonly used. But in these instances, as in so many others, the light of modern revelation clears up the darkness of ancient passages; and the Lord has in this day and age made plain the fact, beyond all question, that there is a distinction between the kingdom of God and the kingdom of heaven. The kingdom of God is the Church of Christ; the kingdom of heaven is that system of government and administration which is operative in heaven, and which we pray may some day prevail on earth. The kingdom of heaven will be established when the King shall come, as come He shall, in power and might and glory, to take dominion in and over and throughout the earth (CR, Apr. 1917, 65).

Strength of the Church. Today the Church of Jesus Christ of Latter-day Saints is stronger than ever before; and the people are confident that it is at its weakest stage for all time to come. It lives and thrives because within it are the elements of thrift and the forces of life. It embraces a boundless liberality of belief and practise; true toleration is one of its essential features; it makes love for mankind second only to love for Deity. Its creed provides for the protection of all men in their rights of worship according to the dictates of conscience. It contemplates a millennium of peace, when every man shall love his neighbor and respect his neighbor's opinion as he regards himself and his own—a day when the voice of the people shall be in unison with the voice of God (*SPM,* 108).

MANIFESTATION OF DIVINE COMMISSION

A Living Church. Revelation is God's means of communication with His children, and we deny the consistent and unchangeable character of Deity when we say that God has revealed Himself to man, but cannot or will not do so again. Is it reasonable to hold that in one age the Church of Christ was blessed, enlightened, and guided by direct revelation and that at another time the Church is to be left to itself, sustained only by the dead letter of earlier days? The living Church must be in vital communication with its Divine Head (*VM,* 153).

Revelation Necessary to Know God. Revelation gives to man his surest knowledge of God (*AF,* 36).

Church Led by Revelation. We are tolerant, tolerant in the extreme. We grant unto every man the right to worship after his own conscience, even as we claim it; but we do not compromise by the acceptance of the views of men in an attempt to mingle them with the doctrine of Christ, and call it all the word of God. The Lord has spoken and is speaking. I bear you solemn testimony that ever since the reestablishment of the Church in 1830, this Church of Jesus Christ has been led by inspiration and revelation from the heavens. This is the day in which you witness such. The Lord is not leaving his Church to itself. He is speaking in the ways best known to him, and inspiring and leading those whom you sustain as your leaders. Follow them and be safe (CR, Oct. 1922, 72).

Purpose of Revelation. I rejoice in belonging to a church that is in a measure up to date, and down to date, that gives me news of the present and that gives me the Word of God concerning the affairs of my life and the duties that lie immediately before me. I rejoice in the progressivism of this Church and more particularly in the fact that its progressivism is of the right kind. It is not that so-called progressivism that seeks to belittle or destroy the achievements of the past: it is not a progressivism that seeks to tear down, that says our fathers were wrong and we know more than they did; that they laid a foundation which in its way was good but not sufficient for us to build upon. We have no such spirit of progression as that, for that is destruction. The spirit of advancement and progressivism in the Church of Christ is that which marks the progression from the seed to the blade and from the blade to the ripened ear. It is a constructive progressivism: the past is added to, and every new revelation doth but make the revelations of the past plainer and reveal their sanctity and their sacred origin the better (CR, Oct. 1912, 126).

New Revelation Imperative. We do not believe in living wholly in the past. We believe in an up-to-date doctrine, in an up-to-date church, an up-to-date religion, a religion that is ever enriched by new revelation, a church that is in direct communication with headquarters, a church that is receiving through revelation the word of God today, pertaining to the affairs of today (CR, Apr. 1912, 128).

Need for Revelation. The recreant and unbelieving Jews rejected their Lord because He came to them with a new revelation. Had they not Moses and the prophets? What more could they need? They openly boasted, "We are Moses' disciples," and added, "We know that God spake unto Moses; as for this fellow, we know not from whence he is." (John 9:28–29.) Those who deny the possibility of present day revelation are not distinguished by originality; they follow a beaten path, hard trodden by ignoble feet.

The Apostles ministered under the guiding influence of revelation. Paul writing to the Corinthians said: "But God hath revealed them [Divine truths] unto us by his Spirit: for the Spirit searcheth all things, yea, the deep things of God. For what man knoweth the things of a man, save the spirit of man which is in him? even so the things of God knoweth no man, but the Spirit of God." (1 Cor. 2:10–12.)

The imperative need of continued revelation appears in the fact that new conditions and unprecedented combinations of circumstances arise with the passage of time, and Divine direction alone can meet the new issues.

The Apostle John knew that in the last days, these present days, the voice of God would be heard calling His people from the Babylon of sin to the Zion of safety: "And I heard another voice from heaven, saying, Come out of her, my people, that ye be not partakers of her sins, and that ye receive not of her plagues." (Rev. 18:4; see also 14:6.) (*VM,* 154–55).

Gifts of the Holy Ghost. It has been already affirmed, that all men who would officiate with propriety in the ordinances of the Gospel must be commissioned for their exalted duties by the authority of heaven. When so invested, these servants of the Lord will not be lacking in proofs of their divine commission; for it is characteristic of the ways of God that He manifests His power by the bestowal of a variety of ennobling graces, which are properly called gifts of the Spirit. These are oftentimes exhibited in a manner so different from the usual order of things as to be called miraculous and supernatural. In this way did the Lord make Himself known in the early times of scriptural history; and from the days of Adam until the present, prophets of God have generally been endowed with such power. Whenever the power of Priesthood has operated through an organized Church on the earth, the members have been strengthened in their faith and otherwise blessed in numerous related ways, by the possession of these gifts. We may safely regard the existence of these spiritual powers as one of the essential characteristics of the Church; where they are not, the Priesthood of God does not operate (*AF,* 217).

Gift of Prophecy. The Gift of Prophecy distinguishes its possessor as a prophet—literally, one who speaks for another, specifically, one who speaks for God. It is distinguished by Paul as one of the most desirable of spiritual endowments, and its preeminence over the gift of tongues he discusses at length. To prophesy is to receive and declare the word of God, and the statement of His will to the people. The function of prediction, often regarded as the sole essential of prophecy, is but one among many characteristics of this divinely given power. The prophet may have as much concern with the past as with the present or the future; he may use his gift in teaching through the experience of preceding events as in foretelling occurrences. The prophets of God are entrusted with His confidences, being privileged to learn of His will and designs. The statement appears that the Lord will do nothing except He reveal His secret purposes unto His servants, the prophets. These oracles stand as mediators between God and mortals, pleading for or against the people.

No special ordination in the Priesthood is essential to man's receiving the gift of prophecy; bearers of the Melchizedek Priesthood, Adam, Noah, Moses, and a multitude of others were prophets, but not more truly so than others who were specifically called to the Aaronic order, as exemplified in the instance of John the Baptist. The ministrations of Miriam and Deborah show that this gift may be possessed by women also. In the time of Samuel the prophets were organized into a special order, to aid their purposes of study and improvement.

In the current dispensation this gift is enjoyed in a fulness equal to that of any preceding time. The Lord's will concerning present duties is made known through the mouths of prophets, and events of great import have been foretold. The fact of the present existence and vitality of the Church is an undeniable testimony of the actuality of latter-day prophecy. The Church today constitutes a body of witnesses, numbering hundreds of thousands, to the effect of this, one of the great gifts of God (*AF*, 228–29).

PRIESTHOOD

Levitical Priesthood. The *Aaronic Priesthood* is named after Aaron, who was given to Moses as his mouthpiece, to act under his direction in the carrying out of God's purposes respecting Israel. For this reason it is sometimes called the Lesser Priesthood; but though lesser, it is neither small nor insignificant. While Israel journeyed in the wilderness, Aaron and his sons were called by prophecy and set apart for the duties of the priest's office.

At a later period the Lord chose the tribe of Levi to assist Aaron in the priestly functions, the special duties of the Levites being to keep the instruments and attend to the service of the tabernacle. The Levites were to take the place of the firstborn throughout the tribes, whom the Lord had claimed for His service from the time of the last dread plague in Egypt whereby the firstborn in every Egyptian house was slain while the eldest in every Israelitish house was hallowed and spared. The commission thus given to the Levites is sometimes called the *Levitical Priesthood;* it is to be regarded as an appendage to the Priesthood of Aaron, not comprising the highest priestly powers. The Aaronic Priesthood, as restored to the earth in this dispensation, includes the Levitical order. The Aaronic Priesthood holds the keys of the ministering of angels, and the authority to attend to the outward ordinances, the letter of the Gospel; it comprises the offices of deacon, teacher, and priest, with the bishopric holding the keys of presidency (*AF*, 204–5).

Melchizedek Priesthood. The *Melchizedek Priesthood* is named after the king of Salem, a great High Priest before whose day it was known as "the Holy Priesthood, after the Order of the Son of God. But out of respect or reverence to the name of the Supreme Being, to avoid the too frequent repetition of his name, they, the Church, in ancient days, called that priesthood after Melchizedek." This Priesthood holds the right of presidency in all the offices of the Church; its special functions lie in the administration of spiritual things, comprising the keys of all spiritual blessings of the Church, the right "to have the heavens opened unto them [the bearers of this Priesthood], to commune with the general assembly and Church of the Firstborn, and to enjoy the communion and presence of God the Father, and Jesus the mediator of the new covenant." The special offices of the Melchizedek Priesthood are those of apostle, patriarch or evangelist, high priest, seventy, and elder. Revelation from God has defined the duties associated with each of these callings; and the same high authority has directed the establishment of presiding officers appointed from among those who are ordained to the several offices in these two Priesthoods (*AF*, 205–6).

Melchizedek Priesthood Administers the Ordinances of the Temple. The Temples of today are maintained and the distinctive ordinances pertaining thereto are administered under the authority of the Higher or Melchisedek Priesthood, the greatest and highest commission ever conferred upon man (*HL,* 237).

Authority Necessary to Speak in God's Name. Religion is more than the confession and profession of the lips. Jesus averred that in the day of judgment many would pretend allegiance to Him, saying: "Lord, Lord, have we not prophesied in thy name? and in thy name have cast out devils? and in thy name done many wonderful works? And then will I profess unto them, I never knew you: depart from me, ye that work iniquity." Only by doing the will of the Father is the saving grace of the Son obtainable. To assume to speak and act in the name of the Lord without the bestowal of authority, such as the Lord alone can give, is to add sacrilege to hypocrisy. Even miracles wrought will be no vindication of the claims of those who pretend to minister in the ordinances of the gospel while devoid of the authority of the Holy Priesthood (*JTC,* 245–46).

Priesthood Line of Authority. No one may officiate in any ordinances of The Church of Jesus Christ of Latter-day Saints unless he has been ordained to the particular order or office of Priesthood, by those possessing the requisite authority. Thus, no man receives the Priesthood except under the hands of one who holds that Priesthood himself; that one must have obtained it from others previously commissioned; and so every bearer of the Priesthood today can trace his authority to the hands of Joseph Smith the Prophet, who received his ordination under the hands of the apostles Peter, James, and John; and they had been ordained by the Lord Jesus Christ (*AF,* 189).

Shaking Dust from the Feet. To ceremonially shake the dust from one's feet as a testimony against another was understood by the Jews to symbolize a cessation of fellowship and a renunciation of all responsibility for consequences that might follow. It became an ordinance of accusation and testimony by the Lord's instructions to His apostles as cited in the text. In the current dispensation, the Lord has similarly directed His authorized servants to so testify against those who wilfully and maliciously oppose the truth when authoritatively presented (see Doc. and Cov. 24:15; 60:15; 75:20; 84:92; 99:4). The responsibility of testifying before the Lord by this accusing symbol is so great that the means may be employed only under unusual and extreme conditions, as the Spirit of the Lord may direct (*JTC,* 345).

Church and State Should Be Kept Separate. It is a fundamental necessity that laws shall be established among men for general governance; and obedience to law is the obvious duty of every member of organized society. Violation of the law, therefore, is not only a secular offense but a transgression of the principles of true religion. This world would be a happier one if men carried more religion into their daily affairs—into business, politics, and statesmanship. Mark you, I say religion, not church. Under existing conditions it is imperative that State and Church be kept separate; and this segregation must be maintained until the inauguration of Christ's personal reign.

Loyal citizenship is at once a characteristic and a test of a man's religion; and as to the incumbent duties of citizenship, the voice of the people, as expressed through the established channels of government, must determine (*VM,* 180–81).

Church versus Secular Law. A question has many times been asked of the Church and of its individual members, to this effect: In the case of a conflict between the requirements made by the revealed word of God, and those imposed by the secular law, which of these authorities would the members of the Church be bound to obey? In answer, the words of Christ may be applied—it is the duty of the people to render unto Caesar the things that are Caesar's, and unto God the things that are God's. At the present time the kingdom of heaven as an earthly power, with a reigning King exercising direct and personal authority in temporal matters, has not been established upon the earth. The branches of the Church as such, and the members composing the same, are subjects of the several governments within whose separate realms the Church organizations exist. In this day of comparative enlightenment and freedom there is small cause for expecting any direct interference with the rights of private worship and individual devotion; in all civilized nations the people are accorded the right to pray, and this right is assured by what may be properly called a common law of humankind. No earnest soul is cut off from communion with his God; and with such an open channel of communication, relief from burdensome laws and redress for grievances may be sought from the power that holds control of nations (*AF,* 422–23).

Church and Politics. Only the other day I was asked, in the course of conversation with an intelligent gentleman, not a member of our Church: "Is the 'Mormon' Church in politics?"

I answered him: "Most assuredly it is in politics, and also in business, in statesmanship, in all the affairs of life, teaching the people to do what is right so far as it possibly can."

"Well, has the Church any candidates in the pending election?"

"Yes, indeed," said I, "the Church has a full ticket, and is counseling its members just how to vote."

Now, let me tell you just how you should vote, just as I told him. The Church is telling its members to look upon the franchise as a sacred gift, to exercise it according to their very best judgment before the Lord, and the Church's ticket is the ticket of the best men, according to the best judgment of the people, to whichever party they belong. Vote the party ticket if you honestly feel that to be best, or vote for the men you think will most effectively subserve the needs of country, state, and people (CR, Oct. 1920, 66).

Saints Are to Obey the Laws of Their Country. Pending the overruling by Providence in favor of religious liberty, it is the duty of the saints to submit themselves to the laws of their country. Nevertheless, they should use every proper method, as citizens or subjects of their several governments, to secure for themselves and for all men the boon of freedom in religious service. It is not required of them to suffer without protest imposition by lawless persecutors, or through the operation of unjust laws; but their protests should be offered in legal and proper order (*AF*, 423).

MILLENNIAL GOVERNMENT

Millennial Reign of the Son of God. We have seen that, according to the words of holy prophets ancient and modern, Christ is to come in a literal sense and so manifest Himself in person in the last days. He is to dwell among His saints. "Yea, even I will be in the midst of you," He declared to the people on this continent, whom He promised to establish in the land of the New Jerusalem; and similar assurances were given through the prophets of the east. In this prospective ministration among His gathered saints, Jesus Christ is to be at once their God and their King. His government is to be that of a perfect theocracy; the laws of righteousness will be the code, and control will be administered under one authority, undisputed because indisputable (*AF*, 363).

Best Form of Government. The best form of government possible unto man is a monarchy with the right kind of a monarch, who will do only justice, full justice, and with due regard to the claims of mercy, give unto every man his right. Such a government will be democracy and monarchy combined, and such is the government of the kingdom of heaven (CR, Apr. 1917, 66).

9

Principles and Ordinances of the Gospel

FIRST PRINCIPLES

First Principles. Faith in God leads to repentance of sin; this is followed by baptism in water for the remission of sins, and this in turn by the bestowal of the Holy Spirit, or the right and title to the personal association and inspiring ministration of the Holy Ghost, through whose power come sanctification and the specific gifts of God (*AF,* 164).

Fundamental Principles of the Gospel. Nevertheless, the Gospel, comprising not alone precepts but the accompanying authority of the Holy Priesthood to administer ordinances, was preached to men in the earliest period of human history. The necessity of (1) faith in the then unembodied but chosen and ordained Savior of mankind, (2) the indispensability of repentance as a means leading to remission of sins, (3) the Divine requirement of baptism by immersion in water, and (4) spiritual baptism through the power of the Holy Ghost—which

239

constitute the fundamental principles and ordinances of the Gospel—was preached and administered to Adam, the patriarch of the race, and by him to his posterity (*VM,* 293–94).

FAITH

Faith in God Brings Spiritual Blessings. In a theological sense faith includes a moving, vital, inspiring confidence in God, and the acceptance of His will as our law and of His words as our guide in life. Faith in God is a principle of power, for by its exercise spiritual forces are made operative. By this power phenomena that appear to be supernatural, such as we call miracles, are wrought. Even the Lord Jesus was influenced and in a measure controlled by the lack of faith or the possession thereof by those who sought blessings at His hands. We are told that at a certain time and place Jesus "could there do no mighty work" because of the people's unbelief, which was so dense that He marveled at it. (Mark 6:5, 6.) Repeatedly did the Lord rebuke and admonish with such reproofs as "O ye of little faith," "Where is your faith?" and "How is it that ye have no faith?" In glorious contrast rang out His words of benediction to those whose faith had made it possible for Him to heal and to save: "Thy faith hath made thee whole" and "According to your faith be it unto you."

Read the record of the youthful demoniac whose agonized father brought his son to the Master, pleading pitiably "If thou canst do any thing, have compassion on us and help us." To this qualified intercession Jesus replied "If thou canst believe" and added "All things are possible to him that believeth." (Read Mark 9:14–29.) The faith requisite to the healing was not that of the Healer alone, but primarily faith on the part of the suppliant.

If through faith Divine interposition may be secured to the accomplishment of what we call material or physical miracles, and of this the Scriptures contain copious testimony (read Hebrews, chapter 11), is it consistent to doubt that faith is the appointed agency for invoking and securing spiritual blessings, even to the attainment of salvation in the eternal worlds?

As shown in earlier articles, redemption from the power of death is assured to all through the victory achieved by Jesus Christ; but salvation is an individual gift, provided for all who shall establish claim thereto through obedience to the laws and ordinances of the Gospel. Faith in God the Eternal Father, and in His Son Jesus Christ as the Redeemer and Savior of the race, and in the Holy Ghost, is essential to the securing of individual salvation. Paul forcefully declares "But without faith it is impossible to please him: for he that cometh to God must believe that he is, and that he is a rewarder of them that diligently seek him." (Heb. 11:6.) (*VM*, 78–79).

Faith Helps Us Move Forward. Long after midnight the train arrived, in a terrific whirl of wind and snow. I lingered behind my companions, as they hurriedly clambered aboard, for I was attracted by the engineer, who, during the brief stop, while his assistant was attending to the water replenishment, bustled about the engine, oiling some parts, adjusting others, and generally overhauling the panting locomotive. I ventured to speak to him, busy though he was. I asked how he felt on such a night,—wild, weird, and furious, when the powers of destruction seemed to be let loose, abroad and uncontrolled, when the storm was howling and when danger threatened from every side. I thought of the possibility—the probability even—of snow-drifts or slides on the track; of bridges and high trestles, which may have been loosened by the storm; of rock-masses dislodged from the mountain-side;—of these and other possible obstacles. I realized that in the event of accident through obstruction on or disruption of the track, the engineer and the fireman would be the ones most exposed to danger; a violent collision would most likely cost them their lives. All of these thoughts and others I expressed in hasty questioning of the bustling, impatient, engineer.

His answer was a lesson not yet forgotten. In effect he said, though in jerky and disjointed sentences: "Look at the engine head-light. Doesn't that light up the track for a hundred yards or more? Well, all I try to do is to cover that hundred yards of lighted track. That I can see, and for that distance I know the road-bed is open and safe. And," he added, with what, through the swirl and the dim lamp-lighted darkness of the roaring night, I saw was a humorous smile on his lips, and a merry twinkle of his eye, "believe me, I have never been able to drive this old engine of mine, God bless her! so fast as to outstrip that hundred yards of lighted track. The light of the engine is always ahead of me!"

As he climbed to his place in the cab, I hastened to board the first passenger coach; and, as I sank into the cushioned seat, in blissful enjoyment of the warmth and general comfort, offering strong contrast to the wildness of the night without, I thought deeply of the words of the grimy, oil-stained engineer. They were full of faith—the faith that accomplishes great things, the faith that gives courage and determination, the faith that leads to works. What if the engineer had failed; had yielded to fright and fear; had refused to go on because of the threatening dangers? Who knows what work may have been hindered; what great plans may have been nullified; what God-appointed commissions of mercy and relief may have been thwarted, had the engineer weakened and quailed?

For a little distance the storm-swept track was lighted up; for that short space the engineer drove on!

We may not know what lies ahead of us in the future years, nor even in the days or hours immediately beyond. But for a few yards, or possibly only a few feet, the track is clear, our duty is plain, our course is illumined. For that short distance, for the next step, lighted by the inspiration of God, go on (*PJT,* 20–22).

Faith a Principle of Power. Observe the significant assertion, "Thy faith hath made thee whole." Faith is of itself a principle of power; and by its presence or absence, by its fulness or paucity, even the Lord was and is influenced, and in great measure controlled, in the bestowal or withholding of blessings; for He ministers according to law, and not with caprice or uncertainty. We read that at a certain time and place Jesus "could there do no mighty work" because of the people's unbelief. Modern revelation specifies that faith to be healed is one of the gifts of the Spirit, analogous to the manifestations of faith in the work of healing others through the exercise of the power of the Holy Priesthood (*JTC,* 318–19).

Faith Must Center in Jesus Christ. Faith in the Lord Jesus Christ is the fundamental principle of the Gospel, the first letter in the alphabet of salvation with which are spelled the words of life eternal. Yet who can have faith in aught of which he knows nothing? Knowledge is essential to faith, and faith impels its possessor to seek further knowledge, and to make of that knowledge, wisdom, which is but knowledge applied and put to use. To preach Christ and Him crucified is the one and only way by which faith in Him may be taught through the medium of either precept or example. While knowledge and faith are thus closely associated, the two are not identical, nor is the one an assured outgrowth of the other. A man may have learned the truth, and yet may ignore it. His knowledge, far from developing within his soul the faith that leads to right action, may but add to his condemnation, for he sins without even the mitigation of ignorance. Evil spirits have testified of their knowledge that Jesus is the Christ, nevertheless they remain the fallen followers of Satan. As living faith develops within the soul of man it leads its possessor to seek a means whereby he may rise from the thraldom of sin; and the very thought of such emancipation inspires a loathing for the evil contamination of the past. The natural fruitage of that glorious growth is repentance (*HL,* 66).

Gifts Given to Those Who Have Faith in Christ. These gifts have been promised of the Lord unto those who believe in His name, and are to follow obedience to the requirements of the Gospel. Among believers they are to serve for encouragement, and as incentives to higher communion with the Spirit (*AF,* 219).

Faith a Gift of God. Though within the reach of all who diligently strive to gain it, faith is nevertheless a divine gift. As is fitting for so priceless a pearl, it is given to those only who show by their sincerity that they are worthy of it, and who give promise of abiding by its dictates. Although faith is called the first principle of the Gospel of Christ, though it be in fact the foundation of religious life, yet even faith is preceded by sincerity of disposition and humility of soul, whereby the word of God may make an impression upon the heart. No compulsion is used in bringing men to a knowledge of God; yet, as fast as we open our hearts to the influences of righteousness, the faith that leads to life eternal will be given us of our Father (*AF,* 107).

Peter Walked on Water. The return by boat proved to be a memorable journey for the disciples. They encountered a boisterous headwind, which of course rendered impossible the use of sails; and though they toiled heavily at the oars the vessel became practically unmanageable and wallowed in the midst of the sea. Though they had labored through the night they had progressed less than four miles on their course; to turn and run before the wind would have been to invite disastrous wreck; their sole hope lay in their holding the vessel to the wind by sheer power of muscle. Jesus, in His place of solitary retirement, was aware of their sad plight, and along in the fourth watch, that is, between three and six o'clock in the morning, He came to their assistance, walking upon the storm-tossed water as though treading solid ground. When the voyagers caught sight of Him as He approached the ship in the faint light of the near-spent night, they were overcome by superstitious fears, and cried out in terror, thinking that they saw a ghostly apparition. "But straightway Jesus spake unto them, saying, Be of good cheer; it is I; be not afraid."

Relieved by these assuring words, Peter, impetuous and impulsive as usual, cried out: "Lord, if it be thou, bid me come unto thee on the water." Jesus assenting, Peter descended from the ship and walked toward his Master; but as the wind smote him and the waves rose about him, his confidence wavered and he began to sink. Strong swimmer though he was, he gave way to fright, and cried, "Lord, save me." Jesus caught him by the hand, saying: "O thou of little faith, wherefore didst thou doubt?"

From Peter's remarkable experience, we learn that the power by which Christ was able to walk the waves could be made operative in others, provided only their faith was enduring. It was on Peter's own request that he was permitted to attempt the feat. Had Jesus forbidden him, the man's faith might have suffered a check; his attempt, though attended by partial failure, was a demonstration of the efficacy of faith in the Lord, such as no verbal teaching could ever have conveyed (*JTC,* 336–37).

REPENTANCE

Meaning of Repentance. The term repentance is used in the scriptures with several different meanings, but, as representing the duty required of all who would obtain forgiveness for transgression it indicates a godly sorrow for sin, producing a reformation of life, and embodies (1) a conviction of guilt; (2) a desire to be relieved from the hurtful effects of sin; and (3) an earnest determination to forsake sin and to

PRINCIPLES AND ORDINANCES OF THE GOSPEL

accomplish good. Repentance is a result of contrition of soul, which springs from a deep sense of humility, and this in turn is dependent upon the exercise of an abiding faith in God. Repentance therefore properly ranks as the second principle of the Gospel, closely associated with and immediately following faith. As soon as one has come to recognize the existence and authority of God, he feels a respect for divine laws, and a conviction of his own unworthiness. His wish to please the Father, whom he has so long ignored, will impel him to forsake sin; and this impulse will acquire added strength from the sinner's natural and commendable desire to make reparation, if possible, and so avert the dire results of his own waywardness. With the zeal inspired by fresh conviction, he will crave an opportunity of showing by good works the sincerity of his newly developed faith; and he will regard the remission of his sins as the most desirable of blessings. Then he will learn that this gift of mercy is granted on certain specific conditions. The first step toward the blessed state of forgiveness consists in the sinner confessing his sins; the second, in his forgiving others who have sinned against him; and the third in his showing his acceptance of Christ's atoning sacrifice by complying with the divine requirements (*AF*, 109).

Repentance. Repentance, which stands eternally established as an indispensable condition of salvation, is today proclaimed anew under the authority of the restored Priesthood, and the call is to every nation, kindred, tongue, and people. The second advent of the Christ is near, and but little time remains to prepare for His coming, which shall be in power and great glory, to the accompaniment of the resurrection of the righteous dead, the glorification of the worthy who are still in the flesh, and the destruction of the wilfully and hopelessly wicked.

Repentance, as the ordained requirement whereby remission of sins may be attained, consists essentially in a genuine sorrow for sin and comprises: (1) a personal conviction of guilt; (2) an earnest desire to secure forgiveness; and (3) a resolute determination to forsake sin and follow the path of righteous living. The first step in the course of effective repentance consists in the acknowledgment or confession of sin before God; the second in the sinner forgiving those who have sinned against him; and the third in his acceptance of Christ's atoning sacrifice as shown by a willingness to obey the further requirements embodied in the Gospel of salvation.

1. Without sincere confession of sin repentance is impossible. The Apostle John declared the solemn truth:

"If we say that we have no sin, we deceive ourselves, and the truth is not in us. If we confess our sins, he is faithful and just to forgive us our sins, and to cleanse us from all unrighteousness." (1 John 1:8, 9.)

In this modern age the voice of the Lord Jesus Christ has been heard to the same effect:

"Verily I say unto you, I, the Lord, forgive sins unto those who confess their sins before me and ask forgiveness, who have not sinned unto death."

And further:

"By this ye may know if a man repenteth of his sins. Behold, he will confess them and forsake them." (Doctrine and Covenants 64:7; and 58:43.)

2. The sinner must be willing to grant forgiveness to others if he

would secure that boon to himself. In teaching us how to pray, the Lord specified the condition on which forgiveness may rationally be asked: "Forgive us our debts as we forgive our debtors." No hope of forgiveness is justified if in our hearts we are unforgiving, "For," said the Christ, "if ye forgive men their trespasses, your heavenly Father will also forgive you: But if ye forgive not men their trespasses, neither will your Father forgive your trespasses." (Matt. 6:14, 15.)

Through His revelations to the restored Church in the current age, the Lord has emphasized this essential element of repentance:

"Wherefore I say unto you, that ye ought to forgive one another, for he that forgiveth not his brother his trespasses, standeth condemned before the Lord, for there remaineth in him the greater sin. I, the Lord, will forgive whom I will forgive, but of you it is required to forgive all men." (Doctrine and Covenants 64:9, 10.)

3. Contrite repentance will naturally lead the penitent to do all he can to make amends for past offenses, and to comply with the conditions on which forgiveness is predicated (*VM*, 81–82).

Repentance Is a Resolute Determination. Repentance, to be worthy of its name, must comprise something more than a mere self-acknowledgment of error; it does not consist in lamentations and wordy confessions, but in the heartfelt recognition of guilt, which carries with it a horror for sin and a resolute determination to make amends for the past and to do better in the future. If such a conviction be genuine it is marked by that godly sorrow which, as Paul has said, "worketh repentance to salvation, not to be repented of; but the sorrow of the world worketh death." Apostle Orson Pratt has wisely said: "It would be of no use for a sinner to confess his sins to God unless he were determined to forsake them; it would be of no benefit to him to feel sorry that he had done wrong unless he intended to do wrong no more; it would be folly for him to confess before God that he had injured his fellow man unless he were determined to do all in his power to make restitution. Repentance, then, is not only a confession of sins, with a sorrowful, contrite heart, but a fixed, settled purpose to refrain from every evil way" (*AF,* 112).

Repentance Is a Gift from God. Repentance, as a requirement made of all men, constitutes the second principle of the Gospel of Christ. It comprises a sincere sorrow for the sins of the past, and a resolute turning away therefrom with the solemn determination to endeavor by Divine assistance to return thereto no more. Repentance comes as a gift from God to him who has treasured and nurtured the earlier gift of faith. It is not to be had for the careless asking; it may not be found upon the highway; it is not of earth, but a treasure of heaven, and is given with care, yet with boundless liberality unto those who have brought forth works that warrant its bestowal. That is to say, all who prepare themselves for repentance will, by the humbling and softening influence of the Holy Spirit, be brought to the actual possession of this great gift (*HL,* 66–67).

Do Not Procrastinate. No soul is justified in postponing his efforts to repent because of this assurance of longsuffering and mercy. We know not fully on what terms repentance will be obtainable in the hereafter; but to suppose that the soul who has wilfully rejected the opportunity of repentance in this life will find it easy to repent there is contrary to reason. To procrastinate the day of repentance is to deliberately place ourselves in the power of the adversary (*AF,* 115).

Heaven Rejoices over the Repentant. The three parables, which appear in the scriptural record as parts of a continuous discourse, are as one in portraying the joy that abounds in heaven over the recovery of a soul once numbered among the lost, whether that soul be best symbolized by a sheep that had wandered afar, a coin that had dropped out of sight through the custodian's neglect, or a son who would deliberately sever himself from home and heaven. There is no justification for the inference that a repentant sinner is to be given precedence over a righteous soul who had resisted sin; were such the way of God, then Christ, the one sinless Man, would be surpassed in the Father's esteem by regenerate offenders. Unqualifiedly offensive as is sin, the sinner is yet precious in the Father's eyes, because of the possibility of his repentance and return to righteousness. The loss of a soul is a very real and a very great loss to God. He is pained and grieved thereby, for it is His will that not one should perish (*JTC,* 461).

Parable of the Prodigal Son. We are not justified in extolling the virtue of repentance on the part of the prodigal above the faithful, plodding service of his brother, who had remained at home, true to the duties required of him. The devoted son was the heir; the father did not disparage his worth, nor deny his deserts. His displeasure over the rejoicing incident to the return of his wayward brother was an exhibition of illiberality and narrowness; but of the two brothers the elder was the more faithful, whatever his minor defects may have been. The particular point emphasized in the Lord's lesson, however, had to do with his uncharitable and selfish weaknesses.

Pharisees and scribes, to whom this masterpiece of illustrative incident was delivered, must have taken to themselves its personal application. They were typified by the elder son, laboriously attentive to routine, methodically plodding by rule and rote in the multifarious labors of the field, without interest except that of self, and all unwilling to welcome a repentant publican or a returned sinner. From all such they were estranged; such a one might be to the indulgent and forgiving Father, "this thy son," but never to them, a brother. They cared not who or how many were lost, so long as they were undisturbed in heirship and possession by the return of penitent prodigals. But the parable was not for them alone; it is a living perennial yielding the fruit of wholesome doctrine and soul-sustaining nourishment for all time. Not a word appears in condonation or excuse for the prodigal's sin; upon that the Father could not look with the least degree of allowance; but over that sinner's repentance and contrition of soul, God and the household of heaven rejoiced (*JTC,* 460–61).

BAPTISM

Symbolism of Baptism by Immersion. Baptism has also been very impressively compared to a burial, followed by a resurrection; and in this symbol of the bodily death and resurrection of His Son has God promised to grant remission of sins. In writing to the Romans, Paul says: "Know ye not, that so many of us as were baptized into Jesus Christ were baptized into his death? Therefore we are buried with him by baptism into death: that like as Christ was raised up from the dead by the glory of the Father, even so we also should walk in newness of life. For if we have been planted together in the likeness of his death, we shall be also in the likeness of his resurrection." And again, the same apostle writes: "Buried with him in baptism, wherein also ye are risen with him through the faith of the operation of God, who hath raised him from the dead." Among all the varied forms of baptism practised by man, immersion alone typifies a birth marking the beginning of a new career, or the sleep of the grave with subsequent victory over death (*AF*, 138–39).

Membership in the Church. Baptism is the gateway leading into the fold of Christ, the portal to the Church, the established rite of naturalization in the kingdom of God. The candidate for admission into the Church, having obtained and professed faith in the Lord Jesus Christ and having sincerely repented of his sins, is properly required to give evidence of this spiritual sanctification by some outward ordinance, prescribed by authority as the sign or symbol of his new profession. The initiatory ordinance is baptism by water, to be followed by the higher baptism of the Holy Spirit; and, as a result of this act of obedience, remission of sins is granted.

Simple indeed are the means thus ordained for admission into the fold; they are within the reach of the poorest and weakest, as also of the rich and powerful. What symbol more expressive of a cleansing from sin could be given than that of baptism in water? Baptism is made a sign of the covenant entered into between the repentant sinner and his God, that thereafter he will seek to observe the divine commands. Concerning this fact, Alma the prophet thus admonished and instructed the people of Gideon: "Yea, I say unto you, come and fear not, and lay aside every sin, which easily doth beset you, which doth bind you down to destruction, yea, come and go forth, and show unto your God that ye are willing to repent of your sins and enter into a covenant with him to keep his commandments, and witness it unto him this day by going into the waters of baptism."

The humbled sinner, convicted of his transgression through faith and repentance, will hail most joyfully any means of cleansing himself from pollution, now so repulsive in his eyes. All such will cry out as did the stricken multitude at Pentecost, "What shall we do?" Unto such comes the answering voice of the Spirit, through the medium of scripture or by the mouths of the Lord's appointed servants: "Repent, and be baptized every one of you in the name of Jesus Christ for the remission of sins." Springing forth as a result of contrition of soul, baptism has been very appropriately called the first fruits of repentance (*AF*, 120–21).

Purpose of Baptism. The special purpose of baptism is to afford admission to the Church of Christ with remission of sins. What need of more words to prove the worth of this divinely appointed ordinance? What gift could be offered the human race greater than a sure means of obtaining forgiveness for transgression? Justice forbids the granting of universal and unconditional pardon for sins committed except through obedience to ordained law; but means simple and effective are provided whereby the penitent sinner may enter into a covenant with God, sealing that covenant with the sign that commands recognition in heaven, that he will submit himself to the laws of God; thus he places himself within the reach of Mercy, under whose protecting influence he may win eternal life. Biblical Proofs that baptism is designed as a means of securing to man a remission of his sins are abundant. John the Baptist was the special preacher of this doctrine, and the authorized administrator of the ordinance, in the days immediately preceding the Savior's ministry in the flesh; and the voice of this priest of the desert stirred Jerusalem and reverberated through all Judaea, proclaiming remission of sins as the fruits of acceptable baptism (*AF,* 122).

The Original Sin. The unscriptural and repellent dogma of inherent degeneracy and the contaminating effect of original sin, by which every child is born vile in the sight and judgment of God, long cast its dark shadow over the minds of men. From this conception sprang the practice of infant baptism and the perverted doctrine of assured damnation for all babes who die unbaptized. Even the most radical of churches has modified its teaching on this subject, and today permits its members to believe that children who die without baptism pass to a state of partial happiness and content, though forever denied the beatific vision of God (*VM,* 88).

Baptism of Little Children. As demonstrated in the preceding pages, the law of baptism is of universal application; in short, baptism is required of all who have lived to the age of accountability. Only those who die in infancy are exempt. Children, having no sin to expiate, and being unable to comprehend the nature of the baptismal obligation, are not to be baptized while living, nor is the ordinance to be performed for them should they die before reaching a responsible age and state. As to the child's part in the heritage of mortality incident to the transgression of Adam, the atonement of Christ is of full effect, and the redemption of the child is assured (*HL, 89–90*).

Infant Baptism. The Latter-day Saints are opposed to the practise of infant baptism, which indeed they believe to be a sacrilege. No one having faith in the word of God can look upon the child as culpably wicked; such an innocent being needs no initiation into the fold, for he has never strayed therefrom; he needs no remission of sins for he has committed no sin; and should he die before he has become contaminated by the sins of earth he will be received without baptism into the paradise of God. Yet there are many professedly Christian teachers who aver that as all children are born into a wicked world they are themselves wicked, and must be cleansed in the waters of baptism to be made acceptable to God. Such doctrine is heinous. The child to whom the Savior pointed as an example of emulation for those even who had received the holy apostleship, the Lord's selected type of the kingdom of heaven, the favored spirits whose angels stand forever in the presence of the Father, faithfully reporting all that may be done unto their charges—are such souls to be rejected and cast into torment because their earthly guardians failed to have them baptized? To teach such false doctrine is sin (*AF,* 125–26.)

Repeated Baptisms. Repeated baptisms of the same person are not sanctioned in the Church. It is an error to assume that baptism offers a means of gaining forgiveness of sins however oft repeated. Such a belief tends rather to excuse than to prevent sin, inasmuch as the hurtful effects may seem to be easily averted. Neither the written law nor the instructions of the living Priesthood designate baptism as a means of securing forgiveness by those who are already within the fold of Christ. Unto such, forgiveness of sin has been promised on confession and repentance with full purpose of heart; of them a repetition of the baptismal rite is not required; and, were subjects of this class repeatedly baptized, unto them remission of sins would in no wise come except they repent most sincerely (*AF*, 144).

GIFT OF THE HOLY GHOST

Baptism of Fire. The gift of the Holy Ghost follows baptism by water, and its authoritative bestowal constitutes the next essential ordinance of the Gospel. In both ancient and modern times this endowment has been regarded as a higher baptism, lacking which the baptism of water is incomplete. John, distinctively known as the Baptist, so taught on the very eve of our Savior's personal ministry. Consider well his words: "I indeed baptize you with water unto repentance: but he that cometh after me is mightier than I, whose shoes I am not worthy to bear: he shall baptize you with the Holy Ghost, and with fire." John testifies further that the One who should thus inaugurate the higher baptism was Jesus, Himself. Not until after he had administered the ordinance of water baptism to Jesus, did John recognize Him as the Christ; but immediately after that recognition, the Baptist fearlessly proclaimed his testimony:

"Behold the Lamb of God. . . . This is he of whom I said, After me cometh a man which is preferred before me. . . . And I knew him not: but he that sent me to baptize with water, the same said unto me, Upon whom thou shalt see the Spirit descending, and remaining on him, the same is he which baptizeth with the Holy Ghost" (*HL,* 74–75).

Companionship of the Holy Ghost. And yet the actual companionship of the Holy Ghost, the divinely-bestowed right to His ministrations, the sanctifying baptism with fire, are given as a permanent and personal possession only to the faithful, repentant, baptized candidate for salvation; and with all such this gift shall abide unless it be forfeited through transgression (*AF,* 165).

FORGIVENESS

Forgive. The sinner must be willing to forgive others, if he hopes to obtain forgiveness. A man's repentance is but superficial if his heart be not softened to the degree of tolerance for the weaknesses of his fellows. In teaching His hearers how to pray, the Savior instructed them to supplicate the Father: "Forgive us our debts, as we forgive our debtors." He gave them no assurance of forgiveness if in their hearts they forgave not one another: "For," said He, "if ye forgive men their trespasses, your heavenly Father will also forgive you; But if ye forgive not men their trespasses, neither will your Father forgive your trespasses." Forgiveness between man and man, to be acceptable before the Lord, must be unbounded (*AF,* 110).

How Oft We Should Forgive. Peter here broke in with a question: "Lord, how oft shall my brother sin against me, and I forgive him? till seven times?" He would fain have some definite limit set, and he probably considered the tentative suggestion of seven times as a very liberal measure, inasmuch as the rabbis prescribed a triple forgiveness only. He may have chosen seven as the next number above three having a special Pharisaical significance. The Savior's answer was enlightening: "Jesus saith unto him, I say not unto thee, Until seven times: but, Until seventy times seven." This reply must have meant to Peter as it means to us, that to forgiveness man may set no bounds; the forgiveness, however, must be merited by the recipient (*JTC*, 392–93).

Obedience Brings Forgiveness. There is but one price set on forgiveness for individual transgression, and this is alike to all,—to poor and rich, to bond and free, to illiterate and learned; it knows no fluctuations, it changes not with time; it was the same yesterday as today it is, and even so shall be forever,—and that price, at which may be bought the pearl beyond all price, is *obedience to the laws and ordinances of the Gospel* (*HL*, 65).

The Unmerciful Servant. "Therefore is the kingdom of heaven likened unto a certain king, which would take account of his servants. And when he had begun to reckon, one was brought unto him, which owed him ten thousand talents. But forasmuch as he had not to pay, his lord commanded him to be sold, and his wife, and children, and all that he had, and payment to be made. The servant therefore fell down, and worshipped him, saying, Lord, have patience with me, and I will pay thee all. Then the lord of that servant was moved with compassion, and loosed him, and forgave him the debt. But the same servant went out, and found one of his fellowservants, which owed him an hundred pence: and he laid hands on him, and took him by the throat, saying, Pay me that thou owest. And his fellowservant fell down at his feet, and besought him, saying, Have patience with me, and I will pay thee all. And he would not: but went and cast him into prison, till he should pay the debt. So when his fellowservants saw what was done, they were very sorry, and came and told unto their lord all that was done. Then his lord, after that he had called him, said unto him. O thou wicked servant, I forgave thee all that debt, because thou desiredst me: Shouldest not thou also have had compassion on thy fellowservant, even as I had pity on thee? And his lord was wroth, and delivered him to the tormentors, till he should pay all that was due unto him. So likewise shall my heavenly Father do also unto you, if ye from your hearts forgive not every one his brother their trespasses."

Ten thousand talents are specified as expressive of a sum so great as to put the debtor beyond all reasonable possibility of paying. We may regard the man as a trusted official, one of the king's ministers, who had been charged with the custody of the royal revenues, or one of the chief treasurers of taxes; that he is called a servant introduces no inconsistency, as in an absolute monarchy all but the sovereign are subjects and servants. The selling of the debtor's wife and children and all that he had would not have been in violation of the law in the supposed case, which implies the legal recognition of slavery. The man was in arrears for debt. He did not come before his lord voluntarily but had to be brought. So in the affairs of our individual lives periodical reckonings are inevitable; and while some debtors report of their own accord, others have to be cited to appear. The messengers who serve the summons may be adversity, illness, the approach of death; but, whatever, whoever they are, they enforce a rendering of our accounts.

The contrast between ten thousand talents and a hundred pence is enormous. In his fellowservant's plea for time in which to pay the hundred pence, the greater debtor should have been reminded of the dire straits from which he had just been relieved; the words, "Have patience with me, and I will pay thee all," were identical with those of his own prayer to the king. The base ingratitude of the unmerciful servant justified the king in revoking the pardon once granted. The man came under condemnation, not primarily for defalcation and debt, but for lack of mercy after having received of mercy so abundantly. He, as an unjust plaintiff, had invoked the law; as a convicted transgressor he was to be dealt with according to the law. Mercy is for the merciful. As a heavenly jewel it is to be received with thankfulness and used with sanctity, not to be cast into the mire of undeservedness. Justice may demand retribution and punishment: "With what measure ye mete, it shall be measured to you again." The conditions under which we may confidently implore pardon are set forth in the form of prayer prescribed by the Lord: "Forgive us our debts, as we forgive our debtors" (*JTC*, 393–95).

OBEDIENCE

Obedience Cleanses. Jesus Christ, through whom the plan of salvation has been made available to mankind, has prescribed the conditions under which we may become its beneficiaries—the terms by which citizenship in the Kingdom of God may be secured.

Among these specified conditions is baptism by immersion for the remission of sins. The gross materialist, who wilfully refuses to see or to acknowledge anything beyond the affairs of earth, may ask: How can water wash away sin? In answer be it said, water cannot remove the stain of guilt; nevertheless, obedience to the law of baptism as required by Jesus Christ is truly a means of securing forgiveness. Obedience, not water, is the cleansing unction. . . . Obedience is a source of power, even as is prayer (*VM, 73–74*).

Obedience Brings Liberty and Happiness. The Gospel He offered was and is the embodiment of liberty, untainted by selfish license. True, it entailed obedience and submission; but even if such could be likened unto a yoke, what was its burden in comparison with the incubus under which they groaned?

The offer, the call, the invitation is in full force and effect today. Transgression of the law is primarily or indirectly the cause of all suffering. Obedience to righteous law is the price of liberty. In such obedience lies happiness.

By a government of the people, administered in equity, every man is under wholesome restriction in compliance with which he finds privilege and protection.

Irresponsibility is directly opposed to enduring freedom. But what are the restraints of democracy in contrast with enslavement under autocratic rule? How easy the yoke, how light the burden, and how glorious the blessings of righteous government!

The Gospel of Jesus Christ is the expression of the eternal truth that shall make men free. It prescribes obedience, compliance, voluntary submission as the conditions of enfranchisement in the kingdom of God (*VM, 325*).

Obedience Is a Test. Obedience is the test of allegiance, and he whom we obey, the leader we elect to follow, is the master who directs our destiny, whether in the liberty of righteousness or the serfdom of sin.

"Know ye not," wrote Paul of old to the proud Romans, "that to whom ye yield yourselves servants to obey, his servants ye are to whom ye obey; whether of sin unto death, or of obedience unto righteousness?" (Romans 6:16.) (*VM, 336*).

PRAYER

Personal Prayers. If you would have your personal prayers reach the Divine destination to which they are addressed, see to it that they are transmitted by a current of pure sincerity, free from the resistance of unrepented sin (*PJT, 11*).

Praying to Our Father in Heaven. We, as a people, profess to be a prayerful people. I ask you severally, and you may answer to your own conscience individually, do you pray or do you content yourself with saying your prayers? There is a vital difference between the two processes. Many of us are taught to say prayers and have not learned how to pray. What inconsistency is there, what glaring inconsistency, in the man who kneels and says: "'Our Father, which art in heaven,'" and then proclaims that he is the offspring of the brute and not the child of God; that God is no personage but an influence, an essence, an immaterial nothing—there can't be an immaterial something—and then address that conception of his as "Father" (CR, Oct. 1914, 102).

Latter-day Saints Must Be Prayerful. Latter-day Saints, let us be what we profess to be; let us be genuine; let us live up to the religion and the principles of the gospel of Jesus Christ that we proclaim. We profess to be a prayerful people. Do we pray? Are our homes kept pure by prayer? Prayer is the Lord's great sterilizer against the germs of spiritual disease that make their way into our homes, contaminating the atmosphere, poisoning the food we eat. I don't mean your family prayers only; but do we individually pray? It is possibly that a mass or collective condition may exist which is very different from the individual condition. There may be a home in which prayers are said, but yet perhaps no member of that household is really prayerful. Do you feel urged at times to seek a place where you can be alone with God, where you can pray, pray unto him, not for others to hear, not to conform with some regulation or custom, or even because of counsel or advice, but because you feel the need of communication with God? (CR, Oct. 1921, 188).

Cannot Live with God Unless Prayerful. He who would really pray—pray as nearly as possible as Christ prayed, pray in actual communion with God to whom the prayer is addressed—will seek privacy, seclusion, isolation; if opportunity permits he will retire to his chamber, and will shut the door, that none may intrude; there he may pray indeed, if the spirit of prayer be in his heart; and this course was commended by the Lord. Wordy supplications, made up largely of iterations and repetitions such as the heathen use, thinking that their idol deities will be pleased with their much speaking, were forbidden.

It is well to know that prayer is not compounded of words, words that may fail to express what one desires to say, words that so often cloak inconsistencies, words that may have no deeper source than the physical organs of speech, words that may be spoken to impress mortal ears. The dumb may pray, and that too with the eloquence that prevails in heaven. Prayer is made up of heart throbs and the righteous yearnings of the soul, of supplication based on the realization of need, of contrition and pure desire. If there lives a man who has never really prayed, that man is a being apart from the order of the divine in human nature, a stranger in the family of God's children. Prayer is for the uplifting of the suppliant. God without our prayers would be God; but we without prayer cannot be admitted to the kingdom of God (*JTC*, 237–38).

CHARITY

Spirit of Charity. I trust that the spirit of charity will manifest itself in our souls and that we will be willing to allow unto others those privileges and rights that we ask for ourselves; that we may in very truth be worthy of the measure of liberty which belongs to the Church of Jesus Christ, for if it be what it professes to be, the repository of truth, there must be in it the elements of true liberty and not that false freedom of the spurious kind which is being put forth in an unceasing stream from the devil's factories (CR, Oct. 1912, 128).

TEMPLE ORDINANCES

Purpose of Temples. To the fervent Latter-day Saint, a temple is not simply a church building, a house for general religious assembly. Indeed the "Mormon" temples are rarely used as places of general gatherings. They are in some sense educational institutions, regular courses of lectures and instruction being maintained in some of them; but they are specifically for baptisms and ordinations, for sanctifying prayer, and for the most sacred ceremonies and rites of the Church, particularly in vicarious work for the dead which is a characteristic of the "Mormon" faith (*SPM*, 31).

Endowment. The ordinances of the endowment embody certain obligations on the part of the individual, such as covenant and promise to observe the law of strict virtue and chastity, to be charitable, benevolent, tolerant and pure; to devote both talent and material means to the spread of truth and the uplifting of the race; to maintain devotion to the cause of truth; and to seek in every way to contribute to the great preparation that the earth may be made ready to receive her King,—the Lord Jesus Christ. With the taking of each covenant and the assuming of each obligation a promised blessing is pronounced, contingent upon the faithful observance of the conditions (*HL,* 100).

Celestial Marriage. We believe in the continuation of individual life in the hereafter and in a literal resurrection, in which future state shall be recognized every sanctified and authorized relationship existing here on earth—of parent and child, brother and sister, husband and wife. We believe, further, that contracts, as of marriage, to be valid beyond the veil of mortality must be sanctioned by a power greater than that of earth. With the seal of the Holy Priesthood upon their wedded state, these people believe implicitly in the perpetuity of that relationship on the far side of the grave. They marry not with the saddening limitation *"Until death do you part,"* but *"For time and for eternity."* This constitutes celestial marriage (*SPM,* 101–2).

Marriage for Eternity Requires Priesthood Authority. Jesus stopped not, however, to question the elements of the problem as presented to Him; whether the case was assumed or real mattered not, since the question "Whose wife shall she be?" was based on an utterly erroneous conception. "Jesus answered and said unto them, Ye do err, not knowing the scriptures, nor the power of God. For in the resurrection they neither marry, nor are given in marriage, but are as the angels of God in heaven." The Lord's meaning was clear, that in the resurrected state there can be no question among the seven brothers as to whose wife for eternity the woman shall be, since all except the first had married her for the duration of mortal life only, and primarily for the purpose of perpetuating in mortality the name and family of the brother who first died. Luke records the Lord's words as follows in part: "But they which shall be accounted worthy to obtain that world, and the resurrection from the dead, neither marry, nor are given in marriage: Neither can they die any more: for they are equal unto the angels; and are the children of God, being the children of the resurrection." In the resurrection there will be no marrying nor giving in marriage; for all questions of marital status must be settled before that time, under the authority of the Holy Priesthood, which holds the power to seal in marriage for both time and eternity *(JTC, 548)*.

Contracts of Marriage. Divine revelation in the dispensation of the fulness of times has made plain the fact, that contracts of marriage, as indeed all other agreements between parties in mortality, are of no validity beyond the grave, except such contracts be ratified and validated by the duly established ordinances of the Holy Priesthood. Sealing in the marriage covenant for time and eternity, which has come to be known as celestial marriage, is an ordinance established by divine authority in the restored Church of Jesus Christ" *(JTC, 564)*.

Sanctity of Marriage. There is no sect or people that sets a higher value on virtue and chastity than do the Latter-day Saints, nor a people that visits surer retribution upon the heads of offenders against the laws of sexual purity. To them marriage is not, can never be, a civil compact alone; its significance reaches beyond the grave; its obligations are eternal; and the Latter-day Saints are notable for the sanctity with which they invest the marital state *(SPM, 103)*.

Children Born under the Covenant. This system of holy matrimony, involving covenants for both time and eternity, is known distinctively as *Celestial Marriage,* and is understood to be the order of marriage that exists in the celestial worlds. This sacred ordinance is administered by the Church to those only who are adjudged to be of worthy life, fit to be admitted to the House of the Lord; for this holy rite, together with others of eternal validity, may be solemnized only within the temples reared and dedicated for such exalted service. Children born to parents thus married under the celestial law are heirs to the Priesthood; "children of the covenant" they are called; no ordinance of adoption or sealing is required to give them place in the blessed posterity of promise (*HL*, 105).

LAWS AND ORDINANCES

Ordinances. By way of summary let it be repeated: The Church of Jesus Christ of Latter-day Saints holds as a fundamental doctrine, attested and proved by scripture both ancient and modern, that compliance with *the laws and ordinances of the Gospel* is an absolute and irrevocable requirement for admission into the Kingdom of God, or in other words, for the securing of individual salvation to the souls of men, and that this requirement is universal, applying alike to every soul that has attained to age and powers of accountability in the flesh, in whatever period or dispensation that soul has lived in mortality. It follows as a necessary consequence that if any soul has failed, either through ignorance or neglect, to render obedience to these requirements, the obligation is not removed by death (*HL*, 76).

MANY GOSPEL PRINCIPLES

Many Principles of the Gospel. This gospel is broad enough, and deep enough, and of such towering heights as to surpass the powers of the greatest mind to comprehend, and yet so simple in its fundamentals as to satisfy the honest inquiry of the child. We speak of faith, repentance, baptism, and the laying on of hands, as the first principles and ordinances of the gospel. We have gone so far as to number them—the first, the second, the third and fourth principles, and the first and the second ordinances. Are there others? Verily, verily, yes. What, a fifth? Yes, and a sixth, and a seventh, aye, and a tenth, and a hundredth and a thousandth. There is no end to the principles of truth embodied in the gospel of Jesus Christ, and yet each one is dependent upon the fundamentals, and each one grows out of those that have been given before (CR, Apr. 1918, 163).

10

MISSIONARY WORK

SCATTERING OF ISRAEL

All Israel Scattered. All the Jews in Palestine at the time of Christ's birth constituted but a small remnant of the great Davidic nation. The Ten Tribes, distinctively the aforetime kingdom of Israel, had then long been lost to history, and the people of Judah had been widely scattered among the nations (*JTC,* 61).

DIVINE COMMISSION

Authority. Do you not remember that the risen Lord, in giving his last instructions to the apostles, told them to go into all the world and teach all nations, baptizing them in the name of the Father, and of the Son and of the Holy Ghost? Who dares take unto himself authority to officiate in those names, the names of the Holy Trinity, if he has not been duly commissioned? Who would dare undertake to speak in the name of the Governor of this sovereign State if he were not duly commissioned? The prison bars are ready to open to receive such a one. It would be a crime under the law of the State. Who can speak in behalf of an officer of the law, it he has not been properly deputized, if authority has not been delegated unto him? Now, why shall we use one rule of common sense in dealing with the things of earth and a rule that is not in accordance with common sense in dealing with the authorities and powers of heaven? (CR, Apr. 1924, 67–68).

Missionaries to Warn the World. The faith of the Latter-day Saints teaches that in the day of the Lord's righteous fury safety will be found in Zion. The importance which they associate with the work of gathering, and the fidelity with which they seek to discharge the duty enjoined upon them by divine authority in the matter of warning the world of the impending dangers, as described in the Revelator's vision, are sufficiently demonstrated by the great extent of the missionary labor as at present prosecuted by this people (*AF,* 339).

THE GOSPEL MESSAGE

Missionaries and Their Message. I am well aware of the fact that some people take a little umbrage at what they think is presumption on our part in sending missionaries amongst them. They think that we should labor as some of the churches of the day labor, amongst the semi-civilized people of heathen nations, who have not come yet to recognize a knowledge of the Lord and Savior of men. We send our missionaries not only to such, but also to those who count themselves enlightened

Christians. Our missionaries go with a message, not with a command. They go in the spirit of persuasion, asking only a hearing, a respectful hearing; for they have something of worth to present. Our missionary system would scarcely be justified had we nothing definite to present, nothing more than minor differences in ritual or creed such as distinguishes some of the great denominations of the day. I would not blame people becoming impatient over such relative trifles; but we have something that can be found amongst no other people upon the face of the earth. This is no instance of group egotism, it is a solemn fact.

We proclaim not only that Jesus Christ is the foreordained and actual Savior of the race; not only that, but we proclaim that no ordinance of salvation can be authoritatively administered except under his commission, and that that commission is definite and personal. Hence these men, young, middle aged, sometimes aged, and in smaller number these women, go out to the world with a proclamation that in this day and age, strictly in accordance with the predictions of ancient prophets and with the word of the Lord Christ himself, while he was in the flesh, he has again spoken, and is speaking from the heavens, directing the affairs of the Church that bears his name, the name given by him, not taken by any human assumption, but conferred and bestowed authoritatively. We do not send missionaries out to assail or attack members of other churches, or the sects and denominations as organized bodies. We send them out to preach the positive doctrine of the restored gospel, which is the doctrine of the ancient gospel, speaking thus of the gospel according to the period of its preaching upon the earth. We are remarkable as a people for this missionary work (CR, Oct. 1924, 138–39).

A Greater Light. Among the material things of the past—things that I treasure for sweet memory's sake and because of pleasant association in bygone days—is a lamp. It is of the Argand type, commonly known in the day of its popularity as the "Student's lamp," so named in acknowledgment of its particular and peculiar suitability for the reader's table. Lamps of this kind were among the best in the long-ago. A very few years divide the long-ago from the present as measured in terms of improvement and progress. In the long-ago of which I speak, illuminating gas was known only in large cities or in pretentious towns with a history, and electric light in dwellings was a rare novelty. Candles and oil lamps were the only common means of domestic illumination.

The lamp of which I speak, the student lamp of my school and college days, was one of the best of its kind. I had bought it with hard-earned savings; it was counted among my most cherished possessions. That type of lamp was provided with a small hollow wick, and had a straight cylindrical chimney, with a constriction near the base, where an enlargement adapted it to the burner. It was constructed in accordance with the best knowledge of the day. Its tubular wick, less than a fingerbreadth in diameter, with efficient air inlet at the bottom, insured fairly complete combustion with a minimum loss of energy through useless generation of heat. The oil reservoir was supported on an upright standard, removed by several inches from the place of combustion; and in consequence, the holder cast no shadow upon the printed page or writing tablet, provided, of course, the lamp was properly placed.

I took good care of my lamp. I had in it a pride such as the horseman feels in his favorite mount. He likes personally to groom and feed his steed, and so I allowed none but myself to trim the wick, burnish the chimney, and fill the reservoir of my lamp. When brightly burning, with its deep green opaque shade, brilliantly deflecting and reflecting beneath, it diffused a wholly satisfactory illumination upon my page; and, as I kept vigil night after night, through the late and early hours, my lamp came to be more than a mere physical illuminator—it was a sympathetic companion, an inspiration to mental and spiritual enlightenment. You who have been in stress and strife, you who have had to wrestle with difficulty and contend with seeming fate, you who have been blessed through all such taxing strain with a never-failing friend, an ever-present and ever-ready companion—you may know somewhat of the affection I felt and feel for my faithful lamp.

Compared with waxen candle and ordinary oil burning lamps it was of high efficiency. What matters it today that such a lamp is counted dim? It was the best I knew; it was excellent in its time. Do you ask how much light it gave? I can answer your query with precision, for as early as that time, in the long-ago, I was a student of science: and I had tested my lamp according to the laws of photometry in the improvised laboratory I had contrived. The light was of about twelve candle power, in terms of the generally recognized and standardized rating. It was brilliant in that period—in the long-ago, remember.

One summer evening I sat musing studiously and withal restfully in the open air outside the door of the room in which I lodged and studied. A stranger approached. I noticed that he carried a satchel. He was affable and entertaining. I brought another chair from within, and we chatted together till the twilight had deepened into dusk, the dusk into darkness.

Then he said: "You are a student, and doubtless have much work to do o'nights. What kind of lamp do you use?" And without waiting for a reply, he continued: "I have a superior lamp I should like to show you, a lamp designed and constructed according to the latest achievements of applied science, far surpassing anything heretofore produced as a means of artificial lighting."

I replied with confidence, and I confess not without some exultation: "My friend, I have a lamp, one that has been tested and proved. It has been to me a companion through many a long night. It is an Argand lamp, and one of the best. I have trimmed and cleaned it today; it is ready for the lighting. Step inside; I will show you my lamp, then you may tell me whether yours can possibly be better."

We entered my study room, and with a feeling which I assume is akin to that of the athlete about to enter a contest with one whom he regards as a pitiably inferior opponent, I put the match to my well-trimmed Argand.

My visitor was voluble in his praise. It was the best lamp of its kind he said. He averred that he had never seen a lamp in better trim. He turned the wick up and down and pronounced the adjustment perfect. He declared that never before had he realized how satisfactory a student lamp could be.

I liked the man; he seemed to me wise, and he assuredly was ingratiating. Love me, love my lamp, I thought, mentally paraphrasing a common expression of the period.

"Now," said he, "with your permission I'll light *my* lamp." He took from his satchel a lamp then known as the "Rochester." It had a chimney which, compared with mine, was as a factory smoke-stack alongside a house flue. Its hollow wick was wide enough to admit my four fingers. Its light made bright the remotest corner of my room. In its brilliant blaze my own little Argand wick burned a weak, pale yellow. Until that moment of convincing demonstration I had never known the dim obscurity in which I had lived and labored, studied and struggled.

"I'll buy your lamp," said I; "you need neither explain nor argue further." I took my new acquisition to the laboratory that same night, and determined its capacity. It turned at over forty-eight candle power—fully four times the intensity of my student lamp.

Two days after purchasing, I met the lamp-peddler on the street, about noontime. To my inquiry he replied that business was good; the demand for his lamps was greater than the factory supply. "But," said I, "you are not working today?" His rejoinder was a lesson. "Do you think that I would be so foolish as to go around trying to sell lamps in the daytime? Would you have bought one if I had lighted it for you when the sun was shining? I chose the time to show the superiority of my lamp over yours; and you were eager to own the better one I offered, were you not?"

Such is the story. Now consider the application of a part, a very small part, thereof.

"Let your light so shine before men, that they may see your good works, and glorify your Father, which is in heaven."

The man who would sell me a lamp did not disparage mine. He placed his greater light alongside my feebler flame, and I hasted to obtain the better.

The missionary servants of the Church of Jesus Christ today are sent forth, not to assail or ridicule the beliefs of men, but to set before the world a superior light, by which the smoky dimness of the flickering flames of man-made creeds shall be apparent. The work of the Church is constructive, not destructive (*PJT,* 1–6).

Sacred Truths. These disciples, some of whom were soon to minister in the authority of the Holy Apostleship, were cautioned against the indiscreet and indiscriminate scattering of the sacred truths and precepts committed to them. Their duty would be to discern the spirits of those whom they essayed to teach, and to impart unto them in wisdom. The words of the Master were strong: "Give not that which is holy unto the dogs, neither cast ye your pearls before swine, lest they trample them under their feet, and turn again and rend you" (*JTC,* 244–45).

EFFORT ON THE PART OF THE INVESTIGATOR

Willingly Sacrifice All. Pearls have always held high place among gems, and long before, as indeed ever since, the time of Christ, pearl-merchants have been active and diligent in seeking the largest and richest to be had. Unlike the man in the last parable, who found a hidden treasure with little or no search, the merchant in this story devoted his whole energy to the quest for goodly pearls, to find and secure which was his business. When at last he beheld the pearl that excelled all others, though it was, as of right it ought to have been, held at high cost, he gladly sold all his other gems; indeed he sacrificed "all that he had"—gems and other possessions—and purchased the pearl of great price. Seekers after truth may acquire much that is good and desirable, and not find the greatest truth of all, the truth that shall save them. Yet, if they seek persistently and with right intent, if they are really in quest of pearls and not of imitations, they shall find. Men who by search and research discover the truths of the kingdom of heaven may have to abandon many of their cherished traditions, and even their theories of imperfect philosophy and "science falsely so called," if they would possess themselves of the pearl of great price. Observe that in this parable as in that of the hidden treasure, the price of possession is one's all. No man can become a citizen of the kingdom by partial surrender of his earlier allegiances; he must renounce everything foreign to the kingdom or he can never be numbered therein. If he willingly sacrifices all that he has, he shall find that he has enough. The cost of the hidden treasure, and of the pearl, is not a fixed amount, alike for all; it is all one has. Even the poorest may come into enduring possession; his all is a sufficient purchase price (*JTC*, 293–94).

GATHERING OF ISRAEL

Gathering of Israel Part of the Abrahamic Covenant. No less certain is the realization of the second part of the prediction, that in and through Abraham's descendants should all nations of the earth be blessed. For, by world-wide dispersion the children of Israel have been mingled with the nations; and the blood of the covenant people has been sprinkled among the peoples. And now, in this the day of gathering, when the Lord is again bringing His people together to honor and bless them above all that the world can give, every nation with the blood of Israel in the veins of its members will partake of the blessings (*AF*, 340).

All Israel Will Be Gathered. The day of deliverance for Israel is near at hand; the restoration of the ancient Kingdom of Judah, and of the remnants of all the tribes distributed throughout the earth, as well as bringing forth from their long exile the tribes that have been lost, are particularly specified as events of the current dispensation, directly precedent to the second advent of the Christ (*VM*, 160).

Gathering of Israel in Process. The present is the day of gathering, when Israel are being assembled from even the outermost parts of the earth, when the Lord has reached out his hand again to gather his people. This work is in progress at such a rate that soon shall the ancient prophecy and promise be realized, as voiced by Jeremiah: "Therefore, behold, the days come, saith the Lord, that it shall no more be said, The Lord liveth, that brought up the children of Israel out of the land of Egypt;

"But, the Lord liveth that brought up the children of Israel from the land of the north, and from all the lands whither he had driven them: and I will bring them again into their land that I gave unto their fathers" (*CR*, Apr. 1923, 142).

Summary of the Gathering of Israel. It is evident that the plan of gathering comprises:

1. Assembling in the land of Zion of the people of Israel from the nations of the earth.

2. Return of the Jews to Jerusalem.
3. Restoration of the Lost Tribes.

The sequence of these events as here presented is that of convenience and has no significance as to the order in which the several gatherings are to be accomplished. The division first named constitutes an important part of the current work of the Church, though the labor of assisting in the restoration of the Lost Tribes is included. We are informed by revelation, given in the Kirtland Temple, that the appointment to and the authority for the work were solemnly committed to the Church. And through none could such authority be more fittingly conferred than through him who had received it by divine commission in a former dispensation of united Israel. Moses, who was the representative of Israel's God when the Lord set His hand the first time to lead His people to the land of their appointed inheritance, has come in person and has committed to the latter-day Church the authority to minister in the work now that the Lord has "set his hand the second time" to recover His people (*AF*, 337–38).

God Knows the Location of Israel. Though smitten of men, a large part of them gone from a knowledge of the world, Israel are not lost unto their God. He knows whither they have been led or driven; toward them His heart still yearns with paternal love; and surely will He bring them forth, in due time and by appointed means, into a condition of blessing and influence befitting His covenant people. In spite of their sin and notwithstanding the tribulations that they were bringing upon themselves, the Lord said: "And yet for all that, when they be

in the land of their enemies, I will not cast them away, neither will I
abhor them, to destroy them utterly, and to break my covenant with
them: for I am the Lord their God." As complete as was the scattering,
so shall be the gathering of Israel (*AF,* 328–29).

GENTILES

Parable of the Great Supper. Explication of the parable was left
to the learned men to whom the story was addressed. Surely some of
them would fathom its meaning, in part at least. The covenant people,
Israel, were the specially invited guests. They had been bidden long
enough aforetime, and by their own profession as the Lord's own had
agreed to be partakers of the feast. When all was ready, on the appointed day, they were severally summoned by the Messenger who had
been sent by the Father; He was even then in their midst. But the cares
of riches, the allurement of material things, and the pleasures of social
and domestic life had engrossed them; and they prayed to be excused
or irreverently declared they could not or would not come. Then the
gladsome invitation was to be carried to the Gentiles, who were looked
upon as spiritually poor, maimed, halt, and blind. And later, even the
pagans beyond the walls, strangers in the gates of the holy city, would
be bidden to the supper. These, surprised at the unexpected summons,
would hesitate, until by gentle urging and effective assurance that they
were really included among the bidden guests, they would feel themselves constrained or compelled to come. The possibility of some of the
discourteous ones arriving later, after they had attended to their more
absorbing affairs, is indicated in the Lord's closing words: "For I say

unto you, That none of those men which were bidden shall taste of my supper" (*JTC,* 452).

Invitation Extended to the Gentiles. The great feast by which the Messianic reign was to be ushered in was a favorite theme of jubilant exposition in both synagog and school; and exultation ran high in the rabbinical dictum that none but the children of Abraham would be among the blessed partakers. The king in the parable is God; the son whose marriage was the occasion of the feast is Jesus, the Son of God; the guests who were bidden early, yet who refused to come when the feast was ready, are the covenant people who rejected their Lord, the Christ; the later guests, who were brought in from the streets and the roads, are the Gentile nations, to whom the gospel has been carried since its rejection by the Jews; the marriage feast is symbolical of the glorious consummation of the Messiah's mission (*JTC,* 538).

SPIRIT WORLD

Missionary Work in the Spirit World. It is evident that labor in behalf of the dead is twofold; that performed on earth would remain incomplete and futile but for its supplement and counterpart beyond the veil. Missionary work is in progress there—work compared with which the evangelistic labor on earth is relatively of small extent. There are preachers and teachers, ministers invested with the Holy Priesthood, all engaged in proclaiming the Gospel of Jesus Christ to spirits still sitting in darkness. This great labor was inaugurated by the Savior during the brief period of His disembodiment. It is reasonable and consistent to hold that the saving ministry so begun was left to be continued by others duly authorized and commissioned; just as the work of preaching the Gospel and administering therein among the living was committed to the Apostles of old through their ordination by the Lord Himself.

Missionary service in the spirit world is primarily effective among two classes: (1) those who have died in ignorance of the Gospel—i. e., those who have lived and died without law, and who therefore cannot be condemned until they have come to the knowledge and opportunity requisite to obedience; and (2) those who failed to comply with the laws and ordinances of the Gospel in the flesh, and who through the experiences of the other world have come to the contrite and receptive state.

It is unreasonable and vitally opposed to both letter and spirit of Holy Scripture to assume that neglect or rejection of the call to repentance in this life can be easily remedied by repentance hereafter. Forfeiture through disobedience is a very real loss, entailing deprivation of opportunity beyond all human computation. Refusal to hear and heed the word of God is no physical deafness, but a manifestation of spiritual disease resulting from sin. Death is no cure for such. The unrepentant state is a disorder of the spirit, and, following disembodiment, the spirit will still be afflicted therewith (*VM*, 248–49).

11

SCRIPTURES

BIBLE

Meaning and Content of the Bible. In present usage, the term *Holy Bible* designates the collection of sacred writings otherwise known as the Hebrew Scriptures, containing an account of the dealings of God with the human family; which account is confined wholly, except in the record of antediluvian events, to the eastern hemisphere. The word *Bible,* though singular in form, is the English representative of a Greek plural, *Biblia,* signifying literally *books.* The use of the word probably dates from the fourth century, at which time we find Chrysostom employing the term to designate the scriptural books then accepted as canonical by the Greek Christians. It is to be noted that the idea of a collection of books predominates in all early usages of the word *Bible;* the scriptures were, as they are, composed of the special writings of many authors, widely separated in time; and, from the harmony and unity prevailing throughout these diverse productions, strong evidence of their authenticity may be adduced.

The word *Biblia* was thus endowed with a special meaning in the Greek, signifying the holy books as distinguishing sacred scriptures from other writings; and the term soon became current in the Latin, in which tongue it was used from the first in its special sense. Through Latin usage, perhaps during the thirteenth century, the word came to be regarded as a singular noun signifying *the book;* this departure from the plural meaning, invariably associated with the term in the Greek original, tends to obscure the facts. It may appear that the derivation of a word is of small importance; yet in this case the original form and first use of the title now current as that of the sacred volume must be of instructive interest, as throwing some light upon the compilation of the book in its present form.

It is evident that the name *Bible,* with its current signification, cannot be of itself a Biblical term; its use as a designation of the Hebrew scriptures is wholly external to those scriptures themselves. In its earliest application, which dates from post-apostolic times, it was made to embrace most if not all the books of the Old and the New Testament. Prior to the time of Christ, the books of the Old Testament were known by no single collective name, but were designated in groups as (1) the Pentateuch, or five books of the Law; (2) the Prophets; and (3) the Hagiographa, comprising all sacred records not included in the other divisions. But we may the better consider the parts of the Bible by taking the main divisions separately. A very natural division of the Biblical record is effected by the earthly ministry of Jesus Christ; the written productions of pre-Christian times came to be known as the

Old Covenant; those of the days of the Savior and the years immediately following, as the New Covenant. The term *Testament* gradually grew in favor until the designations *Old* and *New Testaments* became common (*AF*, 237–39).

Summary of the Contents of the Bible. The Church of Jesus Christ of Latter-day Saints accepts the Holy Bible for just what it purports to be, nothing less, nothing more. Taken as a whole the Holy Bible is a collection of sacred and historical writings, depicting though incompletely the Divine dealings with mankind on the Eastern Hemisphere from the creation down to about the close of the first century after Christ. The Old Testament contains a brief record of pre-Mosaic time, but is largely a history of the Semitic people or Hebrews, as they lived under the Law of Moses. The New Testament is distinctively the Scripture of the Gospel as contrasted with the Law, and is devoted to the earthly ministry of the Savior and to the growth of His Church under apostolic administration. The compilation as it now stands is the work of men, and our modern translations from the original Hebrew of the Old Testament and Greek of the New have been made by skilled linguists and learned theologians.

But the wisdom of even the wisest of men may be faulty, and the understanding of the prudent may be biased and dangerously imperfect. The many revisions and successive versions of the Bible, made as the errors of earlier renditions became strikingly apparent, testify to the unreliability of scholarship in the translation of sacred writ. Moreover, it is an indisputable fact that the compilation of books constituting our present version is incomplete; for within the Bible itself more than a score of books, epistles, or other writings not included are mentioned, and generally in such a way as to show that those lost Scriptures were considered authentic and genuine. Furthermore, numerous Biblical passages are tinged with what scholars call "gloss"—that is wording intended to convey the private interpretation of the translator.

The Latter-day Saints openly proclaim their reservation as to incorrect translation. We are in harmony with all able and earnest students of the Scriptures in accepting the Bible as the Word of God, only so far as it is translated correctly (*VM*, 121–22).

Compiling of the Old Testament. Ezra is usually attributed the credit of compiling the books of the Old Testament as far as completed in his day, to which he added his own writings. In this work of compilation he was probably assisted by Nehemiah and the members of the Great Synagogue—a Jewish college of a hundred and twenty scholars (*AF*, 240).

Allegory. Allegories are distinguished from parables by greater length and detail of the story, and by the intimate admixture of the narrative with the lesson it is designed to teach; these are kept distinctly separate in the parable (*JTC*, 299).

A Parable Is a Sketch. Let it not be forgotten that a parable is but a sketch, not a picture finished in detail; and that the expressed or implied similitude in parabolic teaching cannot logically and consistently be carried beyond the limits of the illustrative story (*JTC*, 285).

Parables an Act of Mercy. It is noticeable that the introduction of parables occurred when opposition to Jesus was strong, and when scribes, Pharisees, and rabbis were alert in maintaining a close watch upon His movements and His works, ever ready to make Him an offender for a word. The use of parables was common among Jewish teachers; and in adopting this mode of instruction Jesus was really following a custom of the time; though between the parables He spake and those of the scholars there is possible no comparison except that of most pronounced contrast.

To the chosen and devoted followers who came asking the Master why He had changed from direct exposition to parables, He explained that while it was their privilege to receive and understand the deeper truths of the gospel, "the mysteries of the kingdom of heaven" as He expressed it, with people in general, who were unreceptive and unprepared, such fulness of understanding was impossible. To the disciples who had already gladly accepted the first principles of the gospel of Christ, more should be given; while from those who had rejected the proffered boon, even what they had theretofore possessed should be taken away. "Therefore," said He, "speak I to them in parables: because they seeing see not; and hearing they hear not, neither do they understand." That the state of spiritual darkness then existing among the Jews had been foreseen was instanced by a citation of Isaiah's words, in which the ancient prophet had told of the people becoming blind, deaf, and hard of heart respecting the things of God, whereby though they would both hear and see in a physical sense yet should they not understand.

There is plainly shown an element of mercy in the parabolic mode of instruction adopted by our Lord under the conditions prevailing at the time. Had He always taught in explicit declaration, such as required no interpretation, many among His hearers would have come under condemnation, inasmuch as they were too weak in faith and unprepared in heart to break the bonds of traditionalism and the prejudice engendered by sin, so as to accept and obey the saving word. Their inability to comprehend the requirements of the gospel would in righteous measure give Mercy some claim upon them, while had they rejected the truth with full understanding, stern Justice would surely demand their condemnation (*JTC,* 295–97).

A Parable Is a Comparison. The essential feature of a parable is that of comparison or similitude, by which some ordinary, well-understood incident is used to illustrate a fact or principle not directly expressed in the story. The popular thought that a parable necessarily rests on a fictitious incident is incorrect; for, inasmuch as the story or circumstance of the parable must be simple and indeed common-place, it may be real. There is no fiction in the parables we have thus far studied; the fundamental stories are true to life and the given circumstances are facts of experience. The narrative or incident upon which a parable is constructed may be an actual occurrence or fiction; but, if fictitious, the story must be consistent and probable, with no admixture of the unusual or miraculous. In this respect the parable differs from the fable, the latter being imaginative, exaggerated and improbable as to fact; moreover, the intent is unlike in the two, since the parable is designed to convey some great spiritual truth, while the so-called moral of the fable is at best suggestive only of worldly achievement and personal advantage. Stories of trees, animals and inanimate things talking together or with men are wholly fanciful; they are fables or apologues whether the outcome be depicted as good or bad; to the parable these show contrast, not similarity. The avowed purpose of the fable is rather to amuse than to teach. The parable may embody a narrative as in the instances of the sower and the tares, or merely an isolated incident, as in those of the mustard seed and the leaven (*JTC*, 298–99).

Parables Given by Jesus Christ. The parables of the New Testament, spoken by the Teacher of teachers, are of such beauty, simplicity, and effectiveness, as to stand unparalleled in literature (*JTC*, 299).

Proverb. A proverb is a short, sententious saying, in the nature of a maxim, connoting a definite truth or suggestion by comparison. Proverbs and parables are closely related, and in the Bible the terms are sometimes used interchangeably (*JTC*, 299).

Bible and Book of Mormon. The question, "What is the Book of Mormon?" [is] a very pertinent one on the part of every earnest student and investigator of this phase of American history. . . . The work has been derisively called the "Mormon Bible," a name that carries with it the misrepresentation that in the faith of this people the book takes the place of the sacred volume which is universally accepted by Christian sects. No designation could be more misleading and in every way more untruthful. The Latter-day Saints have but one "Bible" and that the Holy Bible of Christendom. They place it foremost among the standard works of the Church; they accept its admonitions and its doctrines, and accord thereto a literal significance; it is to them, and ever has been, the word of God, a compilation made by human agency of works by various inspired writers; they accept its teachings in fulness, modifying the meaning in no wise, except in the rare cases of undoubted mistranslation, concerning which Biblical scholars of all faiths differ and criticize; and even in such cases their reverence for the sacred letter renders them more conservative than the majority of Bible commentators and critics in placing free construction upon the text. The historical part of the Jewish Scriptures tells of the divine dealings with the people of the Eastern Hemisphere; the Book of Mormon recounts the mercies and judgments of God, the inspired teachings of His prophets, the rise and fall of His people as organized communities on the Western Continent (*SPM*, 18–20).

Bible and Book of Mormon Witnesses of Jesus Christ. Among the outstanding facts of profoundest import recorded in the Bible concerning Jesus Christ and His mission are these:

1. His preexistence and antemortal Godship.
2. His foreordination as the Redeemer and Savior of mankind.
3. Predictions of His embodiment in the flesh, as the Son of the Eternal Father and of mortal woman.
4. The fulfilment of these predictions in His birth as Mary's Child.
5. The sending of a forerunner, John the Baptist, to prepare the way for the Lord's public ministry.
6. Christ's earthly life, covering about a third of a

century, characterized by beneficent service, by authoritative administration, and by unexceptionable example.

7. The establishment of His Church with duly ordained Apostles, who, with other ministers invested with the Holy Priesthood, carried forward the work of salvation after the Lord's departure.

8. The specific and authentic enunciation of the fundamental principles and ordinances of the Gospel, by which the way of salvation has been opened to all, and without which none can abide in the Kingdom of God, these comprising: (1) Faith in Him as the Son of God and the Redeemer of the world; (2) Repentance of sin; (3) Baptism by immersion for the remission of sins; and (4) Bestowal of the Holy Ghost by the authoritative laying on of hands.

9. The Lord's sacrificial and atoning death.

10. His actual resurrection, whereby His spirit was reunited with the crucified body and He became a glorified and immortalized Soul.

11. His ministry as a Resurrected Being among men.

12. His exaltation to the place He had won at the right hand of God the Eternal Father.

13. The general apostasy of mankind from the Gospel of Christ, bringing about an era of spiritual darkness.

14. The restoration of the Holy Priesthood in the latter days, by which the Gospel would be again preached

in power and its ordinances administered for the salvation of men.

15. The assurance of our Lord's yet future return to
earth, in glory and judgment, to inaugurate the predicted Millennium of peace and righteousness.

16. His eternal status as Judge of both quick and dead,
and the eventual Victor over sin and death.

In every particular, even to circumstantial detail, the Scriptures of
the West accord with those of the East in their solemn witness to these
portentous developments of the Divine plan, which has for its purpose
"the immortality and eternal life of man." The voice of the continents,
the independent testimonies of Judah and Ephraim, the Scriptures of
the Jews and those of the Nephites, are heard in tuneful harmony bearing true witness to the world of the everlasting Gospel of Jesus Christ
(*VM,* 147–48).

BOOK OF MORMON

Book of Mormon and Its Place. The Book of Mormon is before the
world. It has been distributed by millions of copies in English and
other modern tongues. Let it be understood that in no sense does the
Book of Mormon profess to be a substitute for the Holy Bible, or to be
in any way related thereto except as a parallel volume of Scripture. The
Bible is essentially a record of the dealings of God with His people of
the East; the Book of Mormon is an embodiment of Divine revelations
to the people of the West. So far as the two books touch common

themes they are in harmony; and in no particular are they contradictory of each other (*VM*, 132).

Coming Forth of the Book of Mormon. The discovery of the ancient record known to mankind as the Book of Mormon was no affair of chance. To the contrary, both the finding of the plates of gold and the translation of the inscriptions were specifically the result of Divine direction (*VM*, 124).

Book of Mormon a New Witness. The Book of Mormon is a new and independent witness of the divinity of Jesus Christ and His Gospel, by which all mankind may be saved through obedience, and without which no man can have place in the Kingdom of God (*VM*, 142).

Book of Mormon Will Strengthen Testimony. To my younger brothers and sisters, to my student friends, I say stand by your testimony. When you have received it from the Lord, let it be your guide. It will be no handicap to you in your researches, your studies, your explorations and investigations. It will not detract from your reputation for learning, if you deserve any such reputation, provided you stand by the truth. As you know, in the Book of Mormon we have that wonderful story of the iron rod seen by Lehi. To those of you who want to explore I say, in all earnestness, tie fast your guide rope to the rod of iron, which is defined as the Word of God. Hold to it firmly, and you may venture out into the region of the unexplored in search of truth if you will; but do not loosen your hold on the rope; and remember that there is very little safety in holding to a rope that is loose at both ends.

By following this course I have had many satisfying explanations of questions that troubled me. Let me illustrate, It has been the general conception that certain animals known to have existed on the eastern hemisphere were not to be found on the western hemisphere in Nephite times; but in the Book of Mormon I find record, positive and simple, that certain of these animals were found by Lehi and his colony. Now, the testimony that the Lord had given me as to the integrity of the Book of Mormon did not furnish me with all details by which I could confront the evidence that was being gathered, which was all of a negative character, relating to the alleged non-existence of the horse and other animals upon the western continent at the time indicated. Some of you may say that as you do not find, ordinarily at least, the bones of buffaloes in this section, that buffaloes never lived here. But go search in the gravels of City Creek, and you may be lucky enough to find, as I have found, the bones and horns of buffaloes. One shred of positive evidence will nullify a volume of negative assumption; and the declarations made in the Book of Mormon, if not already verified, will surely be verified every whit (CR, Apr. 1929, 48).

Internal Message. The internal consistency of the Book of Mormon sustains belief in its divine origin. The parts bear evidence of having been written at different times and under widely varying conditions. The style of the component books is in harmony with the times and circumstances of their production. The portions that were transcribed from the plates bearing Mormon's abridgment contain numerous interpolations as comments and explanations of the transcriber; but in the first six books, which, as already explained, are the verbatim record of the smaller plates of Nephi, no such interpolations occur. The book maintains consistency throughout; no contradictions, no disagreements have been pointed out (*AF*, 278–79).

Book of Isaiah. It has been declared and proclaimed by a certain school of Bible students, commentators and scholars, that the Book of Isaiah was written not entirely by Isaiah the Prophet, the son of Amoz—in many respects the greatest of the prophets of that age but that the book is the work of at least two men, and perhaps of many, part of it written by Isaiah himself, and the other part by another man, without local habitation or name, who lived somewhere, near the end of the period of the Babylonian captivity or exile, fully a century after the death of Isaiah the Prophet. That idea concerning the duality of the Book of Isaiah has been exploited, and there are learned readers of the Bible, who, with superior air, point out certain chapters of the Book of Isaiah which they say were not written by Isaiah the Prophet, but by this "deutero" or second Isaiah. So he is called in view of even the scholars' ignorance as to his true name or place of abode. The claim is made that the chapters of Isaiah from the second to the thirty-ninth inclusive, were really written by Isaiah, and that thence on to the end of the sixty-sixth chapter, the last in the book, the subject-matter is not the writing of Isaiah at all, but that of another man, who falsely ascribed the authorship to the Prophet.

Such is the speculation concerning the duality of authorship in that book; but, once started, these learned investigators have undertaken to dissect Isaiah and to spread before the gaze of the people both his gross and minute anatomy, to the extent of denying his authorship of other parts of chapters, and of certain verses, singling them out from the rest, and they have left to the credit of the Prophet Isaiah only twenty-four and a half chapters of his book.

I well remember when the positive and emphatic denial of the unity of the Book of Isaiah was put forth by the German school of theologians. So too I remember the many questions that arose among our people regarding it, not a few of such questions coming to me personally. To some of the inquirers I said: "Why trouble yourselves about the matter? I know that the claim is false." "Well, have you looked into it?" I was asked. "Sufficiently so," I replied, "for I have received the testimony promised by the Lord through the Prophet Moroni concerning the integrity and genuineness of the Book of Mormon."

In the Second Book of Nephi, I find transcriptions of several chapters of Isaiah, that is to say, chapters as the material is now divided and designated in our Bible—twelve chapters at least, taken from the brass plates of Laban, which plates were brought from Jerusalem to Lehi in the wilderness, as you know, 600 years before the birth of Christ. Laban was a rich man. He could afford to have books made of metal sheets, while others perhaps were content with poorer and less enduring material—just as some people can now afford to have de luxe editions and others are willing to accept poorer paper and bindings. But on those plates of brass, brought from Jerusalem in the year 600 B. C., you will find the writings of Isaiah, not only the early chapters allowed to Isaiah by modern scholars; but the later chapters as well, which are ascribed by the critics to the second or false Isaiah. Let us remember that we have in the Book of Mormon transcriptions from the brass plates of Laban, comprising the record of Isaiah, oft-times word for word the same as the translation appearing in the Bible, chapter after chapter. The entire Book of Isaiah must have been in existence at that time.

Abinadi, a Book of Mormon prophet, quoted from what is now called the fifty-third chapter of Isaiah to the priests of Noah; and the fifty-third chapter comes in that portion which is ascribed to the false Isaiah; but the Nephites had it, Lehi had it, Laban had it six hundred years before Christ; and my testimony as to the genuineness of the Book of Mormon is sufficient to set at rights with me any question as to the authorship of the Book of Isaiah.

Would you have higher authority than that of mortal prophets of Book of Mormon record? Then take the words of the Lord Jesus Christ himself when he appeared a resurrected being amongst the Nephites. In preaching to them he quoted one entire chapter of Isaiah—as we find recorded in the twenty-second chapter of Third Nephi. That quotation by our Lord is practically identical with the fifty-fourth chapter of Isaiah. I speak of the chapters as we now have them. I repeat, Jesus Christ quoted to the Nephites almost word for word what Isaiah had written in what we now know as the fifty-fourth chapter of his book. Then the Lord said: "And now, behold, I say unto you, that ye ought to search these things. Yea, a commandment I give unto you that ye search these things diligently; for great are the words of Isaiah."

This is the testimony of the Lord Jesus Christ (CR, Apr. 1929, 45–47).

Book of Mormon Geography. I sometimes think we pay a little undue attention to technicalities, and to questions that cannot be fully answered with respect to the Book of Mormon. It matters not to me just where this city or that camp was located. I have met a few of our Book of Mormon students who claim to be able to put a finger upon the map and indicate every land and city mentioned in the Book of Mormon. The fact is; the Book of Mormon does not give us precise and definite information whereby we can locate those places with certainty. I encourage and recommend all possible investigation, comparison and research in this matter. The more thinkers, investigators, workers we have in the field the better; but our brethren who devote themselves to that kind of research should remember that they must speak with caution and not declare as demonstrated truths points that are not really proved. There is enough truth in the Book of Mormon to occupy you and me for the rest of our lives, without our giving too much time and attention to these debatable matters (CR, Apr. 1929, 44).

Book of Mormon Is a Guide. I bear you witness, as witness has been borne before, and I speak it to you with all the assurance that the Three Witnesses and the Eight Witnesses put their testimony on record—that the Book of Mormon is just what it claims to be, as set forth by the ancient historian and prophet, the translation of whose words appears on the title page of the current work. There is nothing in the Book of Mormon to be explained away. The Book teaches, explains, and expounds; it will settle many of your problems, it will guide you in the path of truth. I know of what I speak for I have found it to be a reliable guide. Brethren and sisters, hold fast to the iron rod. May God help us so to do, I pray in the name of the Lord Jesus Christ. Amen (CR, Apr. 1929, 49).

Jaredites. "Of the two nations whose histories constitute the Book of Mormon, the first in order of time consisted of the people of Jared, who followed their leader from the Tower of Babel at the time of the confusion of tongues. Their history was written on twenty-four plates of gold by Ether, the last of their prophets, who, foreseeing the destruction of his people because of their wickedness, hid away the historical plates. They were afterward found, 123 B.C., by an expedition sent out by King Limhi, a Nephite ruler. The record engraved on these plates was subsequently abridged by Moroni, and the condensed account was attached by him to the Book of Mormon record; it appears in the modern translation under the name of the Book of Ether.

"The first and chief prophet of the Jaredites is not mentioned by name in the record as we have it; he is known only as the brother of Jared. Of the people, we learn that, amid the confusion of Babel, Jared and his brother importuned the Lord that He would spare them and their associates from the impending disruption. Their prayer was heard, and the Lord led them with a considerable company, who, like themselves, were free from the taint of idolatry, away from their homes, promising to conduct them to a land choice above all other lands. Their course of travel is not given with exactness; we learn only that they reached the ocean, and there constructed eight vessels, called barges, in which they set out upon the waters. These vessels were small and dark within; but the Lord made luminous certain stones, which gave light to the imprisoned voyagers. After a passage of three hundred and forty-four days, the colony landed on the western shore of North America, probably at a place south of the Gulf of California, and north of the Isthmus of Panama.

"Here they became a flourishing nation; but, giving way in time to internal dissensions, they divided into factions, which warred with one another until the people were totally destroyed. This destruction, which occurred near the hill Ramah, afterward known among the Nephites as Cumorah, probably took place at about the time of Lehi's landing in South America—590 B.C." (*JTC*, 16).

Lehi Taken to America. The avowed purpose of Jehovah, in leading Lehi and his colony from Jerusalem and conducting them across the great waters to the American shores, was to separate unto Himself a body of Israelites who would be cleansed from false tradition and the defiling precepts of men respecting the appointed mission of Christ in the flesh. As Moses was led into the desert and later into the mountain top, as Elijah was impelled to seek the cavern's solitude, that each might the better hear the Divine voice—so a nation was sequestered in the New World that they might learn the word of revealed truth in its simplicity and plainness (*VM*, 141).

Mulekites. Mulek was the son of Zedekiah, king of Judah, an infant at the time of his brothers' violent deaths and his father's cruel torture at the hands of the king of Babylon. Eleven years after Lehi's departure from Jerusalem, another colony was led from the city, amongst whom was Mulek. The colony took his name, probably on account of his recognized rights of leadership by virtue of lineage. The Book of Mormon record concerning Mulek and his people is scant; we learn, however, that the colony was brought across the waters to a landing, probably on the northern part of the American continent. The descendants of this colony were discovered by the Nephites under Mosiah; they had grown numerous, but, having had no scriptures for their guidance had fallen into a condition of spiritual darkness. They joined the Nephites and their history is merged into that of the greater nation. The Nephites gave to a part of North America the name Land of Mulek (*AF*, 262).

Location of Nephites. The Nephites lived in cities, some of which attained great size and were distinguished by unique architectural beauty. The people appear to have occupied vast areas in Central and North America, though it is not to be supposed that these regions were all populated by them at any one time (*SPM*, 16).

Nephite Period of Peace Turns into Persecution. The Church of Jesus Christ developed rapidly in the land of Nephi, and brought to its faithful adherents unprecedented blessings. Even the hereditary animosity between Nephites and Lamanites was forgotten; and all lived in peace and prosperity. So great was the unity of the Church that its members owned all things in common, and "therefore they were not rich and poor, bond and free, but they were all made free, and partakers of the heavenly gift." Populous cities replaced the desolation of ruin that had befallen at the time of the Lord's crucifixion. The land was blessed, and the people rejoiced in righteousness. "And it came to pass that there was no contention in the land, because of the love of God which did dwell in the hearts of the people. And there were no envyings, nor strifes, nor tumults, nor whoredoms, nor lyings, nor murders, nor any manner of lasciviousness; and surely there could not be a happier people among all the people who had been created by the hand of God." Nine of the twelve special witnesses chosen by the Lord passed at appointed times to their rest, and others were ordained in their stead. The state of blessed prosperity and of common ownership continued for a period of a hundred and sixty-seven years; but soon thereafter came a most distressing change. Pride displaced humility, display of costly apparel superseded the simplicity of happier days; rivalry led to contention, and thence the people "did have their goods and their substance no more common among them, and they began to be divided into classes, and they began to build up churches unto themselves, to get gain, and began to deny the true church of Christ." Man-made churches multiplied, and persecution, true sister to intolerance, became rampant (*JTC*, 741–42).

Hill Cumorah. Before their more powerful foes, the Nephites dwindled and fled until about the year A.D. 400 they were destroyed as a nation after a series of great battles, the last of which was fought near the hill called Cumorah, in the State of New York, where the hidden record was subsequently revealed to Joseph Smith (*SPM*, 16–17).

Historical Summary. The Book of Mormon contains a history of a colony of Israelites, of the tribe of Joseph, who left Jerusalem 600 B.C., during the reign of Zedekiah, king of Judah, on the eve of the subjugation of Judea by Nebuchadnezzar and the inauguration of the Babylonian captivity. This colony was led by divine guidance to the American continent, whereon they developed into a numerous and mighty people; though, divided by dissension, they formed two opposing nations known respectively as Nephites and Lamanites. The former cultivated the arts of industry and refinement, and preserved a record embodying both history and scripture, while the latter became degenerate and debased. The Nephites suffered extinction about A.D. 400, but the Lamanites lived on in their degraded course, and are today extant upon the land as the American Indians (*JTC*, 49).

Stick of Ephraim. The Book of Mormon contains pointed and specific predictions of its own coming forth in the latter days; and these prophecies harmonize with the Biblical Scriptures. The ancient peoples whose voice is again heard among the living were of the tribes of Ephraim and Manasseh, and therefore of the family of Joseph, son of Jacob. With this fact in mind, the thoughtful student finds profound significance in the otherwise obscure words of Ezekiel (37:15–20): "The word of the Lord came again unto me, saying, Moreover, thou son of man, take thee one stick, and write upon it, For Judah, and for the children of Israel his companions: then take another stick, and write upon it, For Joseph, the stick of Ephraim, and for all the house of Israel his companions: And join them one to another into one stick; and they shall become one in thine hand."

To the puzzled questioners who would ask the meaning of all this, the prophet was told to declare the Lord's purpose in this wise: "Thus saith the Lord God; Behold I will take the stick of Joseph, which is in the hand of Ephraim, and the tribes of Israel his fellows, and will put them with him, even with the stick of Judah, and make them one stick, and they shall be one in mine hand."

Plainly the record of Judah, which we recognize as the Holy Bible, was to be supplemented by the record of Joseph; and the bringing forth of the latter was to be effected by the direct exercise of Divine power, for the Lord said, "I will take the stick of Joseph"; and of the two He averred "they shall be one in mine hand," even as the prototypes had become one in the hand of Ezekiel.

If the testimony of scholars as to Biblical chronology be reliable, Lehi and his colony had already crossed the great waters and become well established in America when Ezekiel voiced this significant prophecy concerning the "stick" or record of Joseph as being distinct from that of Judah. The prediction has been fulfilled. The Holy Bible and the Book of Mormon, the records of Judah and Joseph respectively, are before the world, each attesting the authenticity of the other, and each standing as an irrefutable testimony of the atoning life, death, and resurrection of the Lord Jesus Christ (*VM,* 137–38).

Joseph Smith Translated the Book of Mormon. Joseph Smith, unschooled beyond the rudiments of what we call an education, unversed in any tongue but the vernacular English, was wholly unequipped according to all human standards to translate the language of a nation long extinct, and, except for certain Indian traditions, forgotten. But the operation of a power higher than human, by which the engraved plates were brought forth from the earth, was to be effective in making the long-buried chronicles intelligible to modern readers.

It was no part of the Lord's plan to entrust the translating to man's linguistic skill; and, moreover, at that time the Rosetta Stone still lay buried beneath the debris of ages, and there was not a man upon the earth capable of rendering an Egyptian inscription into English. As the Book of Mormon avers, the original writing was Egyptian, modified through the isolation of the ancient peoples on the Western Continent, and designated Reformed Egyptian.

It was divinely appointed that the sacred archives should be restored to the knowledge of men through the gift and power of God. Had it not been written that in the latter days the Lord would accomplish a marvelous work and a wonder, whereby the wisdom of the wise would fail and the understanding of the learned be hidden? (See Isa. 29: 13, 14.) And this because men would put their dogmas and precepts above the revealed word? (Verse 13.) In the translation of the Book of Mormon there was to be no gloss of fallible scholarship, no attempt to improve and embellish the plain, simple and unambiguous diction of the original scribes who wrote by inspiration. Therefore was the commission laid upon one who was rated among the weak of the earth, but whose ministry, nevertheless, has confounded the mighty. (See 1 Cor. 1:27, 28.) (*VM*, 127–28).

Translation of the Book of Mormon. The translation of the Book of Mormon was effected through the power of God manifested in the bestowal of the gift of revelation. The book professes not to be dependent upon the wisdom or learning of man; its translator was not versed in linguistics; his qualifications were of a different and of a more efficient order. With the plates, Joseph Smith received from the angel other sacred treasures, including a breastplate, to which were attached the Urim and Thummim, called by the Nephites *Interpreters;* and by the use of these he was enabled to translate the ancient records into our modern tongue. The details of the work of translation have not been recorded, beyond the statement that the translator examined the engraved characters by means of the sacred instruments, and then dictated to the scribe the English sentences (*AF*, 267).

Spaulding Manuscript. The Book of Mormon was before the world; the Church circulated the work as freely as possible. The true account of its origin was rejected by the general public, who thus assumed the responsibility of explaining in some plausible way the source of the record. Among the many fanciful theories propounded, perhaps the most famous is the so-called Spaulding story. Solomon Spaulding, a clergyman of Amity, Pennsylvania, died in 1816. He wrote a romance to which no name other than "Manuscript Story" was given, and which, but for the unauthorized use of the writer's name and the misrepresentation of his motives, would never have been published. Twenty years after the author's death, one Hurlburt, an apostate "Mormon," announced that he had recognized a resemblance between the "Manuscript Story" and the Book of Mormon, and expressed a belief that the work brought forward by Joseph Smith was nothing but the Spaulding romance revised and amplified. The apparent credibility of the statement was increased by various signed declarations to the effect that the two were alike though no extracts for comparison were presented. But the "Manuscript Story" was lost for a time, and in the absence of proof to the contrary, reports of the parallelism between the two works multiplied. By a fortunate circumstance, in 1884, President James H. Fairchild, of Oberlin College, and a literary friend of his—a Mr. L. L. Rice—while examining a collection of old papers which had been purchased by the gentleman last named, found the original manuscript of the "Story."

After a careful perusal and comparison with the Book of Mormon, President Fairchild stated in an article published in the New York *Observer,* February 5, 1885:

"The theory of the origin of the Book of Mormon in the traditional manuscript of Solomon Spaulding will probably have to be relinquished. . . . Mr. Rice, myself, and others compared it [the Spaulding manuscript] with the Book of Mormon and could detect no resemblance between the two, in general or in detail. There seems to be no name nor incident common to the two. The solemn style of the Book of Mormon in imitation of the English Scriptures does not appear in the manuscript. . . . Some other explanation of the origin of the Book of Mormon must be found if any explanation is required."

The manuscript was deposited in the library of Oberlin College (*SPM,* 20–23).

DOCTRINE AND COVENANTS

Doctrine and Covenants. The spirit of advancement and progressivism in the Church of Christ is that which marks the progression from the seed to the blade and from the blade to the ripened ear. It is a constructive progressivism: the past is added to, and every new revelation doth but make the revelations of the past plainer and reveal their sanctity and their sacred origin the better. I ask you, have you yet discovered in this volume of modern scripture, the D&C, one utterance that is in any manner opposed to the spirit of the scriptures of the past? It will be time to raise objection to modern revelation when we find that such revelation is in opposition to the spirit of the Word of God of past times: but when the modern utterances are plainly but later works of the same author, why need we complain? (CR, Oct. 1912, 126).

ARTICLES OF FAITH

Articles of Faith. Joseph Smith, the first divinely commissioned prophet and the first president of the Church of Jesus Christ in the latter-day, or current, dispensation, set forth as an epitome of the tenets of the Church the thirteen avowals known as the "Articles of Faith of The Church of Jesus Christ of Latter-day Saints." These include fundamental and characteristic doctrines of the Gospel as taught by this Church; but they are not to be regarded as a complete exposition of belief, for, as stated in Article 9, "We believe all that God has revealed, all that He does now reveal, and we believe that He will yet reveal many great and important things pertaining to the Kingdom of God." From the time of their first promulgation, the Articles of Faith have been accepted by the people as an authoritative exposition; and on October 6, 1890, the Latter-day Saints, in general conference assembled, re-adopted the Articles as a guide in faith and conduct (*AF,* 6).

ADDITIONAL SCRIPTURE

Gospel. One of the inherent weaknesses of the human mind is that of reaching after completeness. We like to feel that we can begin and end a subject of study. We are like those thoughtless students in school who seem to think that all that is known about the subject is to be found within the covers of their text book; and a reprehensible but still somewhat popular custom prevails in some of the colleges on the part of the classes who finish the study of some book, to hold a cremation ceremony and burn up the texts as evidence that they have no further use for them; they think they know the whole thing. We have learned the solemn truth that the gospel is greater than any book, greater than the Bible, indispensable though that volume is; greater than the Book of Mormon, great as is the mission of that Scripture, brought to the world in these latter days by the power and inspiration of God; greater than our current volume of modern revelation, for there is more to come. More is included in the gospel than all Scripture thus far written; and the living oracles are established in the Church to give unto the people from time to time the mind and the will of God in addition to what has been placed upon record with relation to the ages past (CR, Apr. 1918, 160).

Constitution Is Scripture. I would have the Latter-day Saints consider the fact that of all peoples on the face of the earth we are peculiarly interested in the outcome of this struggle. [World War I] Therefore we have a sound foundations in this for our patriotism, for our sacrifice, for our efforts in behalf of this government, for our unqualified allegiance to the Constitution of the United States, which is veritably the scripture of the nation; for upon this Church has been laid the commission to preach the gospel in every nation as a witness (CR, Apr. 1918, 162).

UNDERSTANDING SCRIPTURE

Scriptures Understood by the Power of the Holy Ghost. We Latter-day Saints are peculiarly literal in our acceptance of plain scripture. We believe that the Scriptures are very simple to understand, if we can only get the theologians to leave them alone and not confuse us with explanations. The Spirit of the Lord will enlighten the mind of the earnest reader, and will interpret the Scriptures, for that is the spirit in which the Scriptures were written (CR, Apr. 1917, 66).

12

RESPONSIBILITY OF THE COVENANT PEOPLE

COVENANT NAME

Israel. "Jacob," a name given to the son of Isaac with reference to a circumstance attending his birth, and signifying *a supplanter,* was superseded by "Israel" meaning *a soldier of God, a prince of God;* as expressed in the words effecting the change, "Thy name shall be called no more Jacob, but Israel, for as a prince hast thou power with God and with men, and hast prevailed." (Gen. 32:28; compare 35:9,10.) (*JTC,* 38).

TRUST GOD

Side with God. A remark that is credited to the great Lincoln, and one which, whether made by him or not, is wholly worthy of the man, is perhaps profitable for consideration here. When asked, during the great conflict in which brother was arrayed against brother, whether he felt in his heart that the Lord was on his side, he answered, "I don't know, and as a matter of fact, that does not concern me; what I want to know is, am I on the Lord's side?" It is a great deal better for us, a far loftier conception, I take it, to consider that we are on God's side than to worry ourselves as to whether He is, on our side. In your dealings, my brother, in your barter and your trade, be on the Lord's side; do as He would have you do under those conditions. As a people we profess to be on the Lord's side. It is for us to make good that profession, to live up to it, to avail ourselves of the influences that are at work for our good, and the powers that are operating for the salvation of men (CR, Oct. 1914, 104).

Lesson of the Bee. A wild bee from the neighboring hills once flew into the room; and at intervals during an hour or more I caught the pleasing hum of its flight. The little creature realized that it was a prisoner, yet all its efforts to find the exit through the partly opened casement failed. When ready to close up the room and leave, I threw the window wide, and tried at first to guide and then to drive the bee to liberty and safety, knowing well that if left in the room it would die as other insects there entrapped had perished in the dry atmosphere of the enclosure. The more I tried to drive it out, the more determinedly did it oppose and resist my efforts. Its erstwhile peaceful hum developed into an angry roar; its darting flight became hostile and threatening.

Then it caught me off my guard and stung my hand,—the hand that would have guided it to freedom. At last it alighted on a pendant attached to the ceiling, beyond my reach of help or injury. The sharp pain of its unkind sting aroused in me rather pity than anger. I knew the inevitable penalty of its mistaken opposition and defiance; and I had to leave the creature to its fate. Three days later I returned to the room and found the dried, lifeless body of the bee on the writing table. It had paid for its stubbornness with its life.

To the bee's short-sightedness and selfish misunderstanding I was a foe, a persistent persecutor, a mortal enemy bent on its destruction; while in truth I was its friend, offering it ransom of the life it had put in forfeit through its own error, striving to redeem it, in spite of itself, from the prison-house of death and restore it to the outer air of liberty.

Are we so much wiser than the bee that no analogy lies between its unwise course and our lives? We are prone to contend, sometimes with vehemence and anger, against the adversity which after all may be the manifestation of superior wisdom and loving care, directed against our temporary comfort for our permanent blessing. In the tribulations and sufferings of mortality there is a divine ministry which only the godless soul can wholly fail to discern. To many the loss of wealth has been a boon, a providential means of leading or driving them from the confines of selfish indulgence to the sunshine and the open, where boundless opportunity waits on effort. Disappointment, sorrow, and affliction may be the expression of an all-wise Father's kindness.

Consider the lesson of the unwise bee!

"Trust in the Lord with all thine heart; and lean not unto thine own understanding. In all thy ways acknowledge him, and he shall direct thy paths." (Proverbs 3:5, 6) (*PJT*, 29–31).

SIGNS OF THE COVENANT PEOPLE

Signs of the Covenant People. The Israelites were distinguished in the first place as worshipers of a living God, a personal God, in whose image they had been created and made. No other nation on the face of the earth recognized the living God. That was a sign by which the covenant people, descendants of Abraham, through Isaac and Jacob, were known. Another sign was this, they observed every seventh day as the Sabbath of the Lord their God; and the Lord had said: This shall be a sign between thee and the nations: They shall know that ye are my people, because ye observe my Sabbaths. And the third sign I mention is that they were tithed of all they possessed. Those were set forth prominently as the banners of Israel, by which all nations should know that they were the covenant people of God. Now I repeat, in every dispensation living scriptures are given. The history of the past is of value, but the great principles are restated, the fundamental laws are reenacted. Christ came to fulfil and supersede the law of Moses, and yet with his own lips in the flesh he restated every commandment in the Decalogue, giving it to the new dispensation. He cited prophecies of the past, connecting up the earlier dispensations with that in which he lived and at the head of which he stood in a particular sense, not only as the head of all dispensations, but in the sense of his being there in mortality.

Where do we stand with respect to those signs? Are we worshiping the true and living God, or are we going idolatrously after the gods of gold and silver, of iron and wood, and brass, diamonds and other idols of wealth? Are we worshiping our farms, our cattle and sheep? Who is our God? To whom are we yielding homage, allegiance and worship? Not worship by means of words only, in ritualistic form, but worship in action, devotion, and sacrificial service? (CR, Oct. 1930, 73).

The Sabbath Is a Sign. There were other signs by which these people, who were called after the name of that living God, were distinguished. One of them was that they observed every seventh day as the Sabbath of the Lord. Even the heathen nations had their fast days, but such were instituted by men for the purpose of gratifying the lust of men, and the conceptions of men as to ceremonial and show. The Sabbath of the Lord our God is not a creation of men. Jesus the Christ is Lord of the Sabbath, and Israel amongst the pagan world was characterized as a Sabbath-observing people. Did not the Lord say through Moses, again through Nehemiah, and again through Ezekiel and through others of the prophets—This is a sign between the children of Israel and me? It shall be a sign between me and my children through all generations forever, that they shall observe my Sabbaths.

Pagan sabbaths were holidays, not holy days. Though the two terms come from the same root, there is a vital distinction between them at the present time. The Lord chided the people of old because they had polluted his Sabbaths, and how had they polluted them? Not always by continuing their worldly work, not always because they did not cease their toil, but because they made the Sabbath a day of pleasure and of license and of indulgence that was evil, and forgot to worship the Lord their God specifically on that day of rest. We are not required, nor are we permitted, if we obey the law of God, to be idle. We should be active and in service, but Sabbath-day work should be directly the service of God and not the secular and wage-earning service of man (CR, Apr. 1923, 141).

HEEDING THE PROPHET

Heed the Teachings. I have met here and there a disgruntled one, one who is saying: Why don't we receive further revelation from God today? We are receiving it day by day. I speak of what I know when I say unto you, if ever the Church of Christ was led by a prophet enjoying communion with God, inspiration from the source of divine revelation, from heaven direct—and none of us can doubt such leadership in the past—this day witnesses that condition. I testify unto you that the man who stands at the head of this Church is the mouthpiece of God unto His people, and if we fail to heed his words, his admonitions, his instructions given unto us as they have been, and are, in love and nevertheless with firmness and with no uncertainty of tone, we bring ourselves under condemnation (CR, Apr. 1918, 161).

GIVING SERVICE

Warning to Members. We are doing much now in seeking to improve the condition and the activities of our quorums, the quorums of the Holy Priesthood; and we have some quorums whose records are good as compared with others. With totals of activities high, it may appear that the members are energetic and that they never before have accomplished so much. But look a little deeper and you may find that of a quorum of ninety-six elders, sixteen perhaps have been doing the work and the other eighty have been carried along without much effort on their part.

The Lord has expressed himself forcefully with respect to such conditions, in these last days. In the first section of the Doctrine and Covenants—I pray you read for yourself—after reciting his purposes and plans and the partial realization of such in the bringing forth of this gospel in this age, he speaks of those who were charged with authority in that day to administer the affairs of the Church, those to whom these commandments were given, and explains that the commandments were given that his servants might have power to lay the foundation of this Church and to bring it forth out of obscurity and out of darkness. Please mark his words: "The only true and living church upon the face of the whole earth with which I the Lord am well pleased." But that is not the end of the sentence or paragraph: "with which I the Lord am well pleased, speaking unto the church collectively and not individually."

There lies a vital distinction. It is expressed but we often overlook it. It is a distinction that should be heeded in all our organizations within the Church, and without; the difference between the collective status or conditions or achievements and the work of the individual. A manufacturing plant may turn out a great total of product, it may have an immense output, and you may say that it is doing well; but examine the units, look into the machinery, not simply inspect it in a general way, but test, try every machine, every part; and you may find that not one mechanical unit there is doing more than fifty or sixty per cent of what it could do, and yet the output is big.

A great acreage may result in a very large yield, but when you come to consider the yield per acre you may find that you are gathering only thirty or even twenty fold when you ought to have been reaping seventy and eighty and even an hundred fold.

We as individuals are not doing all that could be done, all that should be done. I have no concern for the Church as a whole; its destiny is foretold, it is going on to glorious victory. But that does not say that each of us who are members of the Church will go on to glorious victory; we may be left behind entirely. What are we doing individually? (CR, Oct. 1928, 118).

Service Requires Sacrifice. To them Jesus testified that the hour of His death was near at hand, the hour in which "the Son of man should be glorified." They were surprised and pained by the Lord's words, and possibly they inquired as to the necessity of such a sacrifice. Jesus explained by citing a striking illustration drawn from nature: "Verily, verily, I say unto you, Except a corn of wheat fall into the ground and die, it abideth alone: but if it die, it bringeth forth much fruit." The simile is an apt one, and at once impressively simple and beautiful. A farmer who neglects or refuses to cast his wheat into the earth, because he wants to keep it, can have no increase; but if he sow the wheat in good rich soil, each living grain may multiply itself many fold, though of necessity the seed must be sacrificed in the process. So, said the Lord, "He that loveth his life shall lose it; and he that hateth his life in this world shall keep it unto life eternal." The Master's meaning is clear; he that loves his life so well that he will not imperil it, or, if need be, give it up, in the service of God, shall forfeit his opportunity to win the bounteous increase of eternal life; while he who esteems the call of God as so greatly superior to life that his love of life is as hatred in comparison, shall find the life he freely yields or is willing to yield, though for the time being it disappear like the grain buried in the soil; and he shall rejoice in the bounty of eternal development. If such be true of every man's existence, how transcendently so was it of the life of Him who came to die that men may live? Therefore was it necessary that He die, as He had said He was about to do; but His death, far from being life lost, was to be life glorified (*JTC,* 518–19).

We May Choose Whom We Will Serve. Had [the gold piece] never been touched by the die in the mint, had it not received the stamp that insures it currency, it would be just as truly gold, intrinsically worth the full ten dollars for the metal of which it consists; but it would be of no ready service, since every time it changed hands the receiver would have to weigh it and determine its composition. Such necessity would involve consideration, test, calculation, and withal, hesitation and caution, with possible failure to meet the exigencies of the time.

How like that precious gift of God—the assurance and testimony of the gospel of Christ, how like the bestowal of the gift of the Holy Ghost by the authoritative imposition of hands, how like the divine call and ordination to the Holy Priesthood, is the stamp on the coin! The soul so impressed, so chosen, so ordained, shows by word and act as well as by silent influence, the touch of the finger of God, even though the divine contact has been but momentary.

Like unto those who are honorable in purpose and honest in heart, yet who have not yet yielded obedience to the requirements of the saving gospel, are the unstamped blanks, good metal though they be.

Their influence is limited, their capacity for service narrowly circumscribed. They await the touch, the impress that shall commission them to testify and minister in the name of the King.

To every sterling piece such as tallies with the law of righteousness, that touch shall come in the present or the hereafter, provided only the piece be ready. But how will the metal receive the imprint? If it be brittle through base alloy, untempered, unannealed and unyielding, it may break under the stress, or even though it hold together it may present but a blurred similitude of the authoritative stamp.

Oh soul! hast thou not yet passed between the dies? Dost thou await the individual impress of divine commission? And is thy lack due to unreadiness? Art thou tempered and annealed to receive the testimony of God's approval?

And thou other soul, bearing the imprint of such testimony, art thou true to the stamp thou bearest? Unlike the inanimate coin, thou hast agency and the ability to choose in what service thou shalt be used. Thou art of divine mintage. Great is thy power. Fail not (*PJT,* 26–27).

Service to God Is a Form of Gratitude. Mr. Romanes, in the course of his customary daily walk, came to a mill-pond. At the edge of the water he saw two boys with a basket. They were obviously engaged in a diverting occupation. As he came up to them Mr. Romanes observed that the youths were well dressed and evidently somewhat refined and cultured. Inquiry elicited the fact that they were upper servants in a family of wealth and social quality. In the basket were three whining kittens; two others were drowning in the pond; and the mother [cat] was running about on the bank, rampant in her distress.

To the naturalist's inquiry the boys responded with a straightforward statement, respectfully addressed. They said their mistress had instructed them to drown the kittens, as she wanted no other cat than the old one about the house. The mother cat, as the boys explained, was the lady's particular pet. Mr. Romanes assured the boys that he was a personal friend of their employer, and that he would be responsible for any apparent dereliction in their obedience to the orders of their mistress. He gave the boys a shilling apiece, and took the three living kittens in charge. The two in the pond had already sunk to their doom.

The mother cat evinced more than the measure of intelligence usually attributed to the animal world. She recognized the man as the deliverer of her three children, who but for him would have been drowned. As he carried the kittens she trotted along.—sometimes following, sometimes alongside, occasionally rubbing against him with grateful yet mournful purrs. At his home Mr. Romanes provided the kittens with comfortable quarters, and left the mother cat in joyful content. She seemed to have forgotten the death of the two in her joy over the rescue of the three.

Next day, the gentleman was seated in his parlor on the ground floor, in the midst of a notable company. Many people had gathered to do honor to the distinguished naturalist. The cat came in. In her mouth she carried a large, fat mouse, not dead, but still feebly struggling under the pains of torturous capture. She laid her panting and well-nigh expiring prey at the feet of the man who had saved her kittens.

What think you of the offering, and of the purpose that prompted the act? A live mouse, fleshy and fat! Within the cat's power of possible estimation and judgment it was a superlative gift. To her limited understanding no rational creature could feel otherwise than pleased over the present of a meaty mouse. Every sensible cat would be ravenously joyful with such an offering. Beings unable to appreciate a mouse for a meal were unknown to the cat.

Are not our offerings to the Lord—our tithes and our other free-will gifts—as thoroughly unnecessary to His needs as was the mouse to the scientist? But remember that the grateful and sacrificing nature of the cat was enlarged, and in a measure sanctified, by her offering.

Thanks be to God that He gauges the offerings and sacrifices of His children by the standard of their physical ability and honest intent rather than by the gradation of His exalted station. Verily He is God with us; and He both understands and accepts our motives and righteous desires. Our need to serve God is incalculably greater than His need for our service (*PJT,* 37–39).

BEARING FRUIT

Fig Tree a Symbol of Judaism. But the fate that befell the barren fig tree is instructive from another point of view. The incident is as much parable as miracle. That leafy tree was distinguished among fig trees; the others offered no invitation, gave no promise; "the time of figs was not yet"; they, in due season would bring forth fruit and leaves; but this precocious and leafy pretender waved its umbrageous limbs as in boastful assertion of superiority. For those who responded to its ostentatious invitation, for the hungering Christ who came seeking fruit, it had naught but leaves. Even for the purposes of the lesson involved, we cannot conceive of the tree being blighted primarily because it was fruitless, for at that season the other fig trees were bare of fruit also; it was made the object of the curse and the subject of the Lord's instructive discourse, because, having leaves, it was deceptively barren. Were it reasonable to regard the tree as possessed of moral agency, we would have to pronounce it a hypocrite; its utter barrenness coupled with its abundance of foliage made of it a type of human hypocrisy.

The leafy, fruitless tree was a symbol of Judaism, which loudly proclaimed itself as the only true religion of the age, and condescendingly invited all the world to come and partake of its rich ripe fruit; when in truth it was but an unnatural growth of leaves, with no fruit of the season, nor even an edible bulb held over from earlier years, for such as it had of former fruitage was dried to worthlessness and made repulsive in its worm-eaten decay. The religion of Israel had degenerated into an artificial religionism, which in pretentious show and empty profession outclassed the abominations of heathendom. As already pointed out in these pages, the fig tree was a favorite type in rabbinical representation of the Jewish race, and the Lord had before adopted the symbolism in the Parable of the Barren Fig Tree, that worthless growth which did but cumber the ground (*JTC*, 526–27).

KNOWING THE DOCTRINE

Test of Our Lord's Doctrine. Any man may know for himself whether the doctrine of Christ is of God or not by simply doing the will of the Father (John 7:17). Surely it is a more convincing course than that of relying upon another's word. The writer was once approached by an incredulous student in college, who stated that he could not accept as true the published results of a certain chemical analysis, since the specified amounts of some of the ingredients were so infinitesimally small that he could not believe it possible to determine such minute quantities. The student was but a beginner in chemistry; and with his little knowledge he had undertaken to judge as to the possibilities of the science. He was told to do the things his instructor prescribed, and he should some day know for himself whether the results were true or false. In the senior year of his course, he received for laboratory analysis a portion of the very substance whose composition he had once questioned. With the skill attained by faithful devotion he successfully completed the analysis, and reported results similar to those, which in his inexperience he had thought impossible to obtain. He was manly enough to acknowledge as unfounded his earlier skepticism and rejoice in the fact that he had been able to demonstrate the truth for himself (*JTC*, 421).

Must Study to Know God. Has he not given us prophets and apostles to teach, patriarchs and high priests, elders and seventies, the Lesser Priesthood, and provisions in the auxiliaries, for the instruction of every soul from the cradle age to the age that is considered as marking the natural end of man's life? The Latter-day Saints are largely a highly educated people, in the things of the Lord; nevertheless, we are not as well educated as we ought to be. We do not read enough, we do not study enough; we do not pray enough: or we would know more of the word of God and of his will concerning the people (CR, Oct. 1921, 189).

KEEPING THE COMMANDMENTS

Greatest Commandment. "Master, which is the great commandment in the law? Jesus said unto him, Thou shalt love the Lord thy God with all thy heart, and with all thy soul, and with all thy mind. This is the first and great commandment. And the second is like unto it, Thou shalt love thy neighbor as thyself. On these two commandments hang all the law and the prophets." The two commandments, here spoken of as first and second, are so closely related as to be virtually one, and that one. "Thou shalt love." He who abideth one of the two will abide both; for without love for our fellows, it is impossible to please God (*AF,* 431).

EXPRESSING GRATITUDE

Sin of Ingratitude. There is a very general tendency today to relegate God to the background in human affairs, to consider that He has no voice in our doings and in this course the Lord hath declared Himself and thus makes plain to us that His anger is aroused against those unfilial children of His who forget Him; for the man who forgets the living God turns to idolatry, and having once known God and turned away from Him he is worse than the heathen who has never known other gods than those of wood and stone. I believe in my heart that many of us are prone to lead relatively Godless lives. I speak of the human family, not of this people distinctively. Many of us, children of God, forget our Father, forget what He has done for us, what He is doing for us; forget how truly we depend upon Him for all that we have and all that we are; and those who do so are great offenders in the eyes of the Lord. For He doth hate ingratitude and He doth hate pride that lifts man in his own estimation and causes him to look around upon the things that God hath given (CR, Oct. 1914, 100).

KEEPING THE SABBATH

Keeping the Sabbath a Commandment. We believe that a weekly day of rest is no less truly a necessity for the physical well-being of man than for his spiritual growth; but, primarily and essentially, we regard the Sabbath as divinely established, and its observance a commandment of Him who was and is and ever shall be, Lord of the Sabbath (*AF,* 452).

Strict Observers of the Sabbath. If we be the people of Israel, the chosen people of God, as is our high profession, we must be thus characterized. Then, whatever shall be the fancies and fantasies of the world, let us be true to the living God, the God who with his Son Jesus Christ, was manifested to the youthful seeker after truth, afterward the Prophet Joseph Smith. We accept the God of our fathers in all literalness. We find that we can come much nearer unto him by that acceptance. We, the chosen of God, must show forth those distinguishing works specified by him. Are we observing his Sabbaths? Where do we stand, oh Israel? Is the reproach to come upon us? Are we polluting that holy day by pandering to our own lust after pleasure, after our own laziness, or perchance, giving ourselves up to the pursuit of wealth on that day? It is the Lord's day, not ours. He has given us six, but the seventh is his, and he demands that we shall recognize it as his and devote every hour of that day to his service. How do we stand, where is that sign showing forth in our lives and in our work as individuals and as families? Is there a sign over your door, oh Latter-day Saints, showing that you are strict observers of the Sabbath, or have you been swept away by this tide of apostasy that is ever seeking to engulf? (CR, Apr. 1923, 143).

Sabbath Observance and the Law of Tithing. Let us lift the banners of Zion, the banner of the true worship of the living God, the banner of Sabbath observance, make it a holy day for the service of the Lord, not a day of idle rest and sleep and inactivity, but a day of activity in the Lord's important service. This he has required of us, and he never has modified the requirement by the slightest amendment. Keep flying the banner of the sacred tithe for the Lord. He would have his people tithed that the land may be sanctified unto them. It is for our good that the law of the tithe has been given. We cannot advance in the knowledge of God and the things pertaining to exaltation in the kingdom of God unless we have that training (CR, Oct. 1930, 74).

PARTAKING OF THE SACRAMENT

A Warning concerning the Sacrament. The divine instructions concerning the sacredness of this ordinance are explicit; and the consequent need of scrupulous care being exercised lest it be engaged in unworthily is apparent. In addressing the Corinthian saints Paul gave solemn warnings against hasty or unworthy action in partaking of the sacrament, and declares that the penalties of sickness and even death are visited upon those who violate the sacred requirements: "For as often as ye eat this bread, and drink this cup, ye do shew the Lord's death till he come. Wherefore whosoever shall eat this bread, and drink this cup of the Lord, unworthily, shall be guilty of the body and blood of the Lord.["] . . . The direct word of the Lord unto the saints in this dispensation instructs them to permit no one in transgression to partake of the sacrament until reconciliation has been made; nevertheless the saints are commanded to exercise abundant charity toward their erring fellows, not casting them out from the assemblies yet withholding the sacrament from them. In our system of Church organization the local ecclesiastical officers are charged with the responsibility of administering the sacrament, and the people are required to keep themselves worthy to partake of the sacred emblems (*AF,* 173–74).

Sacrament. From the scriptural citations already made, it is plain that the sacrament is administered to commemorate the atonement of the Lord Jesus, as consummated in His agony and death; it is a testimony before God that we are mindful of His Son's sacrifice made in our behalf; and that we still profess the name of Christ and are determined to strive to keep His commandments, in the hope that we may ever have His Spirit to be with us. Partaking of the sacrament worthily may be regarded therefore as a means of renewing our avowals before the Lord, of acknowledgment of mutual fellowship among the members, and of solemnly witnessing our claim and profession of membership in the Church of Jesus Christ. The sacrament has not been established as a specific means of securing remission of sins; nor for any other special blessing aside from that of a continuing endowment of the Holy Spirit, which, however, comprises all needful blessings. Were the sacrament ordained specifically for the remission of sins, it would not be forbidden to those who are in greatest need of forgiveness; yet participation in the ordinance is restricted to those whose consciences are void of serious offense, those, therefore, who are acceptable before the Lord, those indeed who are in as little need of special forgiveness as mortals can be (*AF*, 175.)

Symbolism of the Sacrament. But the figure used by Jesus— that of eating His flesh and drinking His blood as typical of unqualified and absolute acceptance of Himself as the Savior of men, is of superlative import; for thereby are affirmed the divinity of His Person, and the fact of His preexistent and eternal Godship. The sacrament of the Lord's supper, established by the Savior on the night of His betrayal, perpetuates the symbolism of eating His flesh and drinking His blood, by the partaking of bread and wine in remembrance of Him. Acceptance of Jesus as the Christ implies obedience to the laws and ordinances of His gospel; for to profess the One and refuse the other is but to convict ourselves of inconsistency, insincerity, and hypocrisy (*JTC*, 343).

PAYING TITHING

A Warning concerning Tithing. I know that this people are the people of the Lord, that they are acceptable unto him, but we are not reaching fully the requirements that the Lord has made upon us; and too many Latter-day Saints are going after strange gods, setting their hearts on their hay and their corn, their bonds and stocks, their automobiles and the luxuries of the world, to the neglect of their duties in the Church. Though I would be no prophet of evil, of disaster, or of calamity, I feel to say that if the Latter-day Saints do not obey the law that God has given with respect to the tithes, they will have less and less to tithe, this in the Lord's own time (CR, Oct. 1930, 74).

Tithing a Law of Gratitude. I would be a hypocrite if I profess to be living the law of the tithe and simply give a little donation to the Lord that bears no proper relation to the blessing he has poured out upon me. I am cheating him—think of it, cheating my landlord who has given me the place I call home, food for my household, clothing for my family, and many blessings of life, and who, moreover, has trusted me to keep the account, and to reckon up how much is due; Who has given me those things on a graded rental, with the understanding that if times are hard and my income be thereby lessened I need not pay him so much, because I do not get as much; and that if times are good and ray income is larger, that I can pay him a little more.

Have you ever found a landlord in mortality who would make any such arrangement? The Lord has said to me in effect: "Now this has been a hard year for you. You have not had as much income as you had last year. I am going to lower your rent. You just pay one-tenth, that is all, but it will be less than you paid me last year." The landlords on earth, at least some, with whom I have had to deal have said: "Look here, times are pretty hard. I must raise your rent; and you must pay it in advance." The Lord says: Pay when you receive the blessing (CR, Oct. 1921, 190–91).

Tithing a Means of Blessing the Saints. As of old, so in the Church of Jesus Christ of Latter-day Saints today, tithing is the divinely established revenue system by which the pecuniary needs of the ecclesiastical community are provided for. And as of old so today, tithe-paying must be a voluntary free-will sacrifice, not to be exacted by secular power nor enforced by infliction of fines or other material penalties. The obligation is self-assumed; nevertheless it is one to be observed with full purpose of heart by the earner who claims standing in the Church and who professes to abide by the revealed word given for the spiritual development of its members.

It is essential that men learn to give. Without provision for this training the curriculum in the school of mortality would be seriously defective. Human wisdom has failed to devise a more equitable scheme of individual contribution for community needs than the simple plan of the tithe. Every one is invited to give in amount proportioned to his income, and to so give regularly and systematically. The spirit of giving makes the tithe holy; and it is by means thus sanctified that the material activities of the Church are carried on. Blessings, specific and choice, are promised the honest tithe-payer; and these blessings are placed within the reach of all. In the Lord's work the widow's penny is as acceptable as the gold-piece of the millionaire (*VM,* 201).

PREPARING FOR THE SECOND COMING

An Eternal Family Unit. One of the fundamental principles under-lying the doctrine of salvation for the dead, is that of the mutual de-pendence of the fathers and the children. Family lineage and the se-quence of generations in each particular line of descent are facts, and cannot be changed by death; on the other hand it is evident from the olden scriptures already cited, and attested by the equally sure word of modern revelation, that the family relationships of earth are recog-nized in the spirit world. Neither the children nor the fathers, neither progenitors nor descendants, can alone attain perfection; and the req-uisite co-operation is effected through baptism and related ordinances, administered to the living in behalf of the dead.

In this way and through this work are the hearts of the fathers and those of the children turned toward each other. As the living children learn that without their ancestors they cannot attain a perfect status in the eternal world, their own faith will be strengthened and they will be willing to labor for the redemption and salvation of their dead. And the dead, learning through the preaching of the Gospel in their world, that they are dependent upon their descendants as vicarious saviors, will turn with loving faith and prayerful effort toward their children yet living.

This uniting of the interests of fathers and children is a part of the necessary preparation for the yet future advent of the Christ as ruling King and Lord of earth (*HL,* 83–84).

Israel Invited to the Feast. Explication of the parable was left to the learned men to whom the story was addressed. Surely some of them would fathom its meaning, in part at least. The covenant people, Israel, were the specially invited guests. They had been bidden long enough aforetime, and by their own profession as the Lord's own had agreed to be partakers of the feast. When all was ready, on the appointed day, they were severally summoned by the Messenger who had been sent by the Father; He was even then in their midst. But the cares of riches, the allurement of material things, and the pleasures of social and domestic life had engrossed them; and they prayed to be excused or irreverently declared they could not or would not come. Then the gladsome invitation was to be carried to the Gentiles, who were looked upon as spiritually poor, maimed, halt, and blind. And later, even the pagans beyond the walls, strangers in the gates of the holy city, would be bidden to the supper. These, surprised at the unexpected summons, would hesitate, until by gentle urging and effective assurance that they were really included among the bidden guests, they would feel themselves constrained or compelled to come. The possibility of some of the discourteous ones arriving later, after they had attended to their more absorbing affairs, is indicated in the Lord's closing words: "For I say unto you, That none of those men which were bidden shall taste of my supper" (*JTC,* 452).

Parable of the Ten Virgins. The Bridegroom is the Lord Jesus; the marriage feast symbolizes His coming in glory, to receive unto Himself the Church on earth as His bride. The virgins typify those who profess a belief in Christ, and who, therefore, confidently expect to be included among the blessed participants at the feast. The lighted lamp, which each of the maidens carried, is the outward profession of Christian belief and practice; and in the oil reserves of the wiser ones we may see the spiritual strength and abundance which diligence and devotion in God's service alone can insure. The lack of sufficient oil on the part of the unwise virgins is analogous to the dearth of soil in the stony field, wherein the seed readily sprouted but soon withered away. The Bridegroom's coming was sudden; yet the waiting virgins were not held blamable for their surprise at the abrupt announcement, but the unwise five suffered the natural results of their unpreparedness. The refusal of the wise virgins to give of their oil at such a critical time must not be regarded as uncharitable; the circumstance typifies the fact that in the day of judgment every soul must answer for himself; there is no way by which the righteousness of one can be credited to another's account; the doctrine of supererogation is wholly false. The Bridegroom's condemnatory disclaimer, "I know you not," was equivalent to a declaration that the imploring but neglectful ones, who had been found unready and unprepared, did not know Him (*JTC,* 578–79).

Royal Wedding. The lessons embodied in this section of the parable may be advantageously considered apart from those of the first division. As was befitting his dignity, the king came into the banquet hall after the guests had taken their places in orderly array. His immediate detection of one who was without the prescribed garment implies a personal scrutiny of the guests. One may be led to inquire, how, under the circumstances of hurried summoning, the several guests could have suitably attired themselves for the feast. The unity of the narrative requires that some provision had been made whereby each one who properly applied was given the garment prescribed by the king's command, and in keeping with the established custom at court. That the unrobed guest was guilty of neglect, intentional disrespect, or some more grievous offense, is plain from the context. The king at first was graciously considerate, inquiring only as to how the man had entered without a wedding garment. Had the guest been able to explain his exceptional appearance, or had he any reasonable excuse to offer, he surely would have spoken; but we are told that he remained speechless. The king's summons had been freely extended to all whom his servants had found; but each of them had to enter the royal palace by the door; and before reaching the banquet room, in which the king would appear in person, each would be properly attired; but the deficient one, by some means had entered by another way; and not having passed the attendant sentinels at the portal, he was an intruder, of a kind with the man to whom the Lord had before referred as a thief and a robber because, not entering by the door, he had climbed up some other way. The king gave a command, and his ministers bound the offender and cast him forth from the palace into outer darkness, where the anguish of remorse caused weeping and gnashing of teeth (*JTC*, 539–40).

Sources

Jenson, Andrew. *Latter-day Saint Biographical Encyclopedia.* 4 vols. 1901–36. Reprint. Salt Lake City: Western Epics, 1971.

Talmage, James E. *The Articles of Faith.* Salt Lake City: The Church of Jesus Christ of Latter-day Saints, 1925.

———. *The Great Apostasy.* Salt Lake City: Deseret Book, 1968.

———. *The House of the Lord.* Salt Lake City: Bookcraft, 1971.

———. *Jesus the Christ.* Salt Lake City: Deseret Book, 1976.

———. *The Parables of James E. Talmage.* Compiled by Albert L. Zobell Jr. Salt Lake City: Deseret Book, 1973.

———. *The Story and the Philosophy of Mormonism.* Salt Lake City: Deseret Book, 1930.

———. *The Vitality of Mormonism.* Salt Lake City: Deseret Book, 1957.

Talmage, John R. *The Talmage Story.* Salt Lake City: Bookcraft, 1972.

Whitney, Orson F. *History of Utah.* 4 vols. Salt Lake City: George Q. Cannon and Sons, 1904.

ABOUT THE COMPILER

CALVIN R. STEPHENS received his master's degree from Brigham Young University in the history and doctrine of The Church of Jesus Christ of Latter-day Saints. He taught at the Ogden, Utah, LDS Institute for many years and at the BYU–Jerusalem Center. Brother Stephens continues to be a popular instructor in adult religious education classes and at BYU Education Week. He served as the president of the California San Bernardino Mission and is a member of the Church's Materials Evaluation Committee. He and his wife, Lynette Davis Stephens, are the parents of four children.